MARINO MARINI

MARINO MARINI

COMPLETE WORKS

INTRODUCTION BY
HERBERT READ

GENERAL TEXT BY
PATRICK WALDBERG

CATALOGUES AND NOTES BY
G. DI SAN LAZZARO

TUDOR PUBLISHING Co.
NEW YORK

TO MARINA MARINI

without whom this book would not have been possible,

to Leon Amiel

who enthusiastically accepted this audacious project; to all those who took part in bringing it to a successful completion — Sir Herbert Read, first of all, who wrote the introduction from his hospital bed shortly before his death, Patrick Waldberg, and all the translators, and art collectors who were good enough to respond to my call, the photographers whose collaboration cannot be praised too highly; — to my valiant assistants who were so valuable to me during the long preparation of this work — Mrs. Maïten Bouisset, Miss Christine Gintz, Mrs. Servane Zanotti and Miss Maud Sissung — at the moment of entrusting its execution to the technical teams of the Pizzi Printing Company in Milan, I address my deepest and most heartfelt gratitude.

G. di San Lazzaro

Paris, February 1, 1970

The Artist and his Wife. (Photo, Herbert List).

MARINO MARINI

was born in Pistoia, Italy, on February 27, 1901. He took courses in painting and sculpture at the Academy of Fine Arts in Florence and, for many years, devoted himself entirely to painting and engraving. This activity was frequently interrupted by trips to Milan. In 1929, the sculptor Arturo Martini, having decided to give up his professorship in sculpture at the School of Fine Arts of the Villa Reale in Monza to settle in Rome, proposed the post to Marino Marini. The latter accepted and installed his studio in the ancient capital of Lombardy. In the following years he visited Paris for long periods of time (1930, 1931, 1936); there, he was in the company of Campigli, De Chirico, Magnelli and De Pisis whom he had known well in Italy, and also met Gonzalez, Kandinsky and Maillol.

He also traveled in northern Europe and went to Germany and England several times, usually alone, wishing to acquire a thorough knowledge of the culture of those countries; he returned frequently to Germany and Holland.

In 1936, thanks to the intervention of Arturo Martini, he received the Quadriennial of Rome Prize, which was Italy's highest artistic award at the time.

Until the declaration of war, he returned to Paris often, thus renewing his contacts with the artists of the capital. In 1936, a monograph, with a preface by Paul Fierens, was written about him in the series "Les Chroniques du Jour" (G. di San Lazzaro, Editor). Although he associated with Picasso, Braque and Laurens during that period, it was always as a spectator.

What interested him above all, was to travel through a country in every direction, to penetrate its culture and civilization. Often he would pass rapidly from one country to another, thus enriching his sensitivity and also his knowledge, superimposing the impressions and images of two neighboring countries such as France and Germany.

During this same period, he stayed in Rome and Florence and in those cities a number of his natural and instinctive possibilities became

Errata

p. 6 - *line 18, for Quadriennial,* read Quadrennial.

p. 371 - *No. 323, for dimensions,* read Height: 3³/₄ in: Length: 4 in: Heigth: 3¹/₈ in:

p. 391 - *No. 18, for title,* read Portrait.

p. 481 - *No. 50, line 4 and « Introduction to Album I », line 40, for an,* read and.

p. 481 - *third column, line 17, for connaisseur,* read connoisseur.

p. 489 - *line 45, for nevere,* read never.

p. 495 - *line 2 (1923), et. al. for Biennal,* read Biennial.

p. 495 - *line 37 (1935), for Quadriennal,* read Quadrennial.

p. 505 - *above photograph, read* The American Ambassador awarding M.M. honorary membership in the « American Academy of Arts and Letters » and in the « National Institute of Arts and Letters » (Florence, 1969).

At Forte dei Marmi. (Photo, Bo Boustedt).

clarified and took form. He led this rapid, feverish way of life constantly, for he was driven by a perpetual need for renewal and knowledge of himself. He undoubtedly continued to meet the artists of his time, but he far preferred solitude to noisy gatherings.

Married only a short time when the war broke out, he and his wife then moved to the Ticino. From there he went frequently to Zurich and Basel, where he met Germaine Richier, Wotruba, Bänninger, Giacometti and Hubacher. In 1944-45, he agreed to present several exhibitions in Basel, Zurich and Bern. When the war ended, he returned permanently to Milan.

In 1948, Curt Valentin, the famous art dealer, introduced himself to Marino Marini after having seen the gallery devoted to the artist in the first exhibition of Italian Art at the New York Museum of Modern Art. This important dealer then began acquiring the works which, in February 1950, made up the Marino Marini exhibition in Valentin's New York Buchholz Gallery. New horizons were opened to the artist in this city: he became acquainted with Lipchitz, Calder, Beckmann, Tanguy, Feininger. This American sojourn corresponds to a period when his forms became freer. The "Riders" lost their static character: a dynamism, a new vitality appeared. After that, exhibitions of the sculptor's works in America, organized by Curt Valentin, followed in rapid succession. On his return to Europe he stopped off in London where the Hanover Gallery exhibited his work; at that time he met Henry Moore. Between 1950 and 1952, a new exhibition toured the most important galleries in Germany. It was in Forte dei Marmi, in the artist's home, that the famous art dealer died in 1954, after which the Pierre Matisse Gallery of New York represented him.

In 1954, Marino Marini was awarded the "Lincei Prize," the most important of Italian artistic distinctions. In 1959, his largest sculpture in bronze was erected in The Hague. Large showings became increasingly common, especially in Germany and the northern European countries; they culminated in the retrospective exhibition of the Kunsthaus in Zurich in 1962, followed by the great retrospective exhibition in Rome in 1966, in the Palace of Venice.

M. Arino 1944

HERBERT READ

INTRODUCTION

The purpose of this brief essay will be to try to define the distinctive qualities of Marino Marini's sculpture, comparing and contrasting his work with that of his predecessors and with the work of certain of his contemporaries. Such a method, which is indeed the general method of art criticism, does not in any way seek to diminish the uniqueness that belongs to the work of a great artist. This uniqueness is essentially a power or energy, what we sometimes call a force of nature, and is something born with the artist, as singular as his physiognomy or temperament. It is, indeed, that temperament or psychic disposition "canalized" and driven in a particular direction, gaining power by the constraint or limitation of its direction.

Every sculptor, if he is to succeed, must possess this elementary "gift," which is not so much a gift as a curse, by which he is impelled to give expression to an inner need by shaping a malleable

9

1934-1935

substance into truthful symbols. Psychologists will explain this impulse as some infantile fixation on the plasticity of the mother's breast, even as an obsessive interest in the child's own faeces, but it needs little more by way of explanation than the general need, in the first months and years of life, for finding some solid ground among the confused impressions that press in upon the senses. We grasp the solid object to assure ourselves of its reality, of reality in general. This sensation, this inner awareness of plastic dimensions, is part of our human development; but we all become, by accident or predisposition, specialists in one or another area of perception; we become visual or aural or haptic types. The sculptor has the haptic sensibility (an inner sense of volume and ponderability) developed in the highest degree.

Once he is consciously aware of his obsession and desires to give it rein, then (unless he falls under influences that distort his choice) he will unconsciously be drawn to certain images, images that have haunted mankind in general and constitute the icons of its myths. The limited number of such images will not be discouraging; rather, the artist takes courage from the fact that he is irresistibly drawn to the major themes of art, and is thereby challenged to rival or excel the deeds of his predecessors. He will find more joy and satisfaction in the variation of a major theme than in the invention of new themes — indeed, inventions, if arbitrary and related only to personal idiosyncrasies, are the sure mark of a minor artist.

The great artist, with what to the uncreative amateur must seem to be a monotonous insistency, will limit himself to a very few motives. Many an ancient sculptor never ventured beyond the human figure itself, and the import of a particular relationship, such as that of mother and child, or rider and horse, was a long cultural development, only coming to perfection in the Renaissance. Complex groups, such as the Parthenon frieze, or the Laocoon, were the exception, regarded as tours de force rather than normal practice.

Marini has conformed to this traditional simplicity. His few portrait-heads apart (a separate aspect of his work which I do not propose to discuss), his work has been almost exclusively limited

10

to two themes: the female figure and the rider and horse, both symbolic. His typical female figure is Pomona, the Roman goddess of fruit trees, a symbol, therefore, of fertility, a local representative of the archetypal Mother Goddess. The rider and horse is a symbol equally universal and is often interpreted as man riding and controlling his instincts, the horse being the symbol of the animal component in man, often specifically the erotic instincts. (¹)

It is not necessary to assume that Marini consciously adopted the theme for its symbolical significance. As a matter of fact, he has confessed that he was first inspired by the equestrian figures he saw on a journey which took him to certain German cathedrals, especially by the famous group at Bamberg cathedral. (²) It would, of course, be completely naïve, even stupid, to suppose that the artist is always motivated by a symbolic intention. Artists in the past have often accepted commissions that have involved symbolic representation (as in every commission to depict, for example, the Madonna and Child) and the artist's integrity will then require him to retreat into his unconscious and make contact with the universal reality of the symbol. But more often, especially in modern art, this contact is made unintentionally: the motivation remains hidden in the artist's unconscious.

In other words, the artist works on a visual, sensuous plane, and is far more likely to be inspired, if not by natural objects, then by other works of art, and especially by the technical methods and inventions of other artists. This is not a question of imitation or plagiarism: it is learning from others the elements of a plastic language, the grammar and syntax without which original composition is impossible. The element of originality in any artist's work is always minimal: what counts is the sensibility and intelligence displayed in realizing an imaginative vision: in giving substantial existence to the intimations of the unconscious. Rodin, basing his craft on his medieval masters, was

(¹) C. G. Jung gives many examples in *Symbols of Transformation*, 2nd edn., Bollingen Series, Princeton University Press, 1967, pages 274-82.

(²) M. Venturoli, "Lo scultore Marino Marini fra Italia ed Europa", in *Le Ore*, n. 6, 10 febbraio, 1966. Quoted by Giovanni Carandente, Catalogue of Mostra di Marino Marini, Rome, 1966. (Edizione de Luca-Toninelli), n. 9, p. 32.

1931

the first modern sculptor to revert to these priorities. Marini, who had direct contact with Rodin, has followed the same procedure.

Whether modelling a woman or a horse, Marini seeks first to identify himself with the life process, the élan vital, characteristic of his subject. His female figure has the ripeness and the rotundity of the Mother Goddess, as she was known in remote antiquity. The same image persists through Greek and Roman art, through Gothic and Renaissance art, and has a more immediate prototype, which may have influenced Marini, in the ripe figures of Renoir. Marini's nudes are nevertheless individual: voluptuous but not elegant, "stocky," as we say in English, implying a close-knit unity of torso and limbs, this effect sometimes being emphasized by the omission of the arms.

The horse and rider is the dominating image in Marini's work, and we must assume that it has some significant appeal to him, but not necessarily an appeal that he could explain. As I have already pointed out, the horse is a symbol of virility, of speed, of controlled strength. The taming of the wild horse marked a definite stage in the evolution of human civilization. But such symbolism apart, the horse, by its animal form, the flexing of its muscles, the grace of its movements, the terror it can inspire when angry or frightened, is in itself a thing of beauty that naturally appeals to the artist. It is the subject of some of the noblest works of art, from the Palaeolithic cave-drawings, the beautiful reliefs from Nineveh, especially those now in the British Museum showing Assurbanipal lion-hunting (9th century B.C.), the sculptured reliefs of the Parthians and Sassanians, the famous horses of the Parthenon frieze, to the many representations of the animal in the Renaissance period. Marini, in selecting this animal as a subject, is showing a predilection as old as art itself. It is all the more amazing, therefore, that he should have given a new treatment to the subject. He begins sedately with the "Cavaliere" of 1936: an animal graceful but sullen, the rider relaxed and formally unified to his mount. So the theme is treated in the "Gentiluomo a cavallo" of 1937. "Il Pellegrino" of 1939, and the "Cavallo" of the same year. Then, eight years later, the animal begins to lose its calm. The muzzle is lifted, the teeth bared, the neck stretched in apprehension; the naked rider also betrays stress ("Cavaliere," 1947). Two years later the rider sits rigidly, at right-angles to the back

12

and outstretched neck of the horse. A phallic significance is given to the tense attitudes of both rider and horse, and this is emphasized in later versions (the "Cavaliere" of 1949-50, which exists in two versions, one in polychrome wood — a unique piece in the collection of Professor Krayenbühl, Zurich — and one in bronze in the collection of Peggy Guggenheim, placed in front of the Palazzo Venier dei Leoni on the Grand Canal of Venice). The horse's neck and head have become phallic in shape, and the image is now manifestly one of erotic potency. Several paintings of the period serve to support this interpretation.

And then, from 1952 onwards, the image begins to disintegrate. A "Cavallo" of this year shows the horse stumbling to its knees, its head drawn back in distress. The final dissolution appears in "Il Miracolo" of 1951-2, of which there are several later versions, all showing the animal in extremis, the rider thrown and falling. The power and the pride of animal and man are lost in a destructive frenzy. The same destructive frenzy is more directly represented in "Il Guerriero" of 1959-60 and "Il Grido" of 1962. It is the final act of a tragedy in which sexual hubris disintegrates into the redemptive harmony of death, represented by abstract forms ("Composizione di Elementi," 1963-4, 1964-5).

It is noteworthy that in the midst of this tragic fury the female form retains its serenity — for example, a drawing of "Pomona" of 1959-60 that echoes the calm figure of 1945.

Perhaps there is a tendency in every great artist to destroy later in life the image of power which he associates with his virile youth — the outstanding example is Michelangelo's assault on his own image of Christ (the Rondanini "Pietà"). Marini's contemporary Henry Moore has shown a similar tendency towards the disintegration of his characteristic formal images — the Reclining Figure of his maturity breaking up into three-piece "bridge-props" and cliff-like promontories. It is a retreat from the organic to the abstract, from the importunity of the senses to a metaphysical harmony, and corresponds to an inevitable physical and psychic development in every individual. The art of the minor artist fails to develop in correspondence with this process — becomes weaker and merely repetitive. In the case of every major artist (Titian, Rembrandt, Goya, Cézanne) the final phase is one of formal compensation, by means of which an impending exhaustion is redeemed by new powers that arise from the hitherto untapped depths of the psyche.

I have perhaps given too much stress to the formal significance of Marini's sculpture, but its technical skill is obvious enough and can only be appreciated in the presence of the work itself. Marini possesses in full power and scope those capacities that constitute and define the art of sculpture — Ruskin described them as "the right placing of masses" and life given "by flexure of surface, not by quantity of detail." His masses have a perfection of ponderability and equipoise, and their surfaces are animated from within — they press with a vital rhythm on the space they occupy. Marini is a master of all the techniques of sculpture, and is distinguished among contemporary sculptors by his bold experiments in colored materials. Many colorful drawings and paintings accompany the sculptures and explore the potentialities of his themes.

Early in his career (1931) Marino Marini used the word "poesia" to describe the quality he wished to render in his sculpture — he was referring more particularly to his portraits. It is a word that will serve to characterize that indefinable personal quality that gives unity to an artist's work — not the formal unity of which enough has been written here and elsewhere, but the unity of a personal vision of reality, a private world of images or symbols that the artist, by his sovereign power of transmutation, embodies in forms that possess not only imaginative power but also visual delights.

Herbert Read

1944

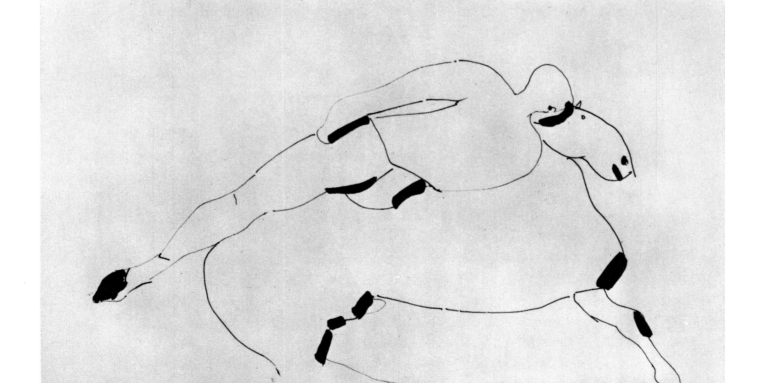

1944

PATRICK WALDBERG

MARINO
MARINI

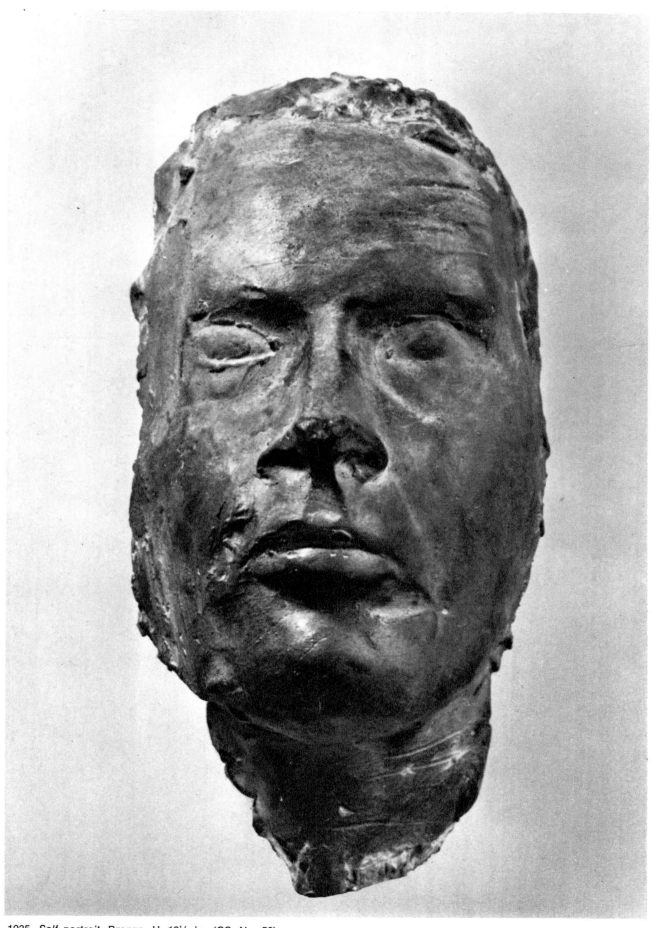

1935. *Self-portrait*. Bronze. H. 10¹/₄ in: (CS. No. 52).

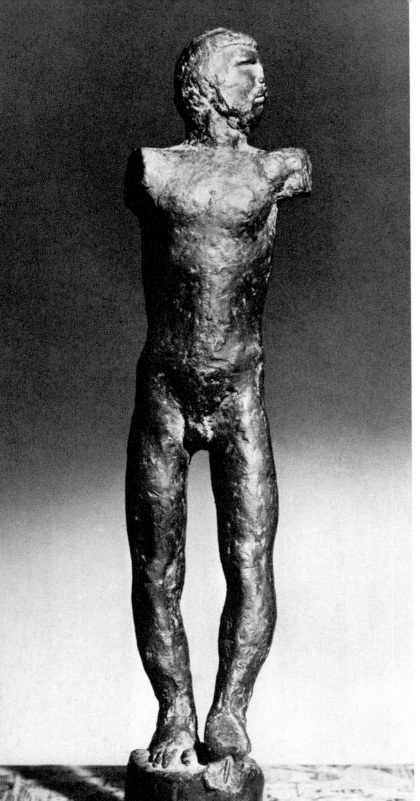

1926. *Small Figure.* Bronze. H. 17¹/₈ in: (CS. No. 2).

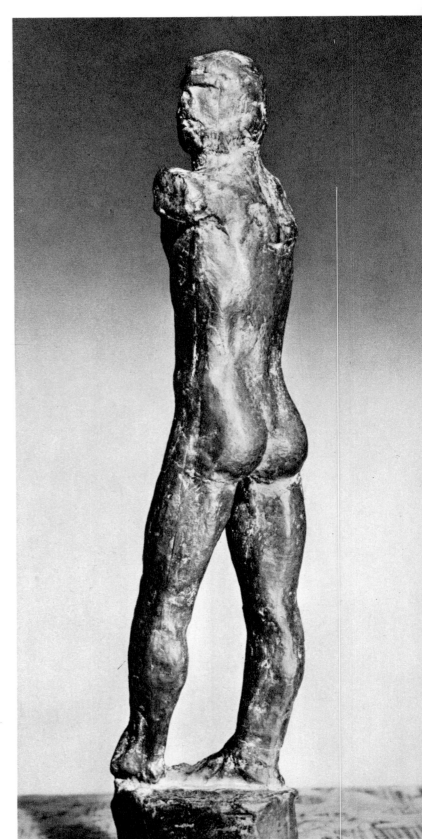

1926. *Small Figure.* Idem. (CS. No. 2a).

1934. *Bather.* Stone.
L. about 59 in: (CS. No. 46).

1926. *Bather.* Terracotta. H. $29\frac{1}{8}$ in: (CS. No. 1).

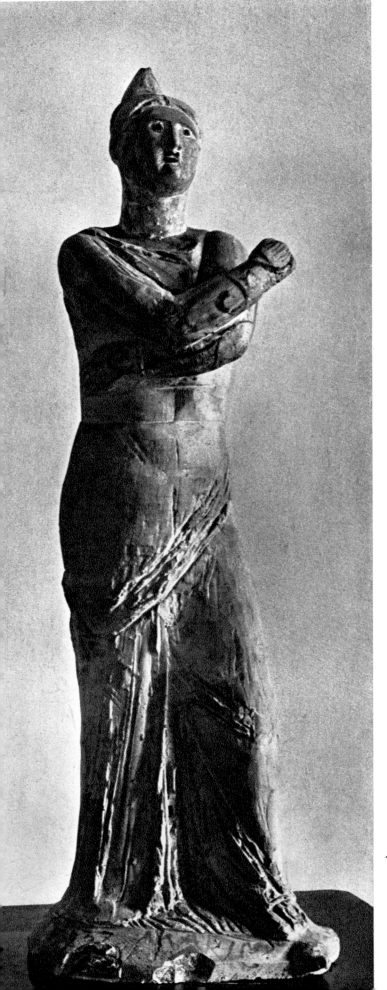

1928. *Victory*. Stone. H. 27½ in: (CS. No. 8a).

1928. *Victory*. Plaster. H. 27½ in: (CS. No. 8).

1929-1930. *Sleeping Woman.* Terracotta. L. 63³/₄ in: (CS. No. 23).

1929. *Female Form.* Terracotta. L. 43¹/₂ in: (CS. No. 24).

1929. *People.* Terracotta.
$26 \times 42^7/_8 \times 17^1/_2$ in: (C.S. No. 16).

1931. *Ersilia.* Polychrome wood $57^3/_4 \times 17^1/_2 \times 26^3/_4$ in: (C.S. No. 31). *Reworked in 1949.*

1929. *People.* Details.
(CS. Nos. 16a, 16b).

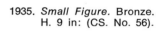
1935. *Small Rider.* Plaster.
H. about 17³/₄ in: (C.S. No. 55).

1935. *Small Figure.* Bronze.
H. 9 in: (CS. No. 56).

1936. *Small Nude.* Terracotta.
H. 9⁷/₈ in: (CS. No. 62).

1933. *Boxer*. Bronze. 32$^{1}/_{4}$×19$^{5}/_{8}$ in: (CS. No. 40).

1932. *Swimmer.* Wood. 45⅝×19⅝ in: (CS. No. 35).

1932. *Swimmer.* Idem. (CS. No. 35a).

1933. *Icarus*. Wood. H. 69$^3/_4$ in: (CS. No. 41).

1932. *Juggler*. Bronze. 11×3$^1/_4$×3$^1/_4$ in: (CS. No. 36).

1934. *Boxer*. Bronze. H. 47$^1/_4$ in: (CS. No. 45)

MARINO MARINI
PUGILE

1935. *Seated Boxer.* Bronze. H. about 26³/₈ in: (CS. No. 54).

1933. *Juggler.* Terracotta. H. 47¹/₄ in: (CS. No. 42).

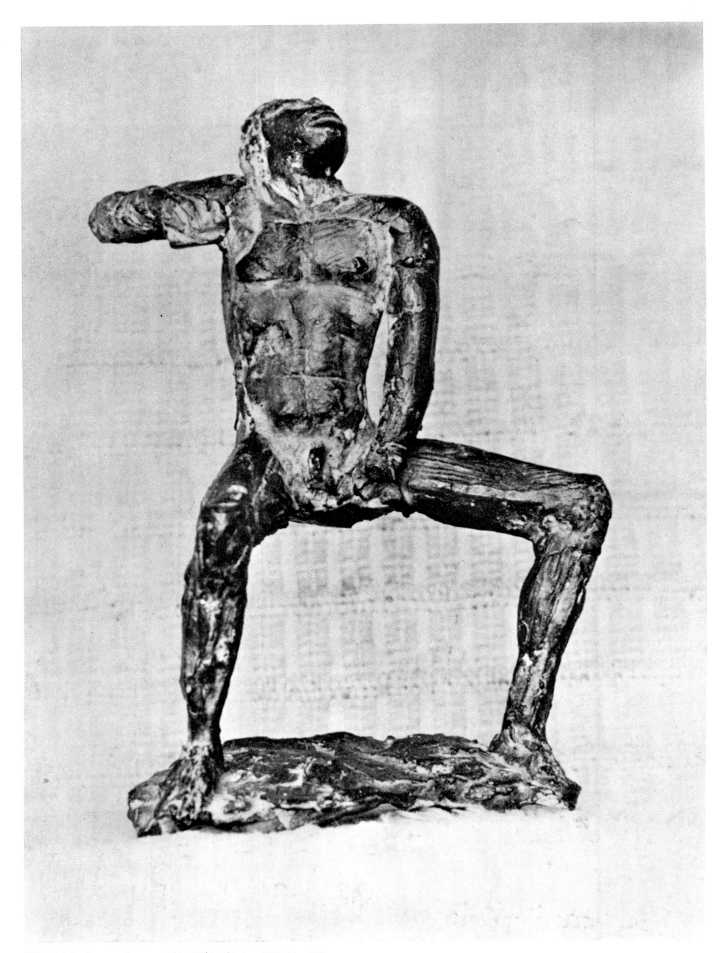

1935. *Little Boxer.* Bronze. 8¹/₄×3¹/₈×5¹/₈ in: (CS. No. 53).

1932

COMING OF AGE

In the course of this century, dominated more than any other by turmoil and upheavals, the spectacle has been of an art which, continually breaking direction, has heaved from weather to lee, swung from bang to whimper, from quaver to catalepsy. We have seen it plunge headlong into the abyss or thrill in the celestial faraway. Between the nether zones of the Surrealist unconscious and the limbo of expurgatory abstraction, we have been treated to every chirp and murmur, every rumble, every polyphony: not one of them have we been spared, neither the hoarse whisper from the depths, the peal of seraphic trumpets, the drumbeat accompaniment to the war-dance, nor the fiddle missing its sound-post and lacking a bow. Amidst the bewildering din of these multitudinous expressions, it was a very practiced ear one needed to recognize the chime of truth. Now and then, from within the tumult, there might indeed arise a winged or solemn voice capable of arresting attention, whether

through the subtlety of its song or by the accents of an inherent nobleness; but while thanks to a few outstanding minstrels we could listen to the moving unfolding of a nocturne, to the arabesques of the gymnopaedic or the play of the fugue, rare are they who have raised us to the level of the symphony, to the level, that is, of epic.

A knight errant in quest of valorous feats and generous adventures, thus does one define the paladin in the role that was his in medieval times. It seems to me that one could justly and without paradox describe Marino Marini as the last paladin of Western sculpture. Not since Rodin has there appeared a body of work where richness and diversity combine with such coherence and rigor, the whole set within such a great respect for life. Indeed, a glance at it is enough to tell that life itself is imaged in his achievement from beginning to end. It shows us that this privileged watcher has from the start bent a constant and loving attention upon the living scene: nude figures, faces, dancers, jugglers, horses, warriors, all of them have been caught at the supreme point where particular form harmonizes with the secret rhythm of the world. We are dealing here with an art that lies as far removed from the expressions of realism as from abstract conceptualism, but whose exemplary virtue, leading the mind forward from the familiar and the everyday, guides it to the confines of the heroic and the legendary. Through deliberate choice, its language is that of tradition, but unattended by any archaism: for if the syntax he employs obeys rules similar to those of the masters of the past, Marini displays a thorough awareness of the parallel explorations and of the concussions which, in his time, have fashioned the new physiognomy of art. His work's altogether modern resonance may finally be owing to its naturalness, to the fact that in it the artist's immediate sensibility, his spontaneity are integrally transmitted. A keen gaze trained upon the world, a gaze synthesized by intelligence into vision, erected by the hand into figure so as to stand, a landmark, upon the shores of time! It is thus that experience, adhering to life, transmutes itself into essence. To the splendid survey Hugo accomplished in his *Légende des Siècles,* ranging from the delicately wrought scene of fine emotion to the apocalypses wherein empires come crashing, Marino seems to offer us

1938. *Bather*. Stone. H. 32⁵/₈ in: (CS. No. 81).

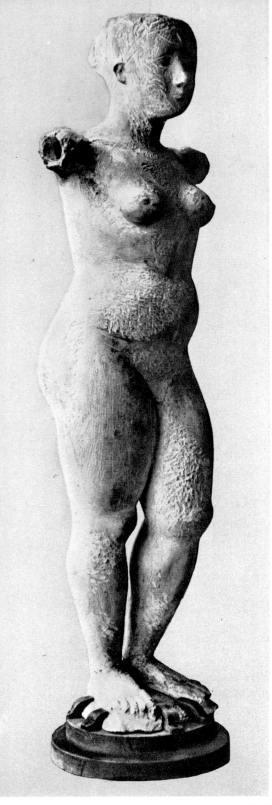

1938. *Young Girl.* Idem. (CS. No. 82a).

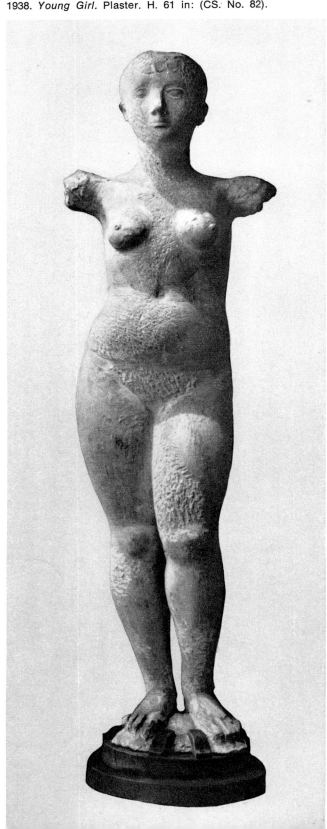

1938. *Young Girl.* Plaster. H. 61 in: (CS. No. 82).

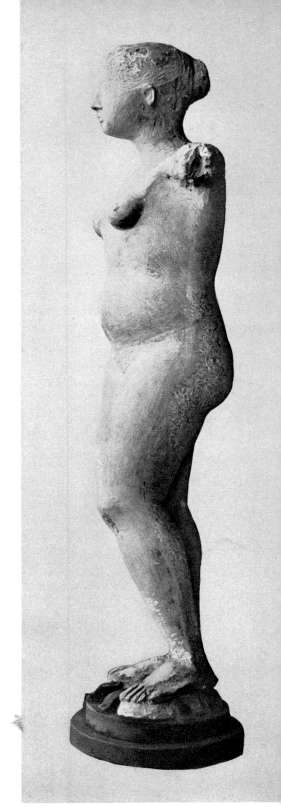

1938. *Young Girl.* Idem. (CS. No. 82b).

1938. *Young Girl.* Detail. Bronze. H. 59⁷/₈ in: (CS. No. 83a).

1939. *Young Girl.* Bronze.
H. 45¼ in: (CS. No. 90).

1942. *The Friends.* Terracotta. 24³/₄×4³/₈×10¹/₄ in: (CS. No. 128).

1942. *Small Boxer.* Plaster 12⁵/₈×17³/₈ in: (CS. No. 130).

1942. *Bather*. Bronze. H. 23¹/₄ in: (CS. No. 129).

1943. *Composition*. Bas-relief. Bronze. $16^7/_8 \times 16^7/_8$ in: (CS. No. 141).

1938

something comparable in the generous *Legend of Forms* his work comprises, joining the baladine's graceful gesture to the agony of the modern warrior stifling upon his death-cry.

The place where Marino Marini's eyes first opened to the world, the surroundings which provided their environment to his childhood and adolescence, doubtless had their influence upon the genesis of an achievement whose growth has the steadiness of that of a tree, inseparable from its roots. He was born on February 27, 1901, in the Tuscan town of Pistoia. Concerning his early years we have the testimony of his twin sister, Egle Marini, who is also a poet. These are the terms in which she describes him then: "An untalkative child, playful, quick to laugh, undisturbed by reprimands, disheartened by the textbook, distracted by the flight of an insect, fascinated by the pattern left in the mud by a tire. At school he takes his shape in solitude. He puts forward no effort, he muses mechanically over the paragraph of Roman history or the strophes which have stuck in his ear, only in his ear."

From this accurate and telling image of Marino as a schoolboy, some constants of temperament and even of character are already to be inferred. He is taciturn, but without that implying anything melancholy in his disposition, for below the surface lies a gaiety which comes forth easily and irrepressibly. One may say that he has remained this way: seldom has he spoken about his life or his art, and then only laconically. However, those who have got near to him know his sense of humor and the mischievous tongue in cheek with which he will tell a story. His solitariness at school reasserts itself in his career, where at an early stage he disencumbers himself of teachers and will go on to remain independent of the influences of his contemporaries. His little taste for schoolbooks will be perpetuated in his distrust of theories, and he has pretty clearly preferred experience to discussion. And the delight he once took in contemplating a flying bug or marks printed in the soil at his feet prefigures the inclination which will carry him every time in the direction of immediate beauty, instantaneously perceptible and palpable beauty. Thus, at the origin of his attitude and approach there is empirical receptiveness and the responding spark, the bases for

43

1948

indispensable decantation and synthesis. Rather than speculate upon the visible world, he moves instinctively toward it, inserts himself in it, conjoins with it, in order next to communicate its forgotten harmonies.

The region where Marino Marini grew up has in many spots retained the look of an Arcadia of ancient days, where shepherds dreamt in innocence and happiness. Not far off, the Tyrrhenian Sea washes the finely sanded fringes of the gulf. Sunlight plays upon the mottled hills' flowered and vineclad slopes. Human gestures, hereabouts, are governed by a rhythm established in a very distant age and the peasant folk, their tools, their flocks belong to their soil, like the mulberry and the green oak. The child's heart fills with these shimmers in which lines and colors blend and breathe in unison. In the house, cosy as a nest, under the bluish glow of the kerosene lamp, he draws, Egle tells us, "with a light hand and amorously." Then the drawings are enhanced by colorings: "close yellow strokes upon a little bird's head; the red and gold meanders of a corolla; emeralds and jades upon insects scrutinized like gems; transparency and airiness of sky..."

At fourteen, Marini's vocation asserts itself. An indocile pupil, with no liking for most of the subjects taught, all his efforts at school go into drawing geography maps, at which he excels; outside school, his best attentions are concentrated upon the familiar flora and fauna, which captivate his eye. Is he already thinking of sculpture? Has he received a sign from the Sibyls of Giovanni Pisano? There are grounds for believing that the decisive impulse will not be felt until a little later, in Florence, where he enrolls at the Beaux Arts Academy in 1917: he is then sixteen years of age.

From somewhat earlier, in 1915, dates an encounter which, brief and silent though it was, cannot be underestimated. Raffaele Carrieri gives us an account of it in one of the subtle analyses he has written of Marino Marini. "Rodin," says Carrieri, "arrived from Rome, where he had finished the portrait of Benedict XV. In Florence he was visiting a favorite pupil of his, and it was the latter who introduced Marino to him. The meeting took place on the Piazza San Marco. Marino did not know a word of French, but even had he spoken it perfectly he would have been incapable of opening his mouth. Rodin had him sit down beside him, as he had done with Nijinsky in Paris after seeing

1947

him dance the *Après-midi d'un faune.* They sat there for a good while, side by side and in silence. Marino resembled a Florentine rustic. Rodin, dressed in black, wearing his mighty beard, was a kind of final incarnation of Moses: the bourgeois Moses of the 19th century. He was to die two years later." This mute contact was doubtless to have major consequences for the taciturn young man.

Depending upon whether one is a native of a country or lands there as a foreigner, the impression it produces will of course be altogether different. We remember Stendhal's excitement when, coming down from the Apennines, he discovered Florence: "My heart was pounding." And, he adds, "I told myself that it was here Dante, Michelangelo, Leonardo da Vinci once lived; in this noble city, queen of the Middle Ages! It was within these walls that civilization began anew..." For the young man from Pistoia—from, that is to say, a neighboring town—the impact must have been less strong. Particularly inasmuch as during his long adolescence Marini remained, as he himself puts it, "like a sealed pebble." This expression, often quoted by his commentators, wonderfully concretizes what he was in those days, withdrawn into himself, receptive to the rays striking upon his surface, to the outside offering the hard contour of his unsubmissive individuality.

Gradually the young artist's spirit wakes to consciousness amidst the soul-palaces of Ghiberti, Brunelleschi and Michelangelo and in the maze of streets and vaults where the echoes of bygone ages converge. "Florence," wrote Renan, "is, after Athens, the city to which the human spirit is most indebted." There, the Platonic dreams of Marsilius Ficinus and of Politian had been materialized by the grace of the builders and the artists—often the same—who ordered space according to the laws of a sacral beauty. The "historic cosmos" of Antiquity, to borrow André Chastel's phrase, is reanimated there through the fervor of the Pollaiuolos, the Donatellos, the Bertoldos, whose style bears the stamp of that "personal energy" without which, Michelangelo maintained, culture is nothing.

Speaking of her brother at this stage of his development, Egle supposes him visited within by "shades of those ancient ragamuffin Mediterraneans who, despite the grave, still preserve the quickness of life...; by intimations of shepherd roughness and nudity...; by fragments of history

1941

—a weighing of history—exhaled by solemn architectures like unto diamonds lying upon the velvet of a jewel-case..." For five years Marino listens, absorbs, draws and paints. Unrelentingly he pursues the task of acquiring the proficiencies his craft demands. "His drawings," Egle writes, "are a chase in the wake of agile thought." Indeed, in his early drawings and paintings one, is struck at once by the mobility and a luminous ease foretokening mastery. Here, figure or object are not at all hemmed in by line; here, line is no more than a light, flowing indication through which, by a kind of osmosis, communication takes place between volumes and the space they move in. A breadth of spirit can already be seen in these early works, and the movement in them is patterned without concern for effect or detail, but in keeping with a rhythmic. The figures deploy in the same dance-like or cere-monial manner as they do upon the curved surfaces of ancient vases or in Roman frescoes. In fact —and this which appears in his first attempts will become one of the constants of Marino's art— each of his drawings or paintings seems charged with a potential for expanse, each is so constructed that, in one's memory, it grows in size, as if the artist's destiny were impelling him, almost in spite of himself, toward the monumental.

For all his wariness of theories and conflicts between schools, Marini was too receptive and sensitive to fail to register and sift the contribution of his contemporaries, whether to decline it, whether to assimilate those of its features which squared with his own temperament. By the time he reaches Florence, Boccioni is dead at thirty-four; and with his disappearance, in 1916, the shroud falls upon Futurism too. Boccioni's *Formes uniques de la continuité dans l'espace* dates from 1913 and constitutes a lone exploit upon a thenceforth unyielding front. The end of the Great War and the period directly after it mark a drying up of inspiration. When in 1922 Marini opts for sculp-ture—albeit without giving up painting—Rodin has been dead for three years. Medardo Rosso is still alive, but he has been inactive for a long while—*Conversation in a Garden* and *The Bookmaker* date from 1893 and 1894; Rodin and Rosso are men belonging to another century. At this point, the only artist who can command Marini's particular attention is Arturo Martini, his elder by twelve years and by now in full possession of his art. The diametrical opposite of Rosso, this many-sided

46

1943. *Suzanne*. Bronze. H. 26⅜ in: (CS. No. 145).

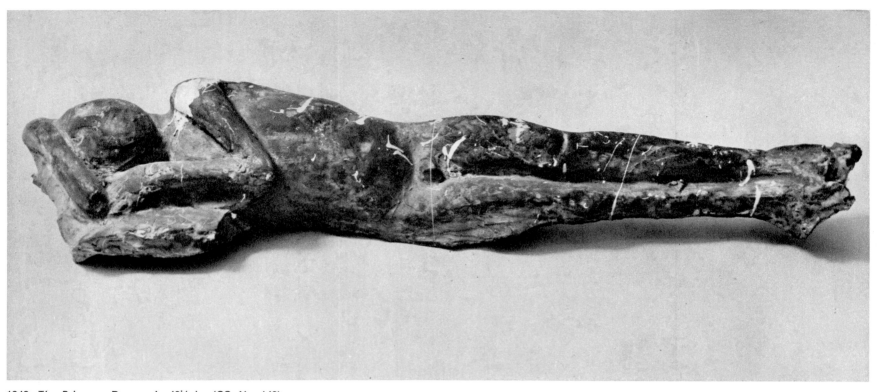

1943. *The Prisoner.* Bronze. L. 42¹/₈ in: (CS. No. 143).

1945. *Small Nude.* Bronze. H. 10³/₄ in: (CS. No. 193).

1943. *Full-length Portrait.* Detail. Polychrome plaster. H. 55¹/₈ in: (CS. No. 142a)

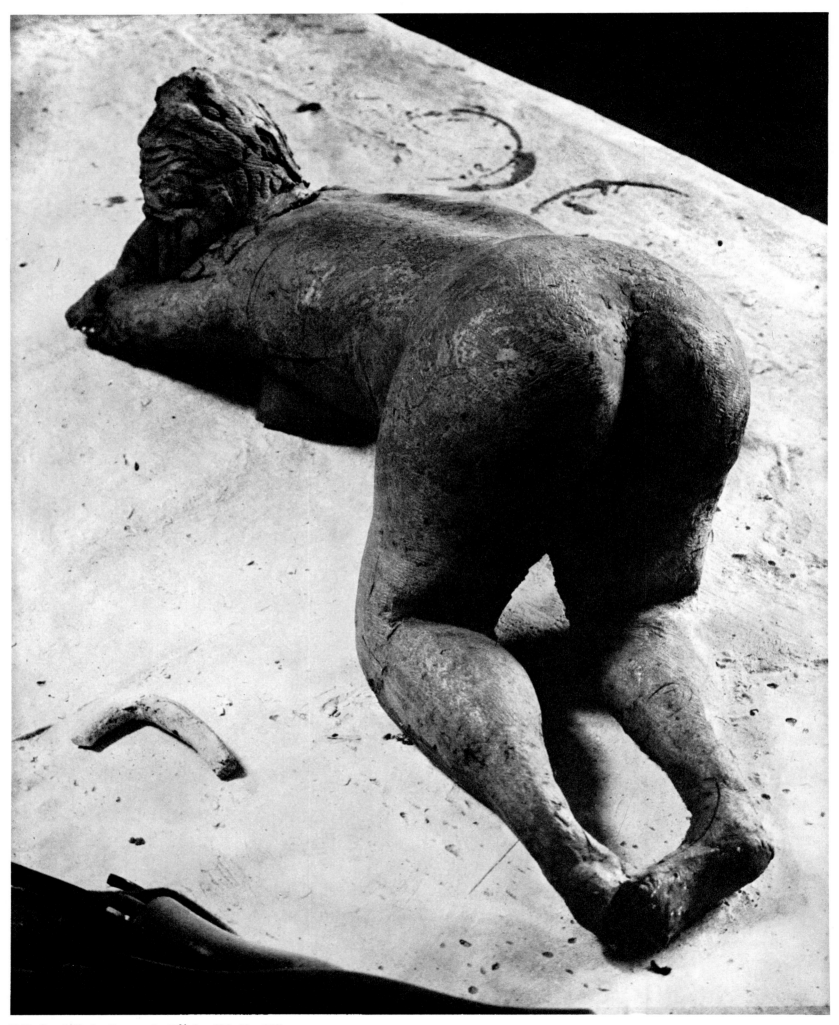

1943. *Small Nude*. Bronze. L. 15³/₄ in: (CS. No. 146).

1943. *Small Nude.* Bronze. 12⁵/₃×7¹/₈ in: (CS. No. 147).

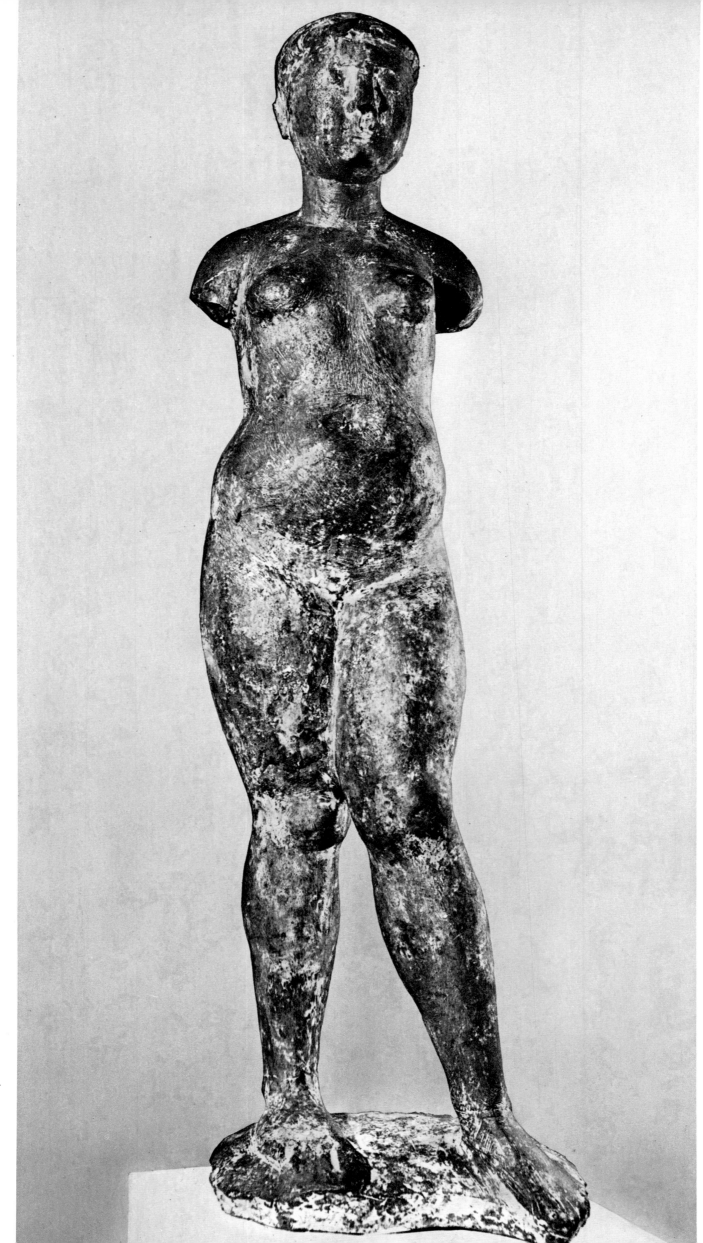

1943. *Young Woman.*
Bronze.
H. 52³/₈ in:
(CS. No. 148).

1945. *Venus.* Terracotta. H. 43¹/₄ in: (CS. No. 195).

1945

1945. *Judith.* Bronze. 53$^1/_8$×20$^1/_8$×25$^5/_8$ in: (CS. No. 196).

artist had received his training in Hildebrandt's Munich atelier. Dazzling technical abilities and unimpeded imaginative verve had led him in the widest variety of directions, from the realism of his prostitutes to the effusiveness of his "young maids in love," from the genre scene to the solemnity of great episodes in civic history. There is no doubt but that the close watch he kept upon Martini helped Marini to resolve a certain number of problems and perhaps also to see the perils inherent in sheer manual dexterity and a too great gift for adopting and transcribing the forms of the past.

Florence and its history, Rodin, Rosso, Martini, they all contributed to the enrichment of his vision, and, in the work he did during his first years, traces of those influences may now and then be detected. However, the springboard by whose means Marini will in one leap attain his natural milieu and climate is the discovery of Etruscan art. Alberti, in the 15th century, had already spoken of it, and not without pride: "...i nostri Toscani antiquissimi furono in Italia maestri in dipignere peritissimi." Pollaiuolo, Donatello too, had been touched by the Etruscan charm, by that enigmatic Tuscan past that Egidus of Viterbo glorified and Piero di Cosimo so sumptuously evoked in his scenes of the hunt. If, as I feel, it is difficult to talk about Marino Marini's *Italianness,* it is perfectly legitimate, on the contrary, to emphasize his *Etruscanness,* and throughout this book I shall have occasion to refer back to that at once plastic, affective and moral heritage. But, before closing these pages devoted to the artist's youth, I would like to cite a passage from Dino Garrone, where he speaks of the Etruscans and of their smile:

"Look at them: their smile does not recall the crescent-shaped smile of mummies, nor has it anything to do with the petrified grin of skulls. It is something alive. It is the initiate's, the magician's smile... Something vibrant, something disturbing and terribly impertinent seems to live on the other side of the protecting glass and to defy the curiosity of peering tourists, the furious probing of specialists..."

From the moment Marino Marini succeeded in recapturing that smile—which yet floats upon his lips today—he became himself at last and, abandoning his patronymic, started signing with his first name: Marino.

1927

1945. *Seated Woman*. Bronze. H. 18¹/₈ in: (CS. No. 192).

1945. *Nude.* Bronze. H. 45$\frac{1}{4}$ in: (CS. No. 191).

1945. *Nude.* Idem. (CS. No. 191a).

1945. *Small Nude.* Bronze. H. 16⅝ in: (CS. No. 190).

1944. *Seated Figure*. Detail. (CS. No. 173a).

1944. *Seated Figure.* Bronze H. 27¹/₂ in: (CS. No. 173).

1943. *Small Nude.* Bronze. H. about 17³/₄ in: (CS. No. 136).

1943. *Small Nude.* Idem. (CS. No. 136a).

1949. *Nude.* Bronze. H. 19¹/₄ in: (CS. No. 241).

1940

THE PORTRAITS

In the sculpture of our century there has been no equivalent, for richness, for diversity, or for strength, to the extraordinary gallery of contemporary portraits Marino has given us. As regards abundance, one might compare him to Despiau; but, despite a great talent and a very sure craft, Despiau remained too much under the sway of bourgeois conventions. Totally the reverse, Giacometti, leaning upon none at all, sought to mould the shape of anguish itself and did without any question attain true greatness, but his efforts were spent upon only a handful of models, most often his brother Diego, his wife, more rarely a friend or a visitor. In contrast to Despiau's, Marino's heads are spiritualized to the point where, all contingency transcended, it seems as though one has been ushered into the very heart of the model: the likeness does not stop at the contour, and the subject looks to us "such as in himself eternity has finally remade him." And unlike Giacometti,

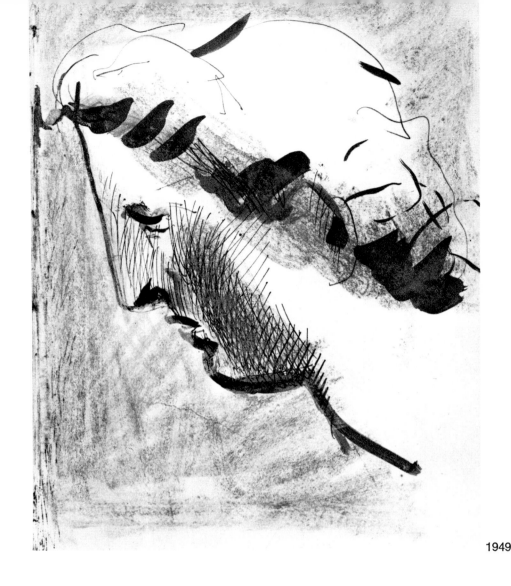

1949

Marino's gaze embraces a far wider horizon, and the vision his hand restores to us, Balzacian in its scope, constitutes, we come to feel, a veritable "human comedy," whence for that matter tragedy is by no means barred.

Each human visage bears the brand of a destiny; joys and sorrows, hopes and disillusionments are limned in its volumes and shadows. From the faces of his friends, Marino has derived types which will survive them still better than Vautrin, Brideau or Madame de Mortsauf perpetuate the creatures who inspired them. Immediate presence and everlastingness: before Marino's portraits it is a dual impression one has, and its origin will be more easily grasped if we listen to the artist himself. "Looking at a form, a profile," he has written, "the first thing is its aspect: round, elongated. Those are essential elements, to be ascertained instantly and to fix in one's brain. Next, I enter into the spirit of the person and the difficult thing here is to imagine this physiognomy within the context of mankind, to imagine what it stands for in the eyes of other men, other human personalities. This once done, everything is done. This truth must live in me the whole while the work is in progress, until the portrait is finished. The result must satisfy me as concerns the vitality of the expressions and the execution of the individual's true and characteristic lines. That task accomplished, the subject once assigned a place in the kingdom of the dead who remain alive, I hand my work over..."

Marino's portraits contain, if I may venture the phrase, *a density of likeness* which, when one happens to be personally acquainted with the model, can be little short of frightening. The reason, I expect, is to be looked for in the fact that this man, this woman, whom one saw, spoke to only the other day, have now suddenly, as Marino puts it, received their "place in the kingdom of the dead," in that realm where, secure from the accidental, they reassume their immanent being. Alberto Magnelli, Filippo De Pisis, Carlo Carrà, Massimo Campigli, Henry Moore, Germaine Richier, Hans Arp—and here I confine myself to those I have come into contact with, some of whom were, or still are, dear friends of mine— it is insufficient to say that in their portraits I *recognize* them, for the truth is that I *discover* them there, and, each time I see the model again, I discern in him aspects I had not detected hitherto, aspects which Marino, however, had succeeded in revealing.

66

A Corner of Marino Marini's Workshop at Milan. (Photo, Herbert List).

1942. *Self-portrait.* Detail. Polychrome plaster. H. 16¹/₈ in: (CS. No. 131a).

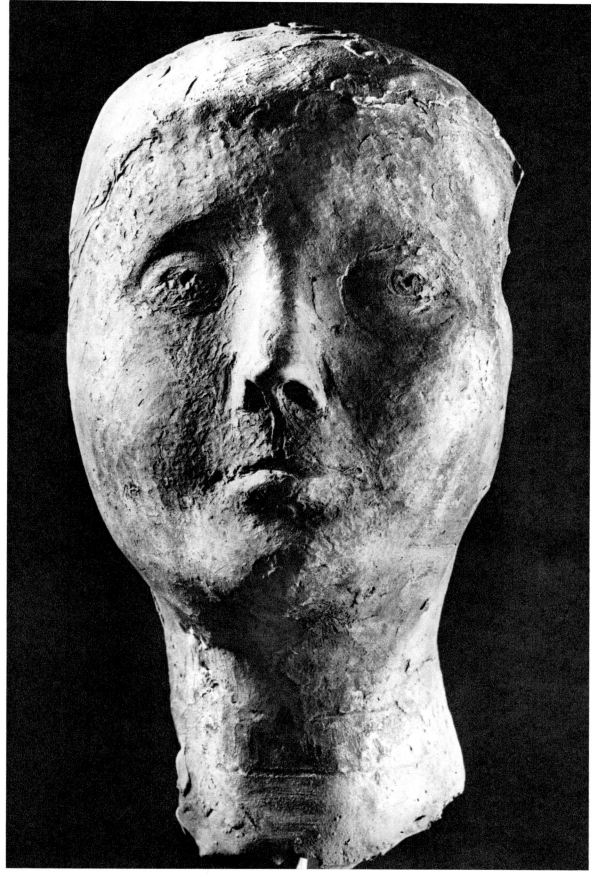

1941. *Donatella.* Terracotta. H. about 15 in: (CS. No. 106).

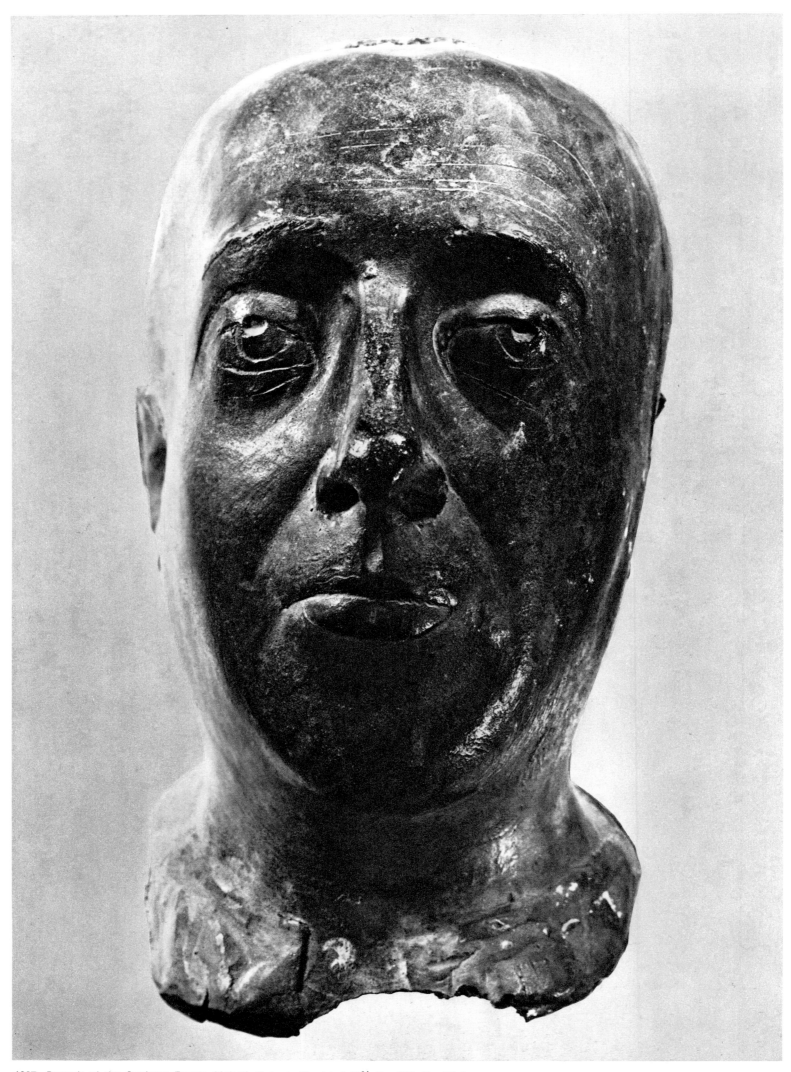

1937. *Portrait of the Sculptor Fausto Melotti.* Bronze. H. about 11³/₄ in: (CS. No. 74a).

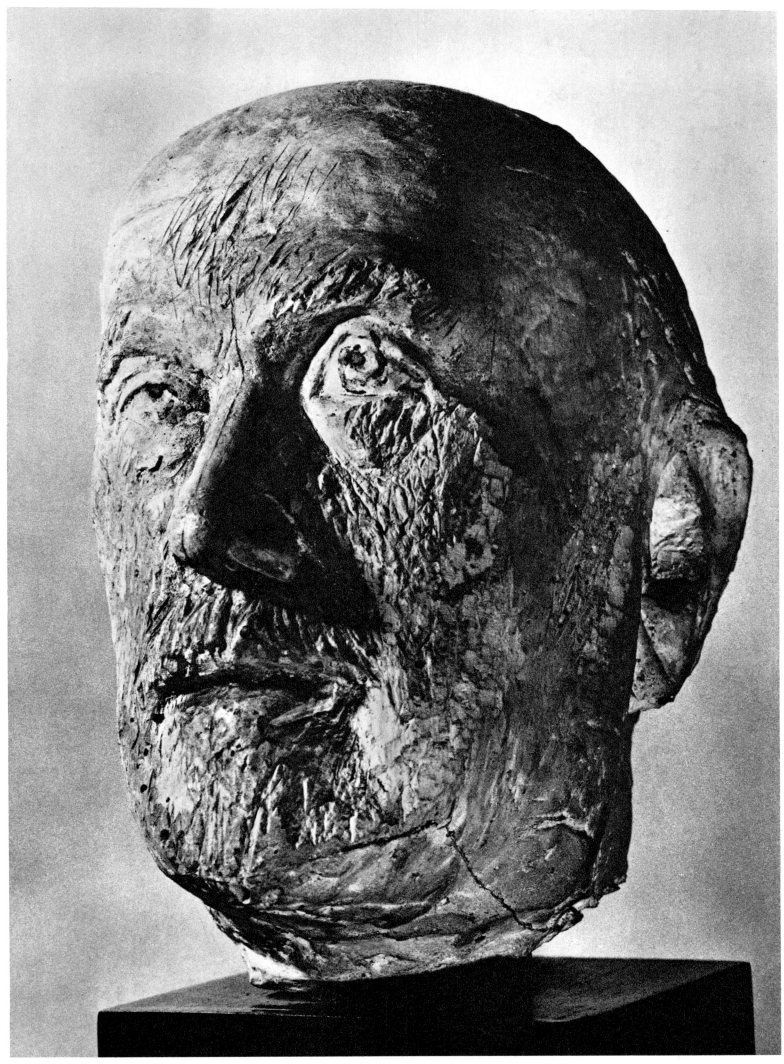

1942. *Portrait of the Painter Arturo Tosi.* Polychrome plaster. H. 9⁷/₈ in: (CS. No. 119a).

1941. *Portrait of the Painter Filippo De Pisis*. Bronze. H. 13³/₄ in: (CS. No. 109).

1947. *Portrait of Emilio Jesi.* Bronze. H. 9¹/₂ in: (CS. No. 225).

1943. *Arcangelo (Archangel)*.
Polychrome plaster.
H. 51³/₄ in: (CS. No. 144).

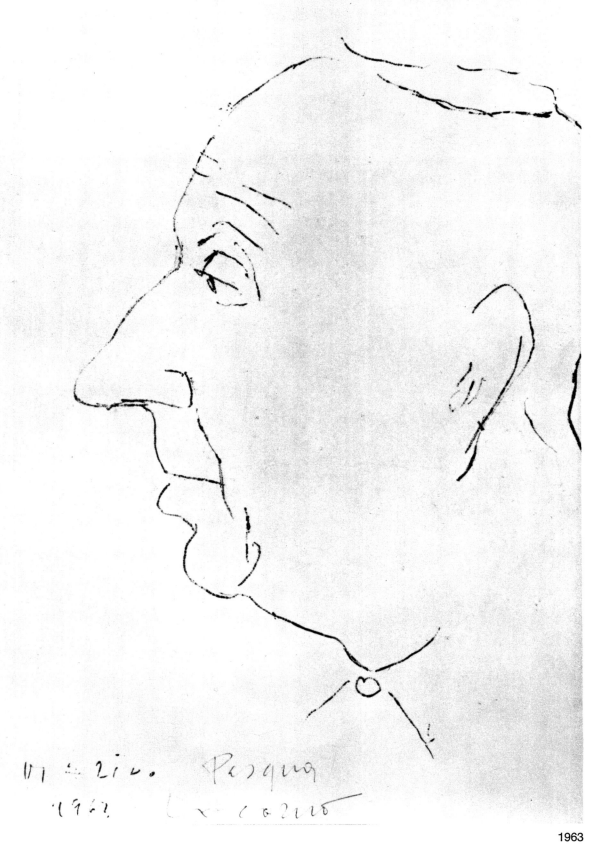

Mario Pasqua
1963 Cascella

1963

Rightly enough, Marino's portraits have been compared to Etruscan figures, but a connection with Roman sculpture may be seen as well. I am thinking in particular of the busts, strikingly alive and powerful, that date from the time of the last Caesars: the bust of Balbinus, those of Caracalla, of Macrinus, or of Septimius Severus, in which the human verity of the subject is transmitted to us entire, and where a startling modernness of conception and treatment is still compelling, even today. In the work of those great anonymous sculptors, as in Marino's, the artist has managed, following Socrates' prescription, "to represent in visible form the workings of the soul." As Carrieri very precisely remarked, "The image is stable and permanent in its autonomy, no matter whose the face that inspired it, masculine or feminine, no matter what its degree of vigorousness or delicacy."

To be sure, an evolution is remarked in Marino's portraits. Until 1940, the retirement in which he kept himself had inflected his work toward a certain classicism. Then, however, as he himself says, "I reacted against the imperialist bombast in Fascism's directives concerning art, inasmuch as I set aside any distinction between my artistic conscience and my private life, and in that I avoided anything representational. So it was I practiced with anonymous busts, similar to those funerary portraits of persons unknown, free of all historic pathos, which after two thousand years still convey their purely human statement to us."

It was in this period that he produced the fine ensembles called *People's Divinity* or *Remembrance of a Faraway Civilization,* works which, more clearly than others, announce the Etruscan upsurge and whose very titles indicate an effort at depersonalization and at the same time a nostalgia for lost worlds. Greek recollections arise at various moments in the portrait series, and there also appear, following trips to Germany, occasional solutions suggested by the masters of the Gothic. Then, and steadily more so, the portraits will affirm their autonomy, each of them being conceived in terms of its own architectonic and of the elementary forms proposed by the subject: round, oval, oblong, square.

"On the farther side of that wall of heads," writes Carrieri, "began the lofty silence where Marino's horses and riders project their massive shadows."

1943

1943. *Arcangelo (Archangel).* Detail of p. 74 Polychrome plaster. H. 51³/₄ in: (CS. No. 144a).

1945. *Portrait of Johann Ulrich Gasser*. Polychrome terracotta. H. 9⁷/₈ in: (CS. No. 204).

1943. *Arcangela (Archangel).*
Bronze. H. 49¹/₈ in: (CS. No. 149).

1942. *Portrait of Massimo Campigli.* Detail. Bronze. H. 15 in: (CS. No. 118a).

1949. *Portrait of Ambassador Dunn*. Detail. Plaster. H. 11³/₈ in: (CS. No. 244a).

1937. *Portrait of Signora Verga.* Polychrome terracotta. H. 9 in: (CS. No. 73).

1943. *Portrait of Marina Marini*. Bronze. H. 11³/₄ in: (CS. No. 150).

1945. *Portrait of Georg Schmidt.* Polychrome plaster. H. 14¹/₄ in: (CS. No. 203)

1944. *Portrait of Hedy Hahnloser.* Plaster. $13^3/_8 \times 7^1/_8 \times 9^7/_4$ in: (CS. No. 181).

1953. *Portrait of Manfred V. Mautner Markhof.* Polychrome plaster. H. 15³/₄ in: (CS. No. 310).

1945. *Portrait of Madame Étienne Grandjean.* Polychrome plaster. H. 13³/₄ in: (CS. No. 201).

1946. *Portrait of Marina Marini*. Polychrome plaster. H. 12$^1/_4$ in: (CS. No. 218).

1937. *Imaginary Portrait.* Terracotta. H. about 9⁷/₈ in: (CS. No. 72).

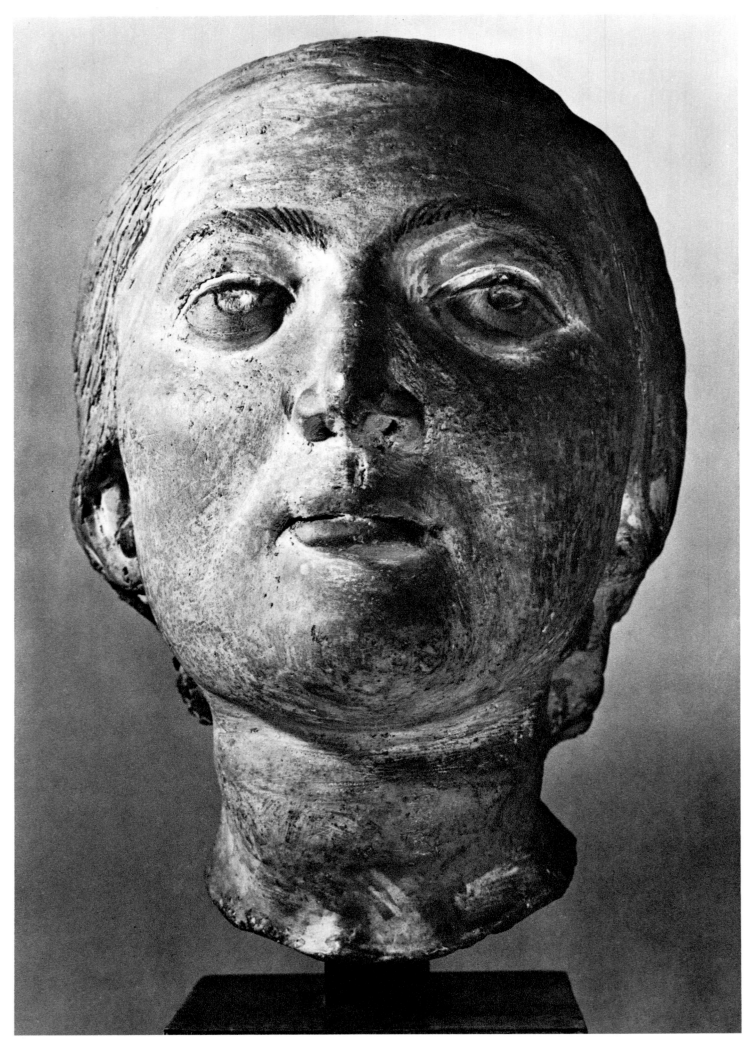

1937. *Portrait of a Woman*. Polychrome terracotta. H. 10⅝ in: (CS. No. 80 x).

1949. *Portrait of Samuel Barber.* Bronze. 11×8⅝ in: (CS. No. 246).

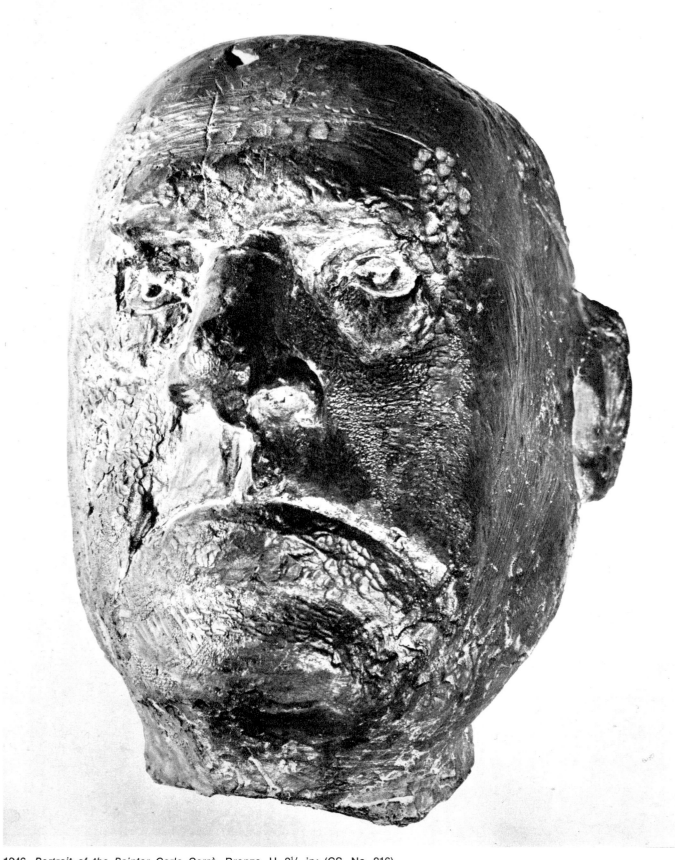

1946. *Portrait of the Painter Carlo Carrà.* Bronze. H. 9$^1/_2$ in: (CS. No. 216).

1943. *Portrait of Ginevra.* Plaster. H. about 23$^5/_8$ in: (CS. No. 151).

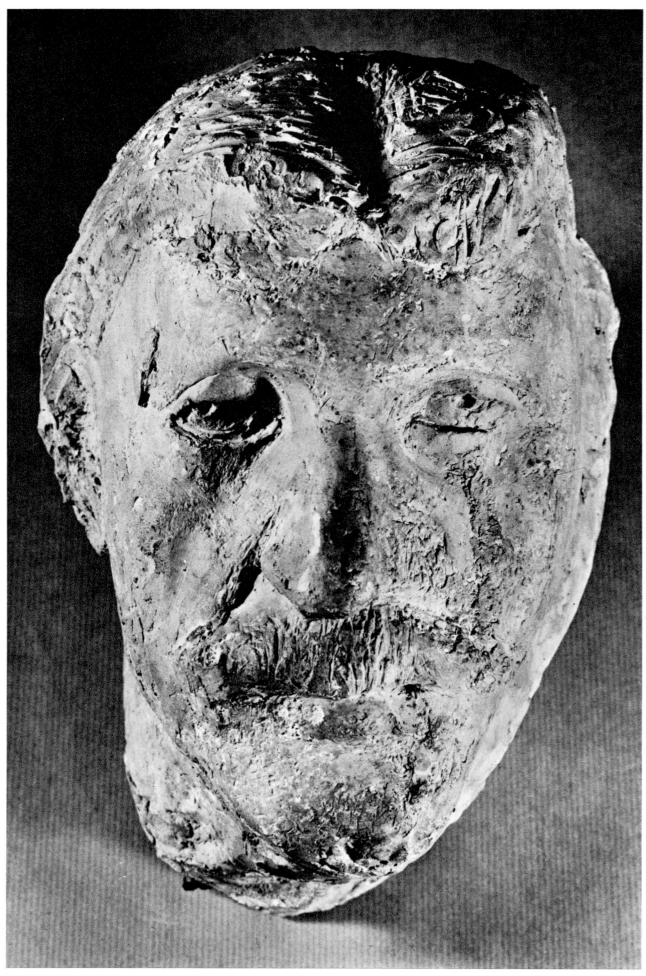

1947. *Portrait of Carlo Cardazzo*. Polychrome plaster. H. 12^1/$_4$ in: (CS. No. 226).

1945. *Portrait of Germaine Richier.* Bronze. H. 13 in: (CS. No. 202).

1949. *Portrait of the Sculptor Hermann Haller.* Polychrome plaster. H. 13⅜ in: (CS. No. 245).

1947. *Portrait of Emma Jeker.* Plaster. H. 13³/₄ in: (CS. No. 219).

1954. *Portrait of Lucy Lambert.* Bronze. H. 15³/₄ in: (CS. No. 324).

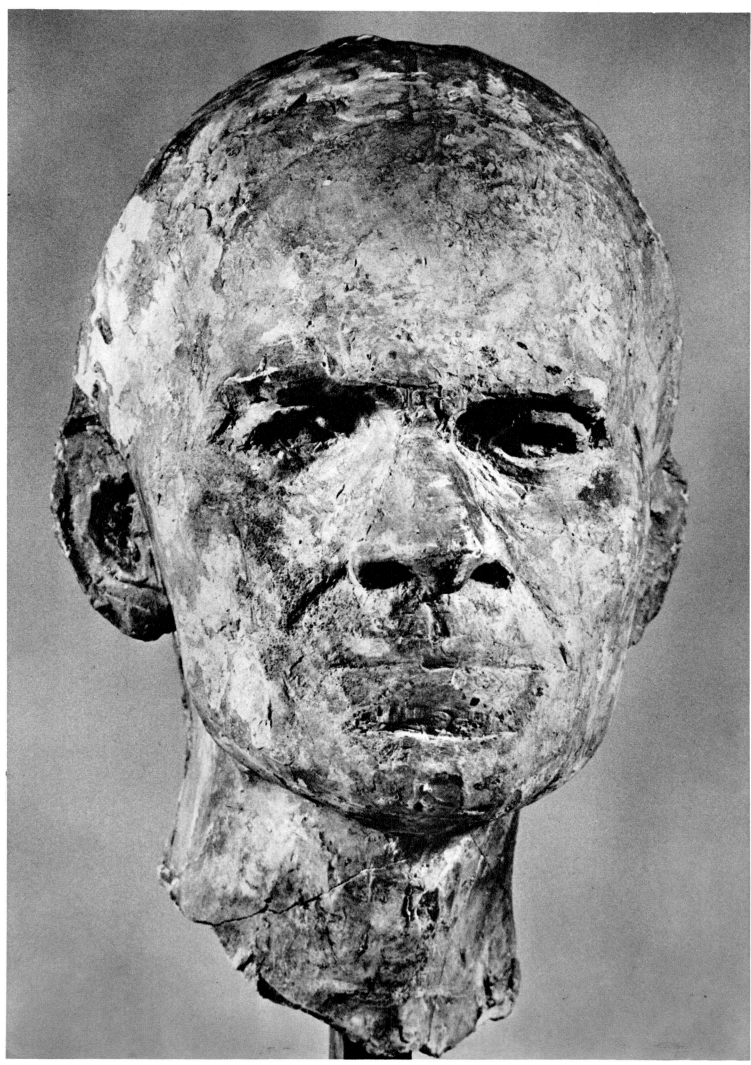

1950. *Portrait of Riccardo Jucker*. Plaster. H. 14¼ in: (CS. No. 261).

1963. *Portrait of Joseph H. Hirshhorn.* Bronze. H. 13³/₄ in: (CS. No. 372).

1954. *Portrait of Curt Valentin.* 2nd version. Bronze. H. 9¹/₄ in: (CS. No. 325).

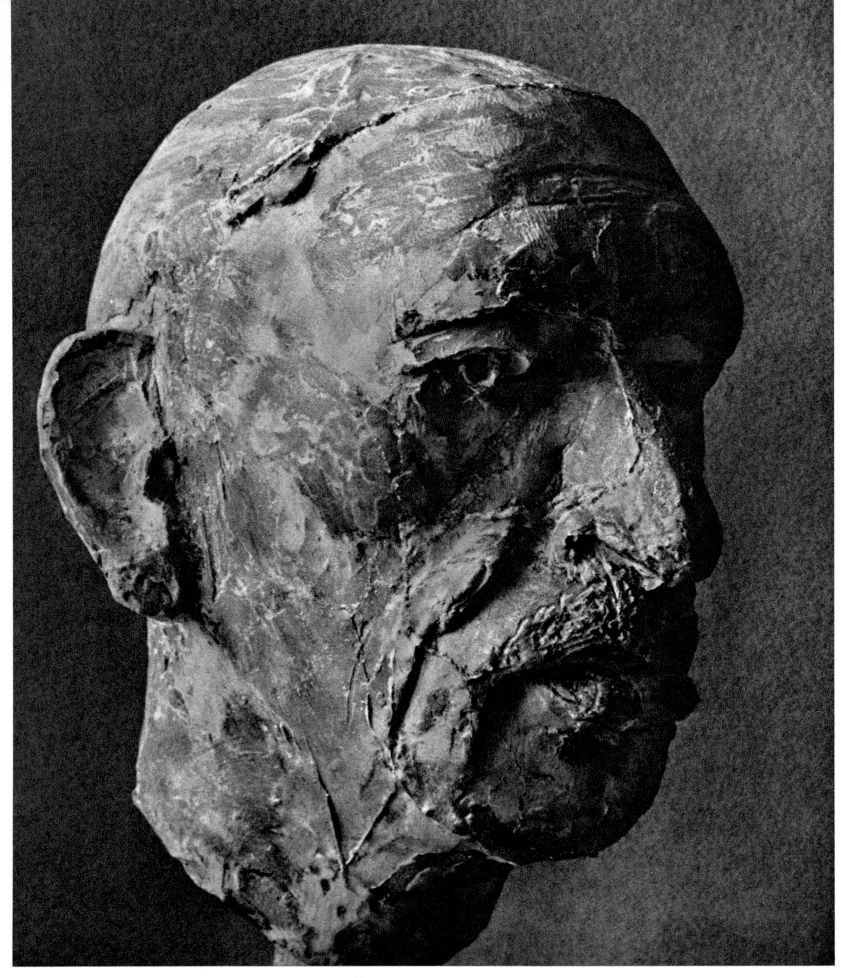

1950. *Portrait of Igor Stravinsky*. 1st version. Bronze H. about 11³/₄ in: (CS. No. 263).

1951. *Portrait of Igor Stravinsky*. 2nd version. Bronze. H. 12⅝ in: (CS. No. 277).

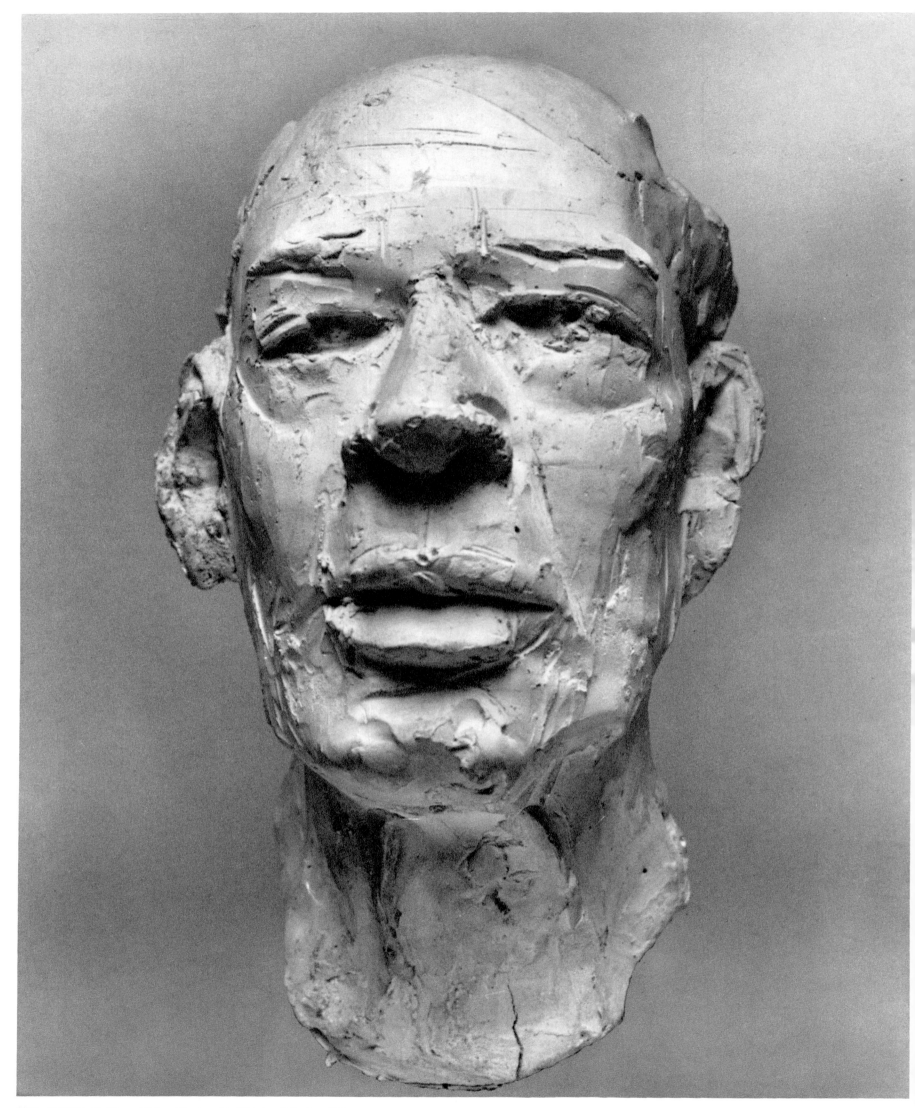

1961. *Portrait of Henry Miller.* Plaster. H. 10⅛ in: (CS. No. 366).

1967. *Portrait of Gottfried B. Fisher*. Bronze. H. 13³/₄ in: (CS. No. 379).

1967. *Portrait of Mies Van Der Rohe.* Final version. Bronze. H. 13 in: (CS. No. 378).

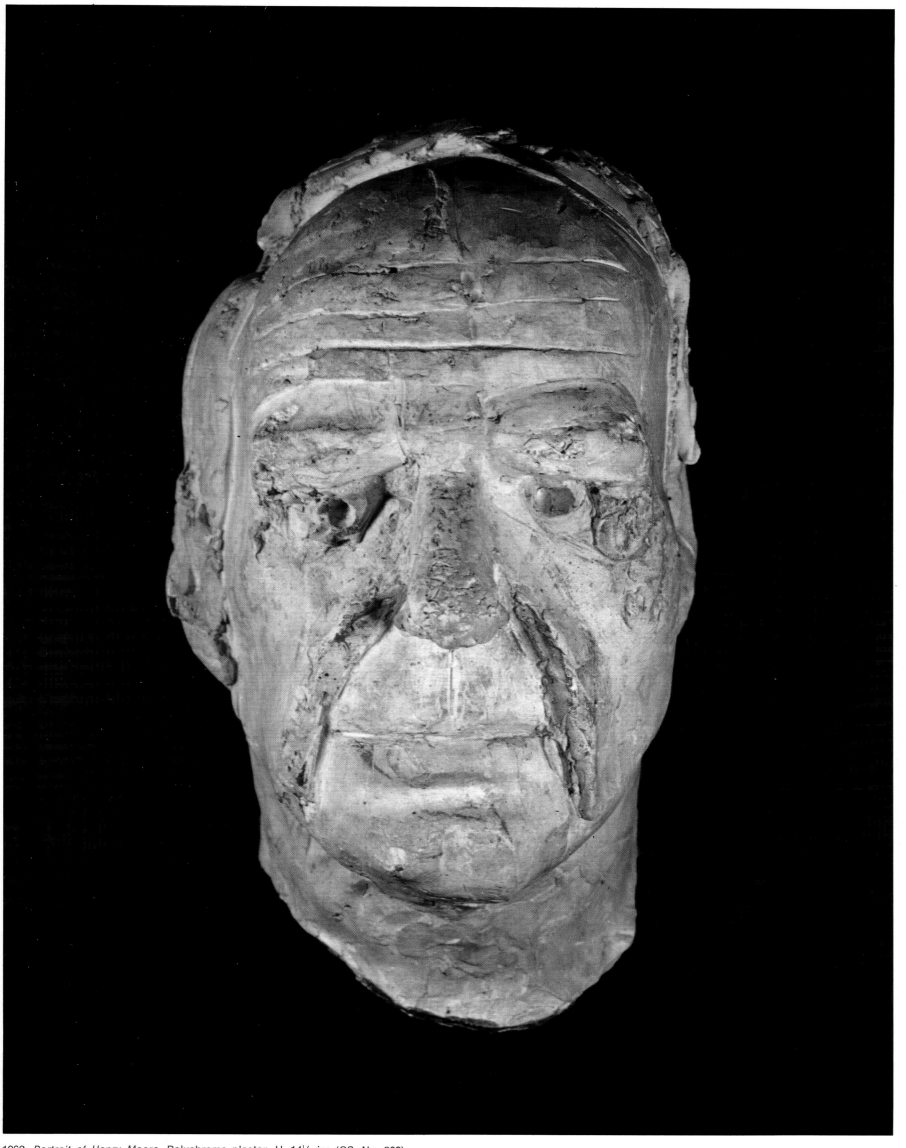

1962. *Portrait of Henry Moore.* Polychrome plaster. H. 14¹/₄ in: (CS. No. 368).

1962. *Portrait of Marc Chagall.* Polychrome plaster. H. 11⁹/₈ in: (CS. No. 369).

1942

THE POMONAS

According to a story that numbers among his confidences, we see Marino, around the year 1924, then at the early stage of his sculptor's career, getting up at night and going in the darkness to feel the work he has under way, and that in order to pursue its completion mentally. There would doubtless be a great deal to say about creative activity's carry-over into sleep and about the emotional crystallizations with which it is enriched in the shadowy zone of unconscious life. The image of Marino letting his hands stray over his creations so as to verify their presence and returning to bed with the tactile sensation that will nourish his dream, this image adds to our understanding of what we sense opposite his achievement: the impression of the artist's close adherence to this work and the feeling that it has been at once lived and dreamt, was at once real and ideal, present and unbounded by time.

109

1935

1939-1940. *Pomona.* Detail. Terracotta. H. 63 in: (CS. No. 92

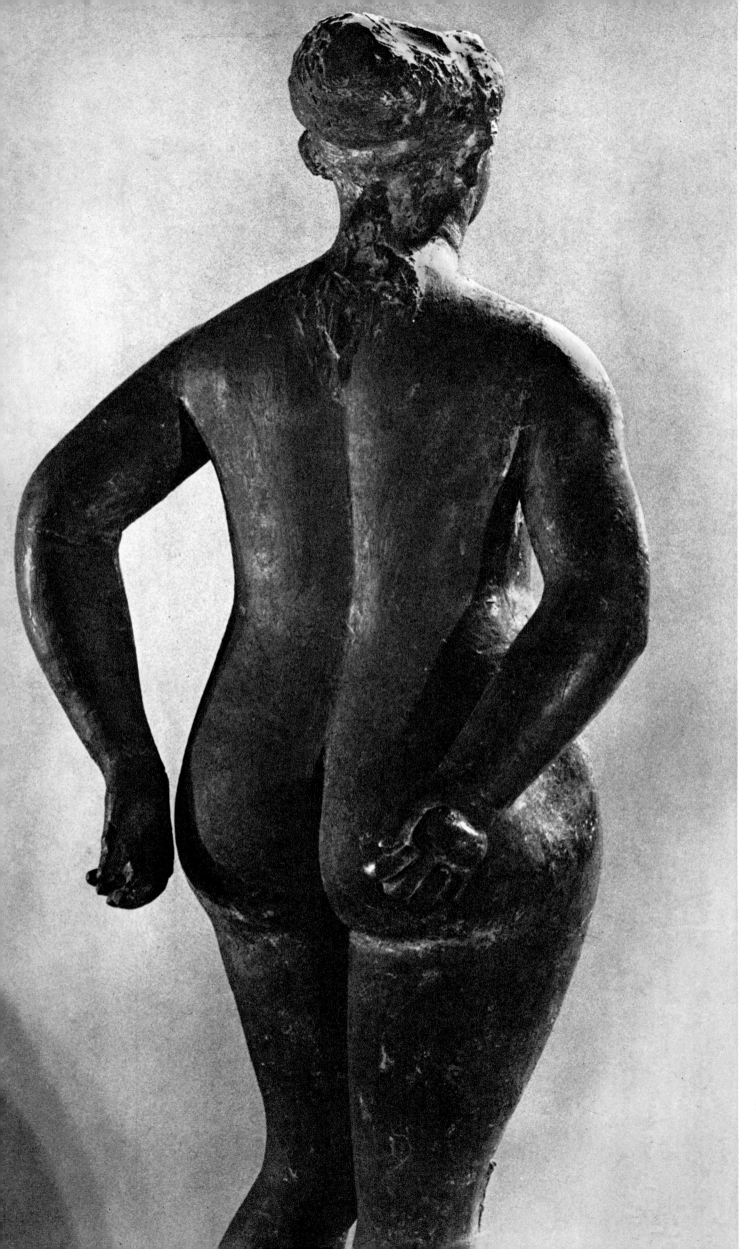

1940. *Pomona*. Back view.
(CS. No. 102a).

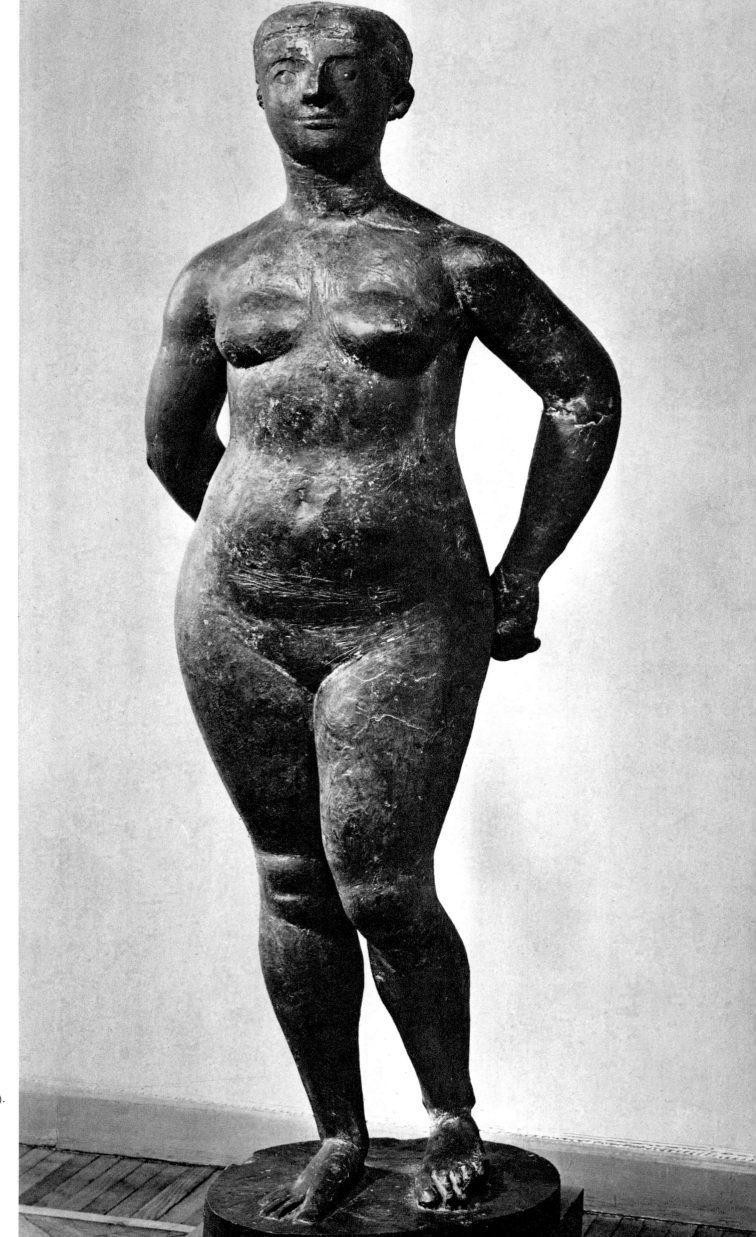

1940. *Pomona*. Bronze.
H. 68⅞ in: (CS. No. 102).

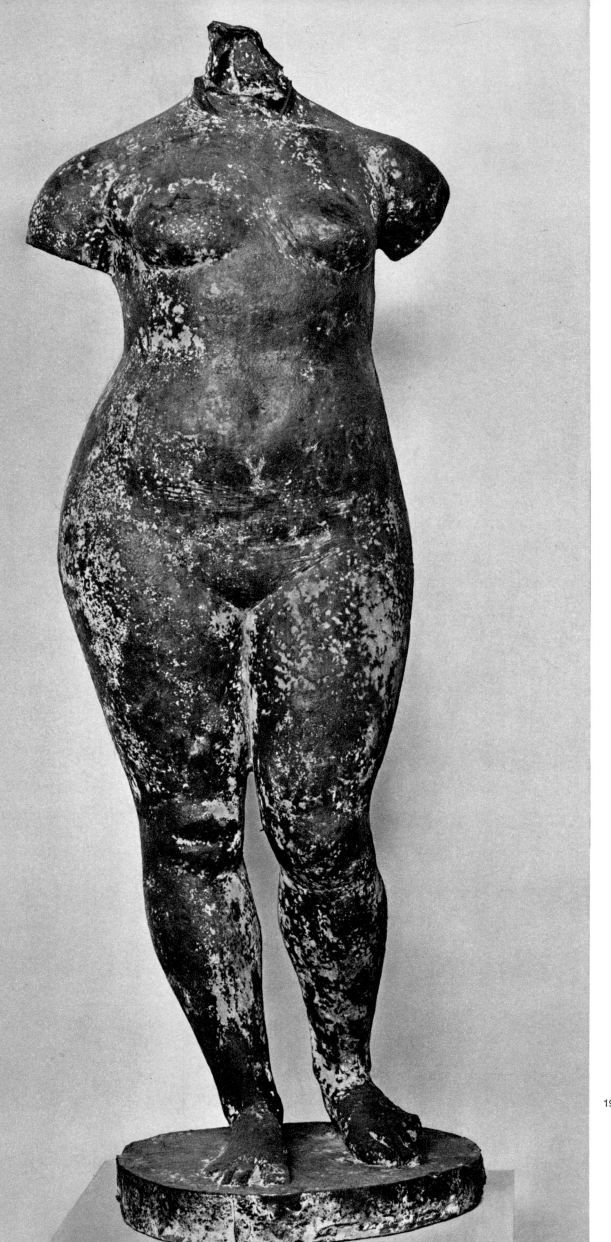

1941. *Pomona*. Bronze.
H. 63 in: (CS. No. 110).

1942. *Pomona*. Polychrome plaster.
H. 27⁷/₂ in: (CS. No. 127).

1943. *Small Pomona*. Bronze. H. 16⁷/₈ in: (CS. No. 140).

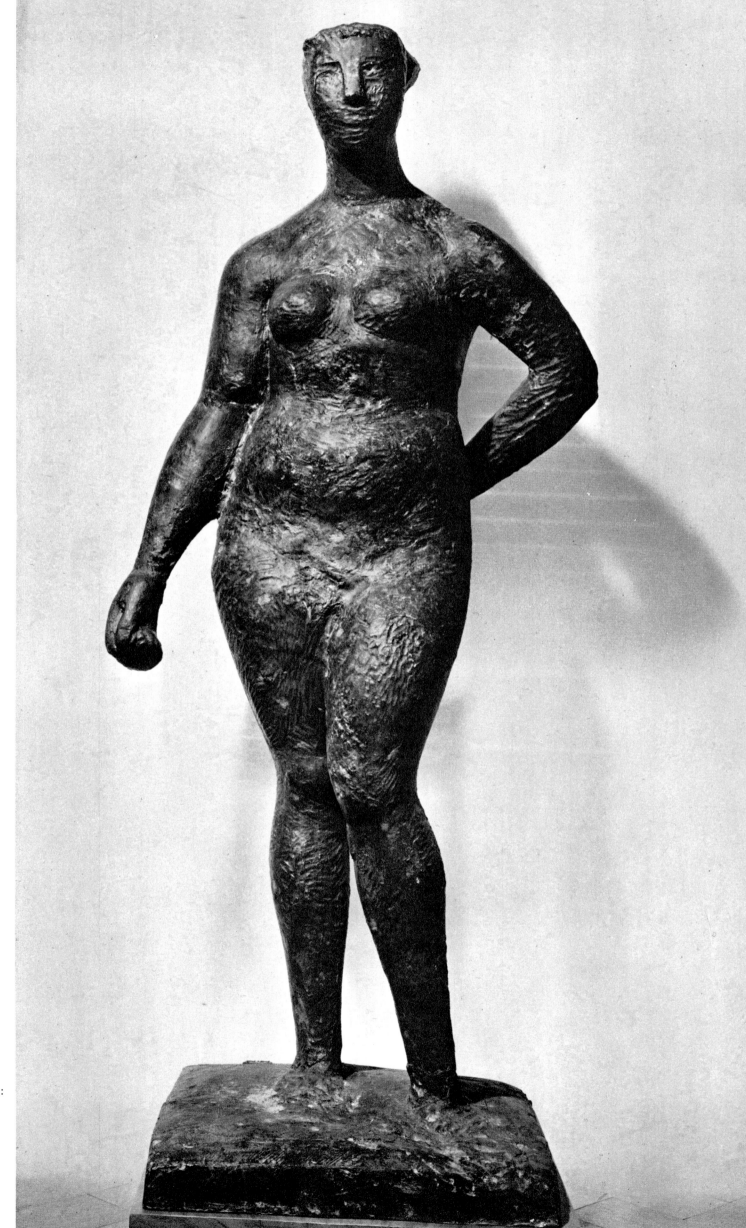

1945. *Pomona*. Bronze.
63×20¹/₈×20¹/₂ in:
(CS. No. 198).

1945. *Pomona*. Detail. Stone. H. 68⁷/₈ in: (CS. No. 197a).

1944

The series of feminine nudes he has titled *Pomonas* would correspond, I believe, to a dream stemming from youth. Later on, *Riders, Warriors, Miracles and Cries* will display the mark of maturity and of the entrance of tragedy among his preoccupations. Pre-Hegelian in their conception, the *Pomonas* emerged from a long pagan revery reflected also in the artist's self-portait, as bland and immaculate as a shepherd out of Propertius, a wreath of flowers crowning his head.

But why from among all available divinities has he chosen Pomona, one of the most unobtrusive of all, in the course of the ages hardly ever represented elsewhere than in allegories? According to tradition, Pomona was the nymph who watched over fruit trees. On a par with Flora, to her service only a minor priest was appointed, for, they used to say, "the fruits of trees are the least voluminous of bounties." In *The Metamorphoses* Ovid presents her as beloved by Vertumnus and becoming his wife. Now, also a fruit deity, Vertumnus is also associated with the cycle of the seasons and the fertility of the soil. In the ancient calendars Flora had her festival, but not Pomona; while it is true that beside the road to Ostia there does exist a sacred wood called the Pomonal, there is no mention anywhere of "Pomonalias." It has been conjectured, and it seems likely, that the worship of Pomona coincided not with any fixed date, but was season-long, keeping pace with the ripening of crops.

All things considered, Pomona's role was so perfectly obvious, so natural that the annals finally did not have much to say in her regard. It was probably owing to these very qualities that she claimed Marino's attention, and because, too, of the season and the fertility rites she was connected with. I shall have occasion, when I come to the horses and riders, to go farther into the mythical aspect of Marino's statuary; but with the *Pomonas* we already notice that which renders his art exceptional in our time. It is as though by way of vision he possessed some lighthouse's far-darting beam, able all at once to seize the reality that is most immediately near and to pierce to the remotest origins in the heart of the night.

These *Pomonas* of Marino, sometimes swelling at the hips like wine-jars, sometimes lithe and slender, things almost of air: might one not imagine them posted at the edge of some orchard, goatherds dreaming at their feet under the starry sky of Latium? They secrete the plenitude of the fruit trees they protect, and may be massive, like sleep, or else in a state of alertness, nigh to trembling on the crest of the heart's delight. It is woman in her eternal youth Marino incarnates in these successive images. One of his commentators—Pica—has contended that there is no sensuality here, and he is wrong; but it is a ritualized sensuality. Exalted in these figures is not the flesh for the flesh's sake, but the tension of forms roused by the caress and love and caught in their hieratic richness. Pica seems to contradict his first assertion when, a little later on, he observes—very correctly, to my mind—that "In all these images"—the *Pomonas*—"femininity is pervaded by all its most remote, most indwelling, most mysterious meanings: as a kind of ineluctable necessity, an unalterable fixedness, primitive and mindless fecundity." To this I would add that woman as sensed, apprehended, conceived of by Marino in his *Pomonas* appears to me beheld in her freedom, in the eternal role that Michelet spoke of when he described her as the mediator between the rational and the sentient.

1940

1944. *Small Pomona*. Polychrome plaster. H. 23⅝ in: (CS. No. 175).

1949. *Pomona, Composition.* Oil on canvas. 63×39³/₈ in: (IP. No. 66).

1946. *Small Seated Pomona.* Bronze. H. 17³/₈ in: (CS. No. 213).

1947. *Pomona*. Bronze.
65¾×17¾×20½ in: (CS. No. 220).

1947. *Pomona.* Detail. (CS. No. 220a).

49. *Pomona*. Bronze.
H. 66¹/₈ in:
(CS. No. 247).

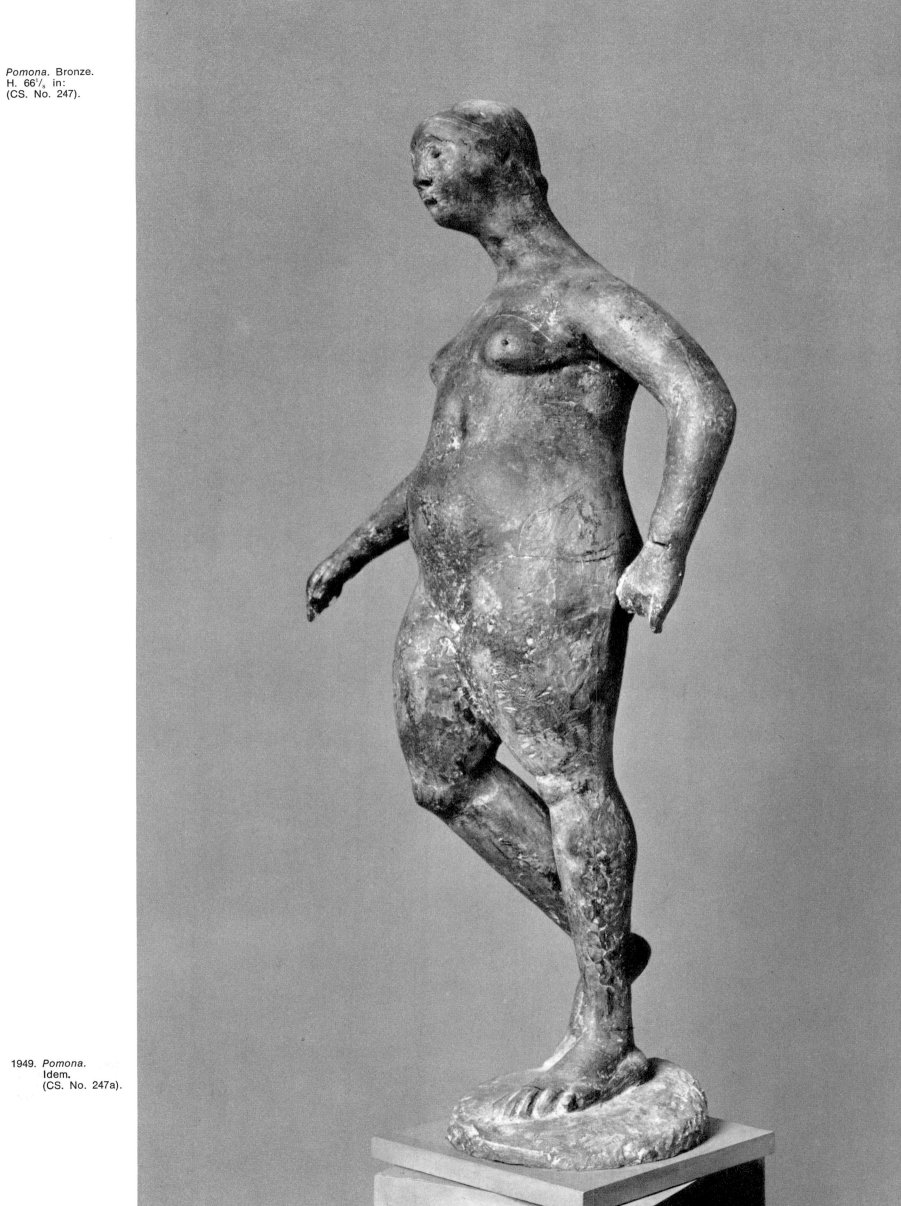

1949. *Pomona*.
Idem.
(CS. No. 247a).

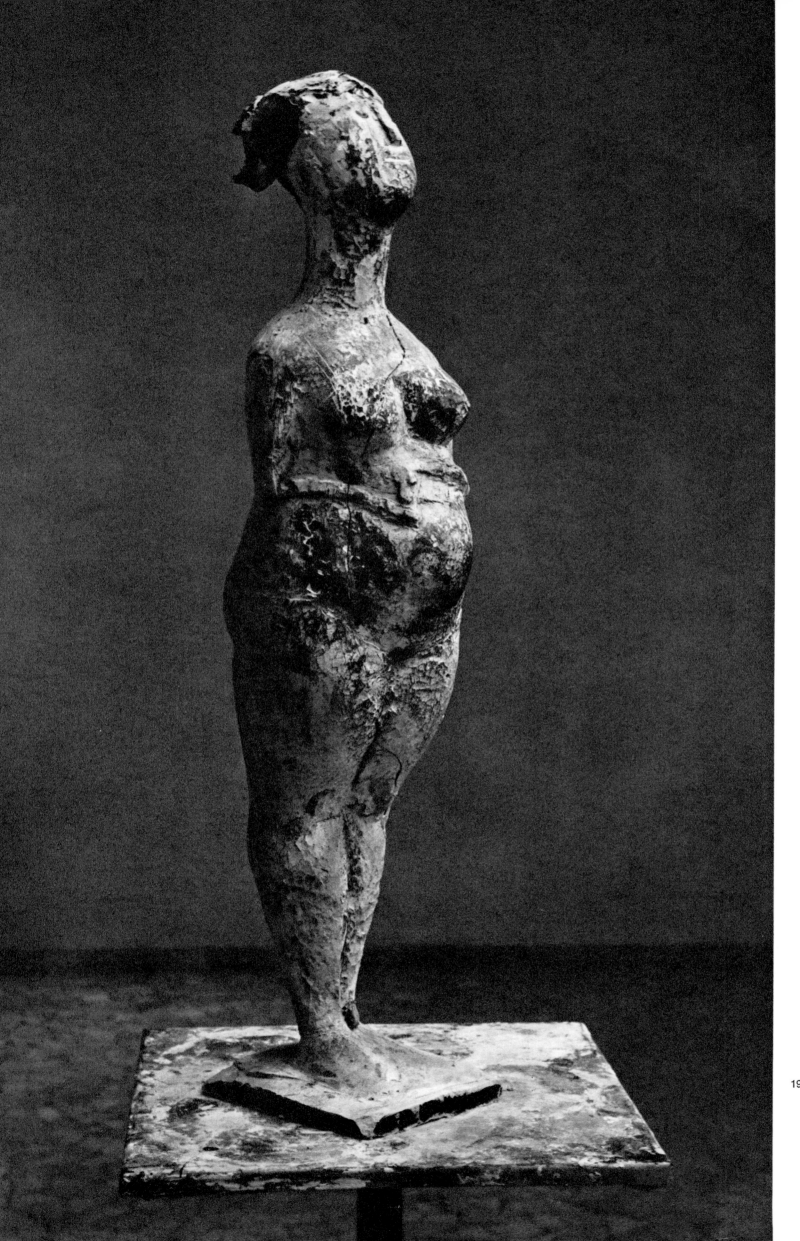

1949. *Small Pomona.*
Study. Bronze.
H. 18⁷/₈ in:
(CS. No. 248).

1950. *Small Pomona.*
Bronze.
H. 5¹/₂ in:
(CS. No. 256).

1948

1957. *The Carriage Builder's Daughters*. Oil on canvas. 59×59 in: (IP. No. 260).

1959. *Three Figures*. Oil on canvas. 59×47¼ in: (IP. No. 283).

1969

DANCERS AND JUGGLERS

In Marino's achievement, the ensemble constituted by his male and female dancers and his jugglers confirms what I noted elsewhere concerning his ability to perceive and to bring to light the very ancient movements by which man attuned his inward self to the universal pulse. From time immemorial the dance and displays of jugglery have been associated with celebrations, with festivals, that is to say with sanctified, exceptional interludes in the ordinary course of affairs. During this time of holiday, Dionysiac moments of collective frenzy or trance aside, the ritual dancing is note-worthy for its methodical deliberateness and the cosmogonic message in its slow unfolding, which seems to retrace the motions of stars and constellations. Whence the very special feeling that comes over us when we watch dancing, a feeling Paul Valéry finely described as "A state which cannot last long, which removes us *outside of* or *far from* ourselves, and where the *unstable* nevertheless

1945

sustains us, while the *stable* figures there only through accident, affording us the idea of another existence altogether capable of the rarest movements in our own, wholly composed of the *values that ultimately limit* our faculties." The same author reminds us that the dance is the art of *voluntary* human movements, and that "it consists in ordering or in organizing our dissipative movements."

It is this very essence of dance that Marino has grasped so well and expressed so masterfully in his often polychromed statues and statuettes whose freedom of execution and naturalness may perhaps be without equivalent save in the little Etruscan bronzes. Futurism, like the earliest cinematography, sought to translate movement by plotting the succession of forms described by a traveling figure: a walking, running or otherwise moving body. Thus were born, the same year and heeding the same imperatives, the *Unique Forms of Continuity in Space* of Boccioni and Marcel Duchamp's *Nu descendant un escalier,* both key achievements of the modern intelligence but which, through their very completeness, seem to rule out any further advance in the same direction. Taking quite the opposite one, Marino, when he presents a dancer or a juggler, stresses not so much the movement itself as the *tension* which renders it possible. The dancer is shown to us, not in repose, for such a thing does not exist in the sphere of dance, but in a state of *suspense,* in that instant of straining stillness where action either emerges or else expires. "State of transition and almost of violence," are Valéry's words for this interval of immobility in dance. It is with an extraordinary economy of means that Marino suggests the effort underlying the dancer's movement: here a faintly bracing leg, there an arm lifting, in another place a foot poised vertically on its tip. Compare if you

134

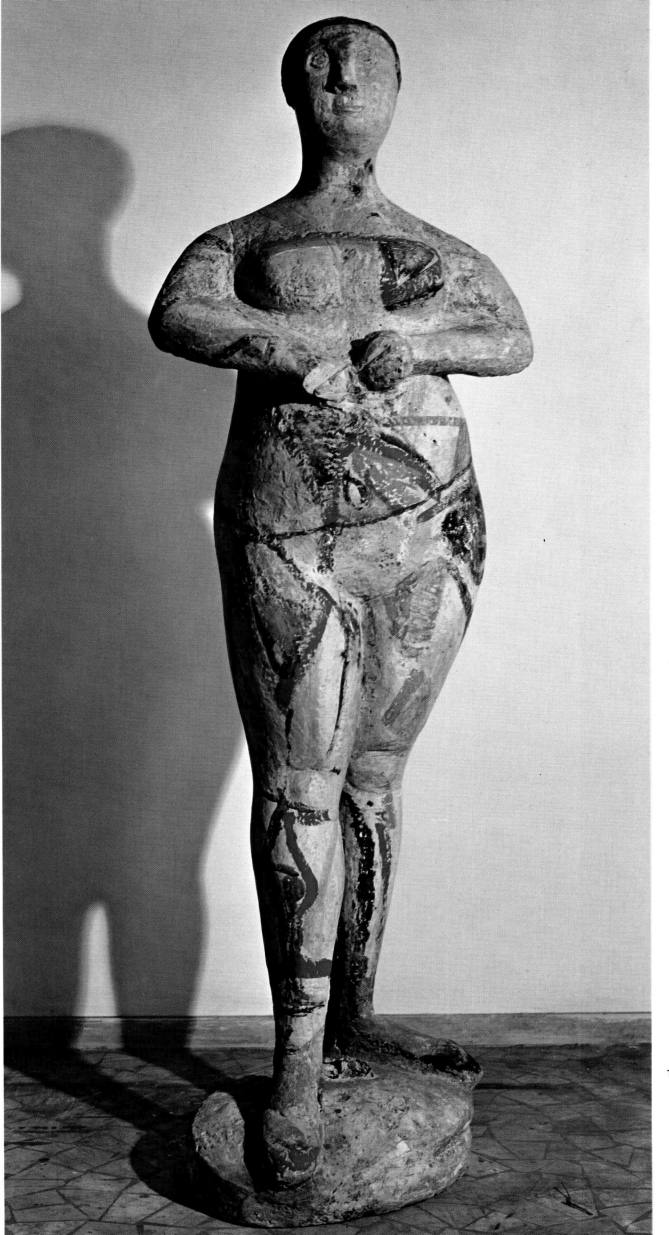

1949. *Dancer.*
Polychrome plaster.
H. 69¼ in:
(CS. No. 242).

1954. *Dancer*. Polychrome plaster. H. 55⁷/₈ in:(CS. No. 322a).

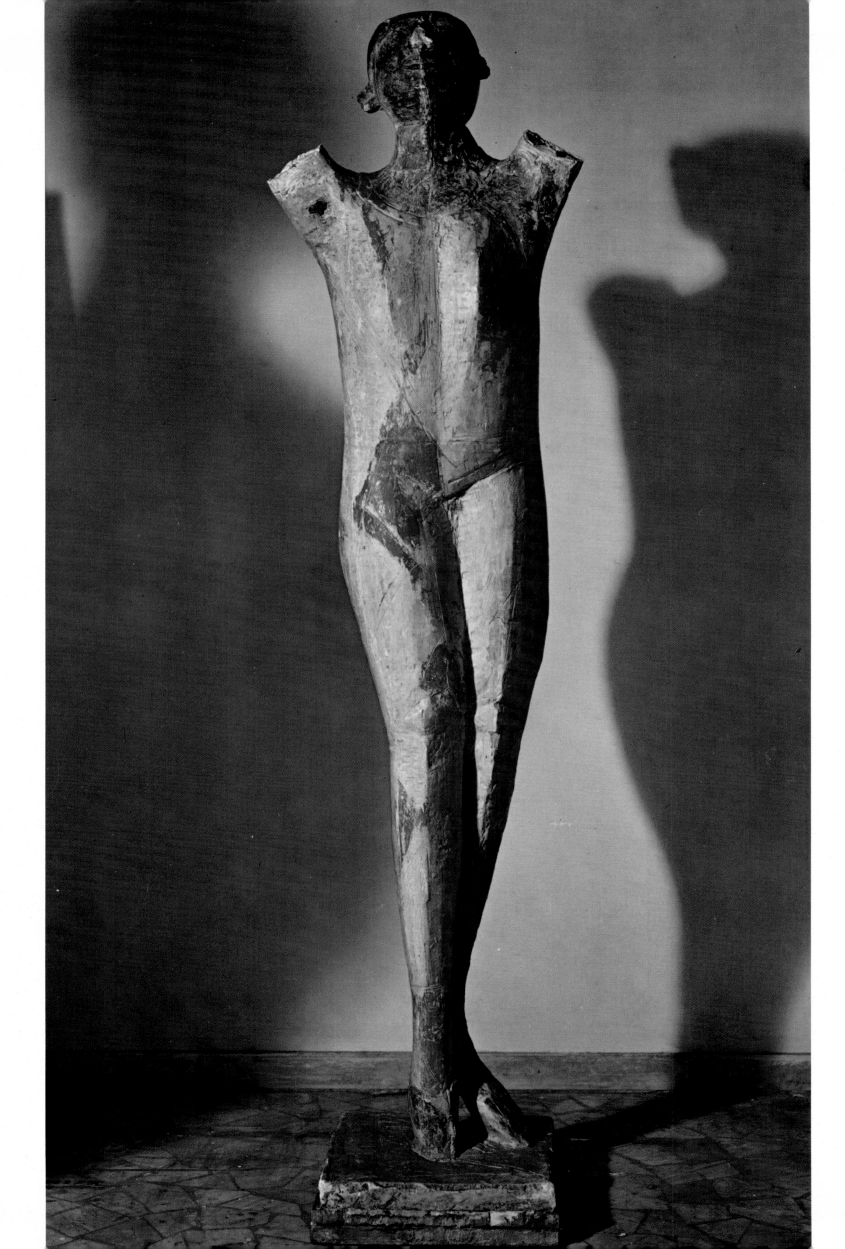

will the *Dancers* and the *Pomonas:* the drifting abandon of the latter, their somewhat heavy passivity stands in utter contrast to the extreme vibrancy of the former, bent upon escape from all the restraints of weight.

What has just been said with respect to the dance applies as well to jugglery and, in a general manner, to all the arts that bring equilibristic skills into play: tightrope walking, acrobatics and the rest. The Codonas and their trapezes, Colléano and his high wire, Enrico Rastelli with his spheres and cylinders, Rich Hays with his white golf-balls, all those breathtaking performers knew how to impart to their bodies the majesty of celestial rhythm. Marino went to watch them, as he watched humbler jugglers, itinerants and at fairs, in whom he recognized the descendants of the officiants at the ancient pagan festivals. If he presents them in the nude, it is in order that nothing localize in time the gesture or the stance, whose immutable character comes through so strongly here.

What with his willowy figure and a facial expression where innocence and a roguish know-ingness are curiously blended, Marino himself has something of the look of a juggler in whom there might also be a little of the magician. The fierce attention a feat of jugglery demands, the strictness governing each gesture, the control needed in handling the objects kept continually in the air... a parallel comes to mind: must not the sculptor be equally attentive, must he not deploy his faculties with equal adroitness and precision in order, within such a complex whole, to isolate the chosen attitude? Slower in its cadence and sustained over a longer period of time, sculpture is also a series of connected operations in which hand and mind work in shifts and together. A superior kind of jugglery, when all is said and done.

1953. *Dancer*. Polychrome plaster. H. 70 in: (CS. No. 302c).

1951

1945. *Dancer.* Bronze.
H. about 57 in:
(CS. No. 194).

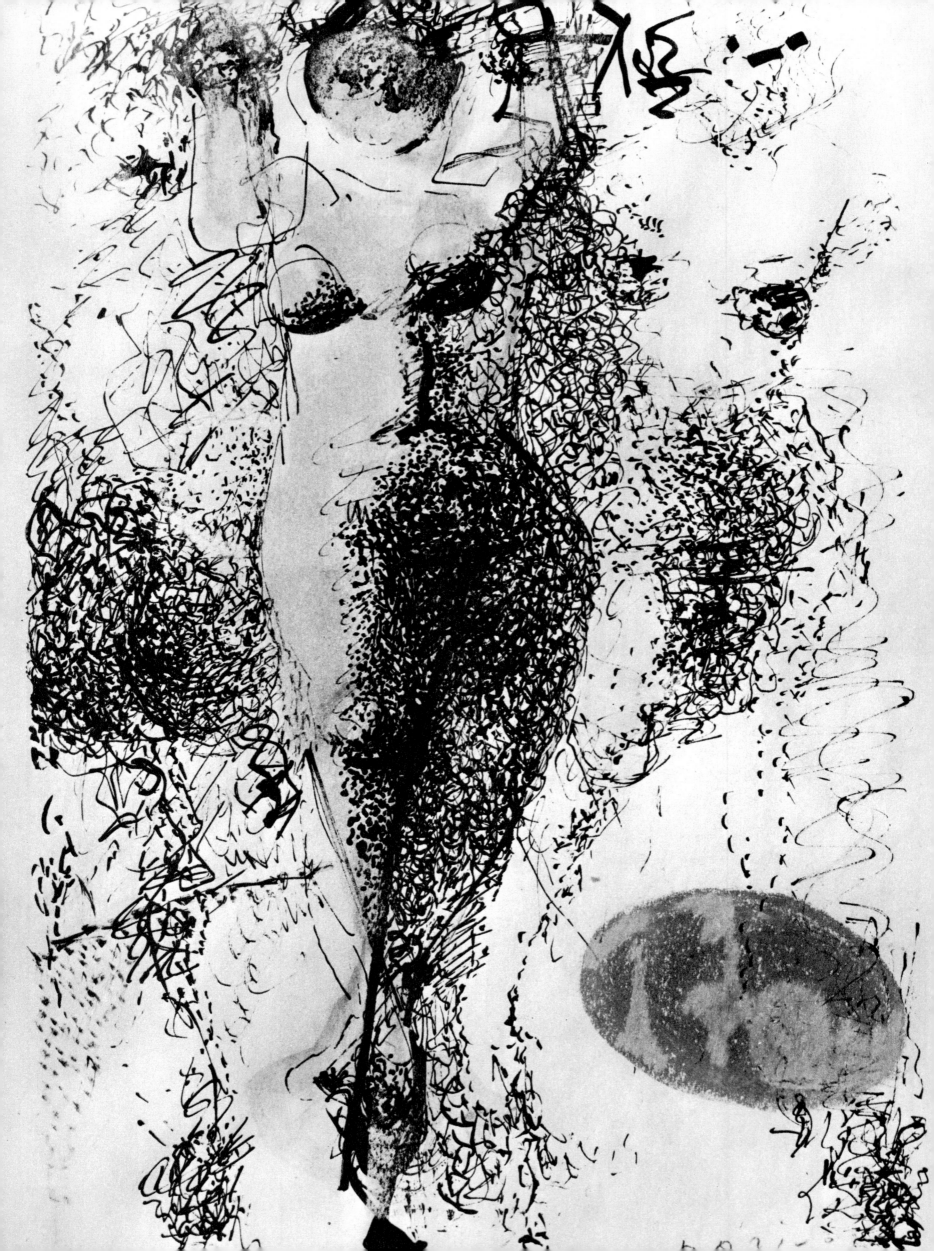

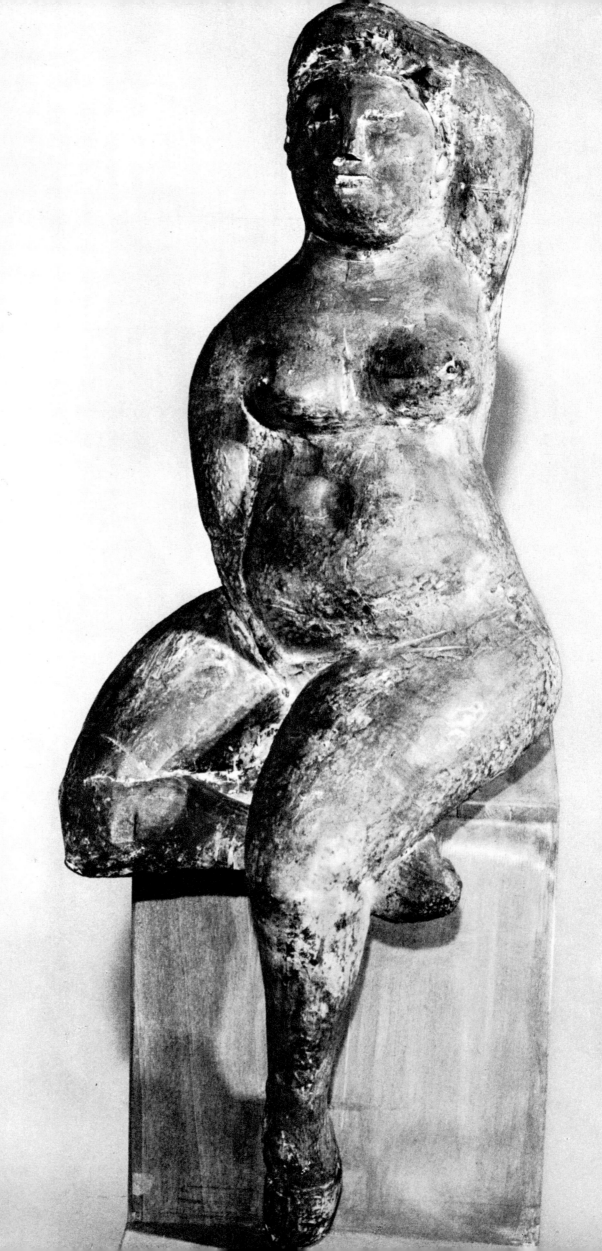

1949. *Dancer*. Bronze.
    H. 46 in:
      (CS. No. 243).

1952-1953. *Dancer.*
Bronze. H. 61 in: (CS. No. 297).

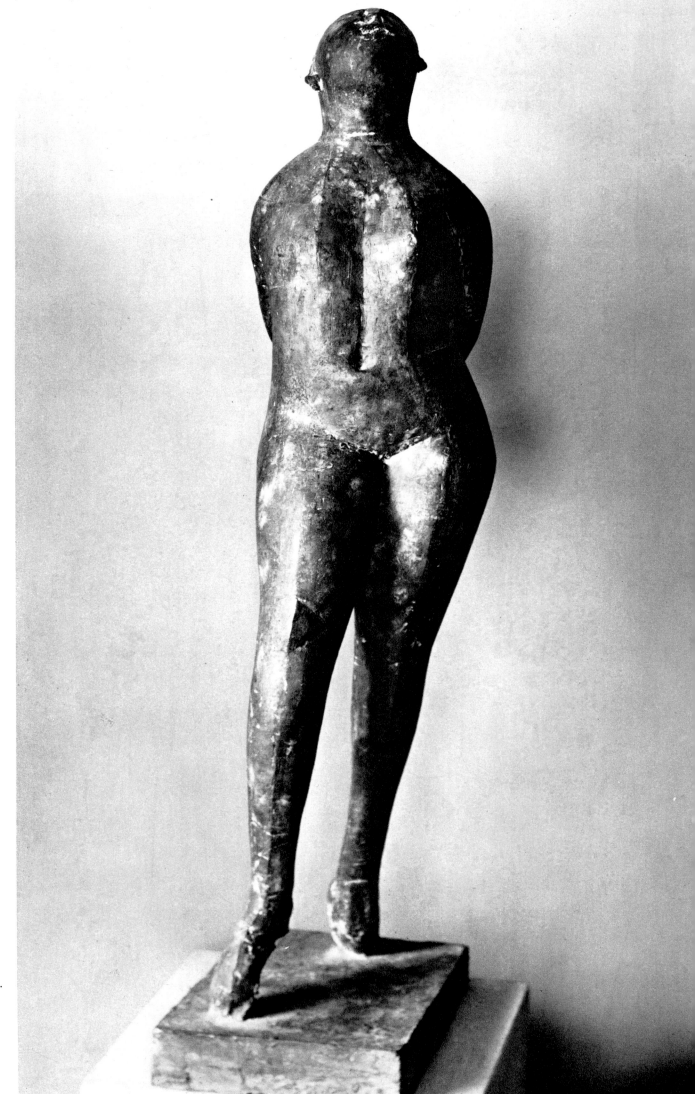

1952-1953. *Dancer*. Idem. (CS. No. 297a).

1953. *Dancer*. Details. Bronze. H. 70 in: (CS. Nos. 302a, 302b).

1953. *Dancer*. Bronze.
61×12⅝×13¾ in: (CS. (CS. No. 298).

1953. *Dancer*. Polychrome plaster. 61×12$^{5}/_{8}$×13$^{3}/_{4}$ in: (CS. 298a).

1959. *Dancer.* Oil on canvas. 59×47¼ in: (IP. No. 284).

1940. *Small Juggler.* Plaster. H. 11 in: (CS. No. 103).

1940. *Juggler.* Bronze. 26×16¹/₈×31¹/₈ in: (CS. No. 104).

1940. *Juggler*. Idem. (CS. No. 104a).

1951. *Juggler.* Bronze. H. 63 in: (CS. No. 270).

1953. *Juggler.* Tempera on paper. 24×16¹/₂ in: (IP. No. 169).

Jugglers on the Mantlepiece (From left to right: CS. No. 308, 320, 304, 309, 341, 306, 300, 305, 307).

1959. *Small Juggler.* Bronze. H. 23⅝ in: (CS. No. 352).

1953. *Small Juggler in Polychrome.* Bronze. H. 18⅞ in: (CS. No. 300).

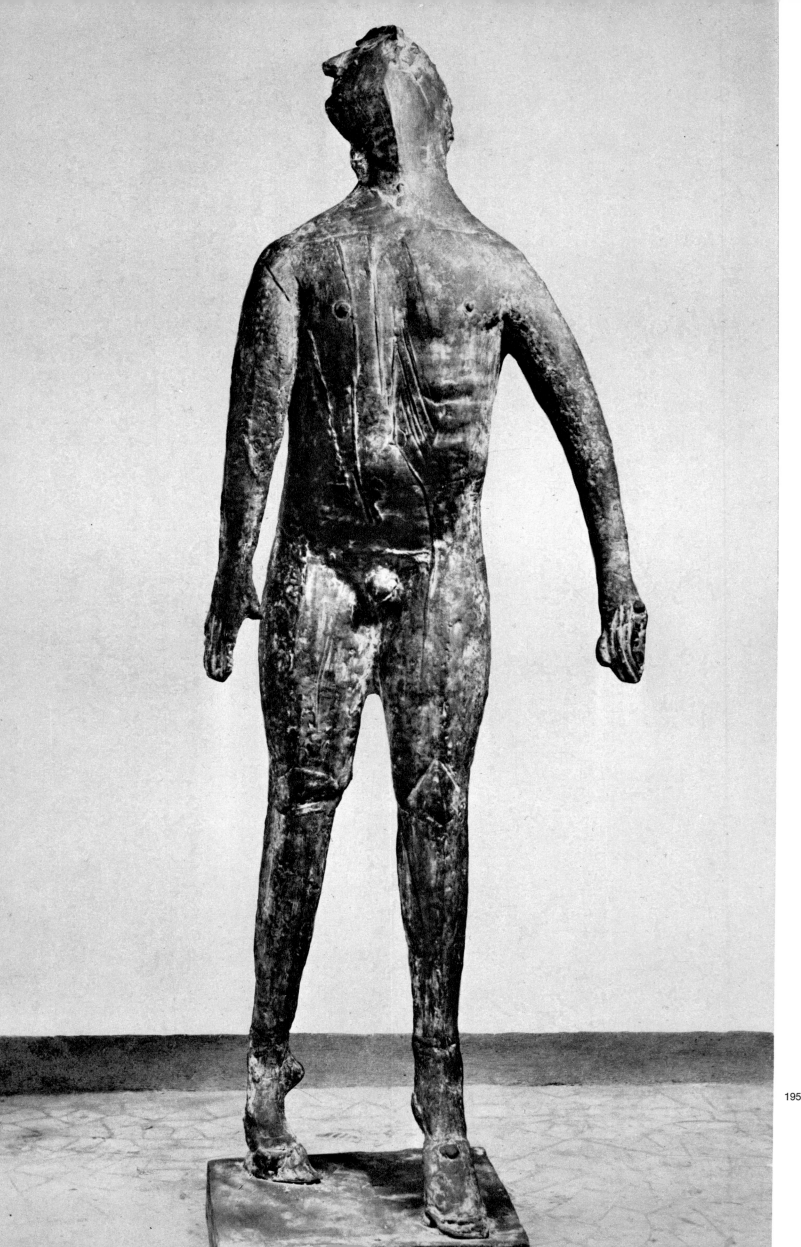

1954. *Juggler*. Bronze.
H. 66¹/₈ in:
(CS. No. 318).

54. *Juggler.* Polychr. plaster.
$66^1/_8 \times 16^5/_8 \times 16^5/_8$ in:
(CS. No. 318a).

1946. *Juggler*. Bronze.
H. 72 in: (CS. No. 214).

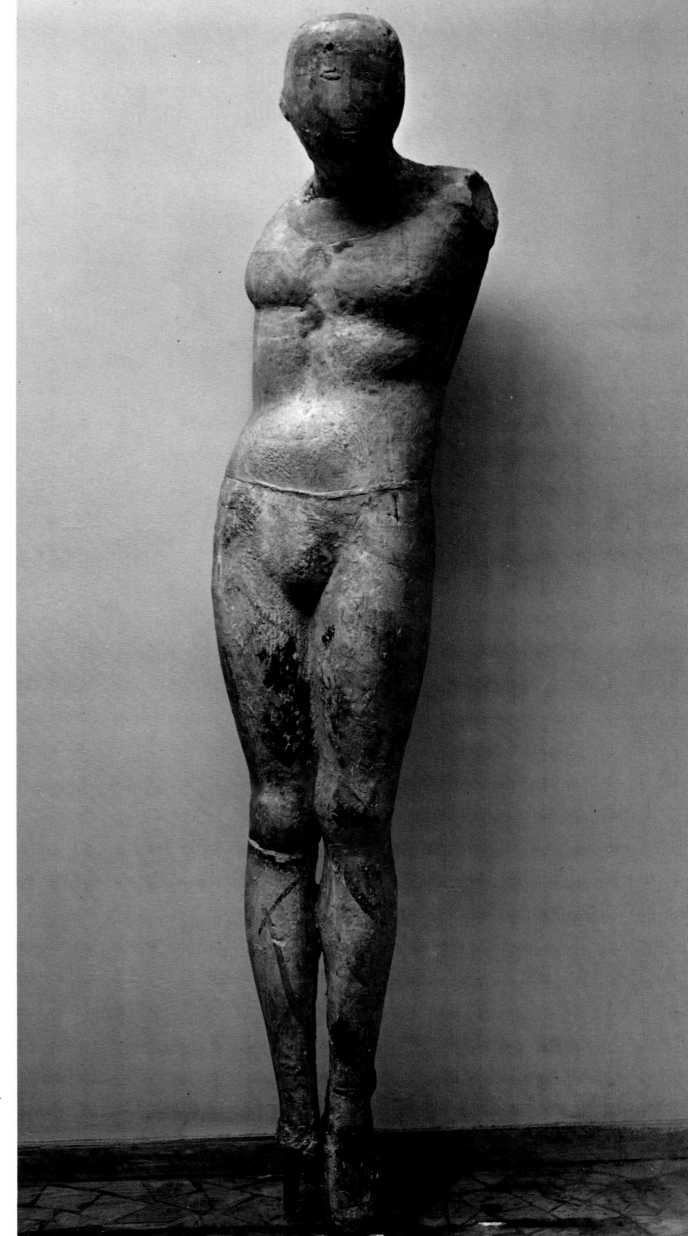

1946. *Juggler*. Polychrome plaster.
H. 72 in: (CS. No 214a).

1957. *Presentation of Jugglers*. Oil. 59×47⅝ in: (IP. No. 261).

MALIVO

1951

1949

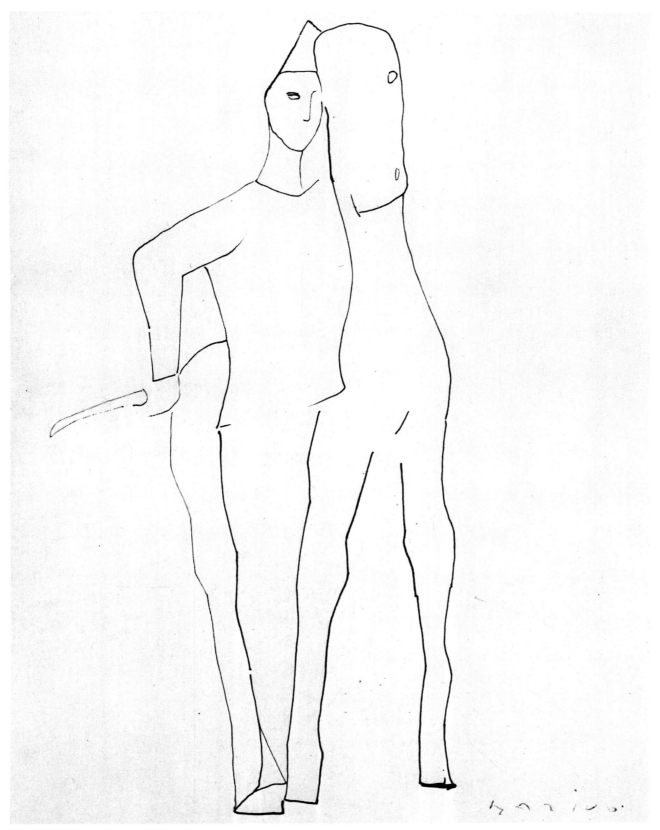

1948

1958. *Juggler*. Oil on canvas. 59×47¹/₄ in: (IP. No. 271).

1952. *Horse and Riders*. Gouache. 36×24 in: (IP. No. 133).

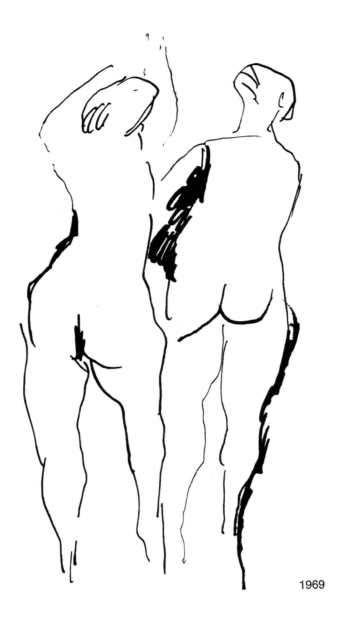

1969

LIMELIGHT

The jugglers and dancers discussed in the preceding chapter have obvious associations with the theater. The place they occupy in Marino's work invites to an examination of the latter from a new viewpoint, in terms of the theatrical world itself.

The domain of the sacred is in the most serious sense a theatrical domain; manifestations of the sacred are bound up with the spectacular. Ceremonies, rites, liturgy, all the gestures and panto-mime enacted in the course of religious solemnities aim at *representing* an ideal order whose special rhythm lies outside the everyday and the ordinary.

In another sense, the profane world, too, may be conceived as a theater, where the effects and themes include illusion, fickle passion, deceiving appearance, the fragility of the instant and dread before oncoming death. Thus was it beheld by the Baroque imagination, which placed itself under

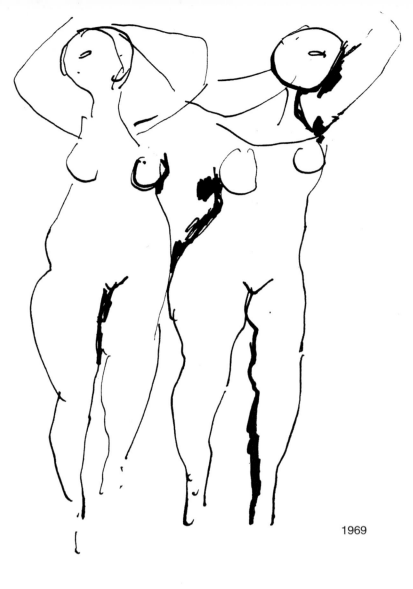

1969

the sign of Circe, queen of metamorphoses, and of Proteus, prince of shifting forms. And thus did Bernini, Borromini or Balthazar Neumann strive to impart to stone or bronze the evanescence of flame, the fugitiveness of wind-flung draperies and of scudding clouds, thus also did they try to fix the human countenance swept by the extremes of suffering or of ecstasy.

Marino's very different aim has been, above all, to transcribe inward movement. He usually bars all apparent dramatization from his figures, and these are shown to us at rest: but it is the rest which is prelude to the leap. Beyond the jugglers and dancers, there are numerous references to the theater to be found in his work, notably in his paintings. *Figurants, Living Theater, Masques,* such titles, which identify works scattered over the course of a great many years, point to a lasting concern. Even as they exist today, and however profoundly detached from their origins they may now be, are not the Theater, the Dance, the Circus the last vestiges of an organic sacred world in which men and the cosmos were once joined in a communion regulated by the rhythm of the seasons and the stars?

Not perhaps in any other aspect of his work is Marino's Etruscan affiliation quite so manifest. Nothing in its nature differs his *Theater* from the theater of the dead that the tombs at Tarquinia or other Etruscan sanctuaries disclose to us. In the unforgettable frescoes the ancient Tuscans left behind, one encounters no suggestion either of distress at the approach of death or of death's terrors. The afterlife depicted there is life such as it could be imagined if lived in this world, at the peak of its equilibrium and harmony. A profound feeling of naturalness animates it, as does a broad, un-failing sympathy with beings and things. Marino is incontestably one of the purest heirs of this direct interpretation of the world. In what he has wrought, there is the same fusion of the familiar and the solemn, the same wedding of naïvely perceived forms within architectonic complexity, the same juxtaposition of hieratic enigma and of the innocent thrust of buoyant life.

Dancers, jugglers, persons of the stage, masqueraders, the whole of Marino's theater sings the nostalgia of a free world where sin is a thing unknown.

170

1951. *The Meeting.*
Oil on canvas.
79$\frac{1}{2}$×47$\frac{5}{8}$ in:
(IP. No. 105).
*Marino Marini
reworked this
painting in 1966.*

1954. *Jugglers*. Oil on canvas. 59×47¹/₄ in: (IP. No. 197).

1951. *The Dream*. Tempera. 59×47¹/₄ in: (IP. No. 106). *Marino Marini reworked this painting in 1966.*

1952. *A Vision*. Tempera. 59×47¼ in: (IP. No. 137). *Marino Marini reworked this painting in 1966.*

1953. *Spectacle.* Oil on canvas. 39⁷/₈×31⁷/₈ in: (IP. No. 177). *Marino Marini reworked this painting in 1966.*

1952. *Performers.* Oil on canvas. 59×47¹/₄ in: (IP. No. 138). *Marino Marini reworked this painting in 1966.*

1959-1960. *Living Theater.* Oil on canvas. 59×59 in: (IP. No. 287).

1956. *Theater with Masked Figures*. Oil on canvas. 78³/₄×94¹/₂ in: (IP. No. 246).

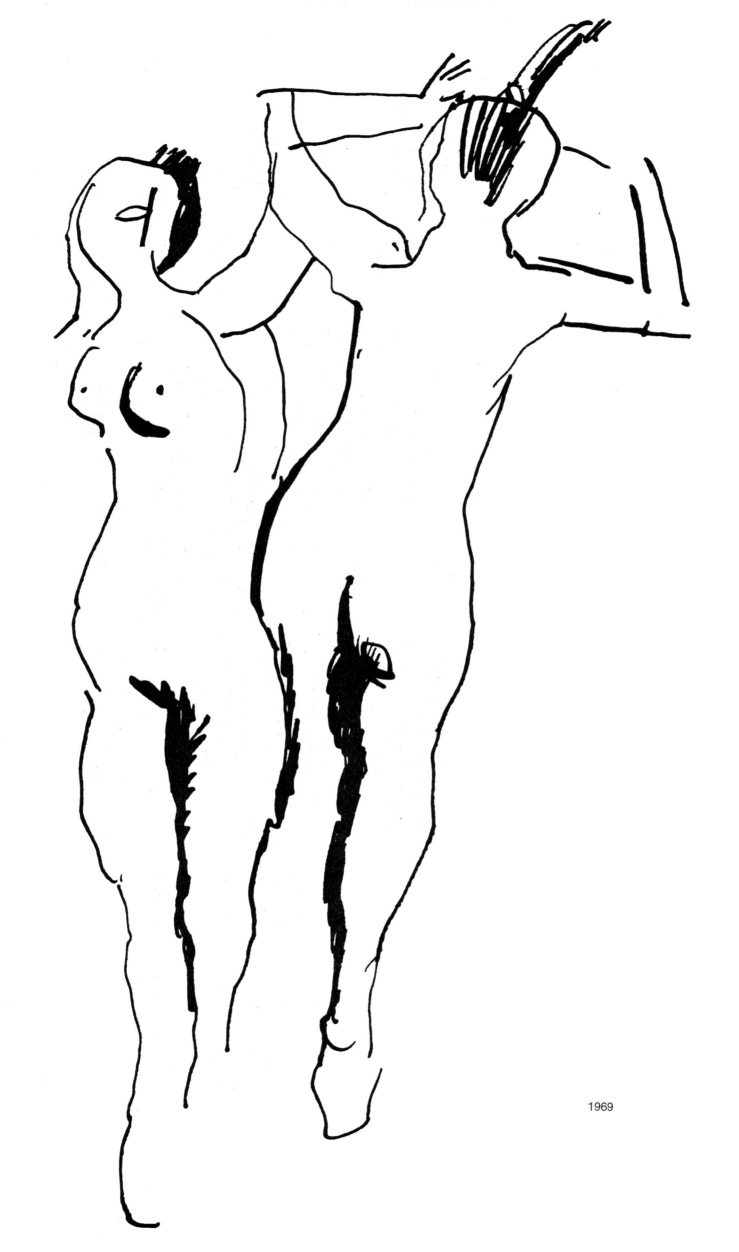

1969

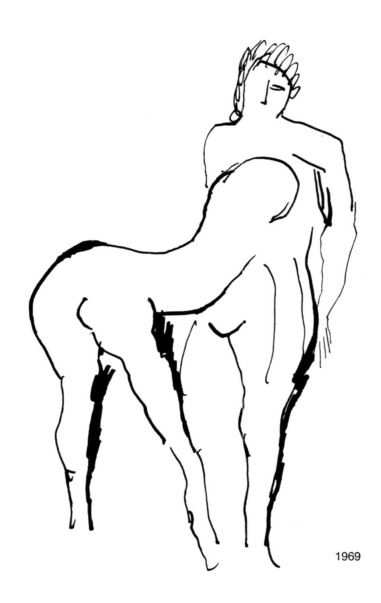

1969

1955

HORSES AND RIDERS

The fact that at one point in his life, as his biographers have noted, Marino chanced to occupy a studio adjoining a riding academy is hardly a very adequate explanation for the monumental importance that horses and horsemen assume in his work. In an interest so constantly and powerfully expressed, I for one would be tempted to see the mark of a predestination seconded by an intuitive understanding of the significance which, since earliest times, has been assigned to the horse and to the symbols connected with it. A consideration of its deployment in Marino's work makes it plain that his approach to this theme differs radically from that of the artists who preceded him. If a past reference suggests itself now and then, it is because there is an eternity of forms and of rhythms; but any such reminder, only fragmentary, is belied at once by the succession of movements and poses, pure Marino through their animation. Nothing here which recalls the equestrian statues

1946

glorifying the personality of a prince or conqueror, nothing either of the elegant courser that captivated a Stubbs, a Géricault, a Degas; with Marino the horse recovers its mythic sense.

From the most ancient times men have associated the horse with the sun and the waters. Diodorus Siculus tells us that the Centaurs were born of Nephele, whose name means cloud. The Dioscuri, we know, were allowed a solar origin: one of them, the red horseman, is in correspondence with the rising sun; the other, the white horseman, with the silvery moon, considered the night-time aspect of the sun. Whenever the horse figures in ritual ceremonies, its function is to assure the fertility of the entire population. It is everywhere the symbol of creation, of inspiration, of movement. Pegasus brings Zeus the thunderbolt, daughter of the clouds. The horse may also be earth, daughter of the sun and the waters: in the grotto at Phigalia stands the mysterious statue of Demeter, its body that of a superb woman surmounted by a mare's head whence flows a river-like mane.

This digression does not lead us away from the subject of Marino's sculpture; quite the contrary, it should help us to penetrate its meaning. Some instinctive clairvoyance enabled Marino to rediscover the mythic association of horse, sun and waters. Remarkable by dint of its well-founded-ness and stability, of the perfection of its balance and the powerful harmony of its curves, Marino's horse divested of its particular determinations, is given to us in its *fullness.* Before it, the words that come to our lips are the very ones Lawrence exclaimed in the painted tombs of Tarquinia: "These archaic horses are so perfectly satisfying *as* horses!"

The very first thing, then, is this ontological consciousness that confers its spiritual dimension upon Marino's horse. But one is struck as well by the perspicacity in the artist who, from beyond the mists of time, has singled out and recaptured the symbol in which the horse was bound up with procreation. The animal's outstretched head continuing the neck, sometimes lying level with its back, the whole tracing one stiff line modified by a barely perceptible camber—that was there for anyone to notice and to reproduce. Little stylization is involved here; it is not uncommon to see

182

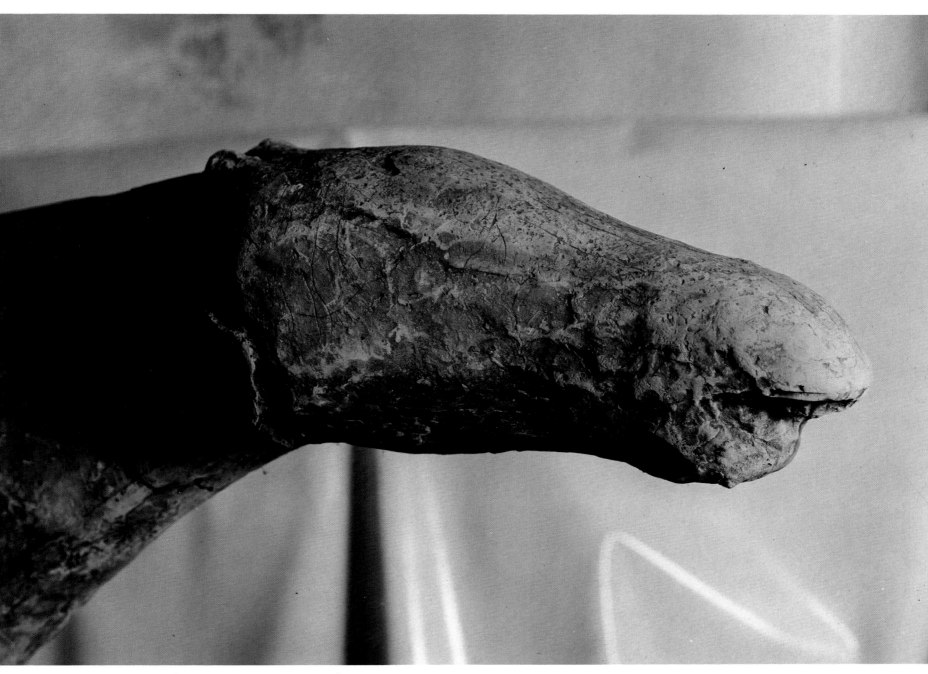

1947. *Head of a Horse.* Detail in cement. L. 19³/₄ in: (CS. No. 229c).

1952. *Red Horse*. Oil on canvas. $78^{3}/_{4} \times 55^{1}/_{8}$ in: (IP. No. 134).

1956. *Idea for the Rider.* Polychrome wood. 77³/₄×36¹/₈×55³/₄ in: (CS No. 332).

1952. *Horse and Rider.* Oil on canvas. 39³/₄×39³/₄ in: (IP. No. 135).

an either harnessed or grazing horse snort in just this way, head stretched forth, ears flattened, from quivering lip to withers a single mass of muscle and tendon, so far simplified in shape as to resemble a projectile. But, from one subject to another, we see Marino, breaking that horizontal, lift that head and neck—and it becomes suddenly clear: the upstraining head and neck of the horse seem to turn into a phallus, a phallus belonging to the rider, himself wonderstruck by this miracle. In passing, we may remark that the phallic notation is not always absent in the rider himself, as in the case of the Venice piece.

I am not convinced that this meaning of the upraised head was, on Marino's part, intentional at the beginning, even if it became obvious in the completed works. In view of the artist's temperament, one might be more correct in saying that he was motivated—*acted upon*—by instinctive forces at work within him. I have already spoken of the spontaneity, the immediacy distinguishing Marino's rapport with the visible world around him. It is as if, in response to an impulse, he has renewed the ancient pact which used once to link Nature and humankind. Previously, he had reactualized the goddess Pomona; to the horse he now restores its ancient significance as a fertilizing force. The rider—naked, plump, unseeing, witless, arms outflung or upraised, wobbling ever more precariously— is the man of today, signifying the opposite. Moreover, horse and rider are soon to undergo progressive emaciation and to become increasingly dramatized, the final collapse coinciding with an extraordinary dereliction of forms. "When," to quote Marino's own words, "you consider one by one my equestrian statues of these past twelve years, you will notice each time that the horseman is incapable of managing his mount, and that the animal, in its restlessness ever more riderless, comes more and more to a rigid standstill instead of rearing. I believe in the most serious way that we are heading toward the end of a world."

1941

1955

1953. *Large Rider*. Polychrome plaster. 83³/₄×81⁵/₈ in: (CS. No. 301).

1949-1951. *Rider.* Polychrome wood. 42⁷/₈×70³/₄ in: (CS. No. 249).

937. *Gentleman on Horseback.* Bronze. H. 61⅜ in: (CS. No. 80).

1945. *Rider.* Polychrome bronze. H. 40⅜ in: (CS. No. 209).

1945. *Horse.* Plaster. 18^1/$_8$×11^3/$_4$ in: (CS. No. 208).

1947. *Horse.* Bronze. H. about 39³/₈ in: (CS. No. 228).

1947. *Rider.* Wood. H. 63³/₄ in: (CS. No. 229).

1947. *Rider*. Detail. (CS. No. 229a).

1947. *Rider.* Bronze. 40⁵/₈×24³/₄ in: (CS. No. 230).

1954. *Resurrection*. Oil on canvas. $43\frac{1}{4} \times 31\frac{1}{2}$ in: (IP. No. 198).

1948. *Rider.* Bronze. 44⅞×48¾ in: (CS. No. 238).

955. *Blue Rider.* Oil on canvas. 55⅛×33¾ in: (IP No. 227).

1947. *Rider.* Detail. Polychrome plaster. H. 40$^{1}/_{8}$ in: (CS. No. 231).

1953. *Large Rider.* Polychrome wood. 83³/₄×81⁵/₈ in: (CS. No. 301a).

1950. *Small Rider*. Bronze. 11×16¹/₂ in: (CS. No. 267).

1936. *Rider.* Bronze. 63×80⁹/₄ in: (CS. No. 64).

1951. *Rider.* Bronze. H. about 45¹/₄ in: (CS. No. 287).

1951. *Rider*. Detail. (CS. No. 287a).

49. *The Town's Guardian Angel.* Bronze. H. 70³/₄ in: (CS. No. 250a).

1949. *Rider* (*The Town's Guardian Angel*). Polychrome wood. H. 70³/₄ in: (CS. No. 250).

1955. *Invocation.* Oil on canvas. 78³/₄×71 in: (IP. No. 228).

1951. *Horse.* Bronze. 90$^1/_2$×82$^5/_8$ in: (CS. No. 282).

1957-1958. *Equestrian Composition*. Bronze. H. 236 in: Monument at The Hague. (CS. No. 348).

1951. *Horse.* Study. Bronze. H. 12³/₄ in: (CS. No. 278).

1952. « *Gertrude* », *The Little Horse.* Bronze. H. 9³/₄ in: (CS. No. 292).

1956-1957. *Rider.* Bronze. 114$^1/_8$×70$^3/_4$ in: (CS. No. 345).

1956-1957. *Composition*. Bronze. 29$^7/_8$ × 50$^3/_4$ in: (CS. No. 346).

1951. *Marino Marini in his Workshop in Milan.* (Photo, Herbert List).

1960. *The Idea, Composition.* Tempera. Paper remounted on canvas. $39^3/_8 \times 28^3/_4$ in: (IP. No. 295

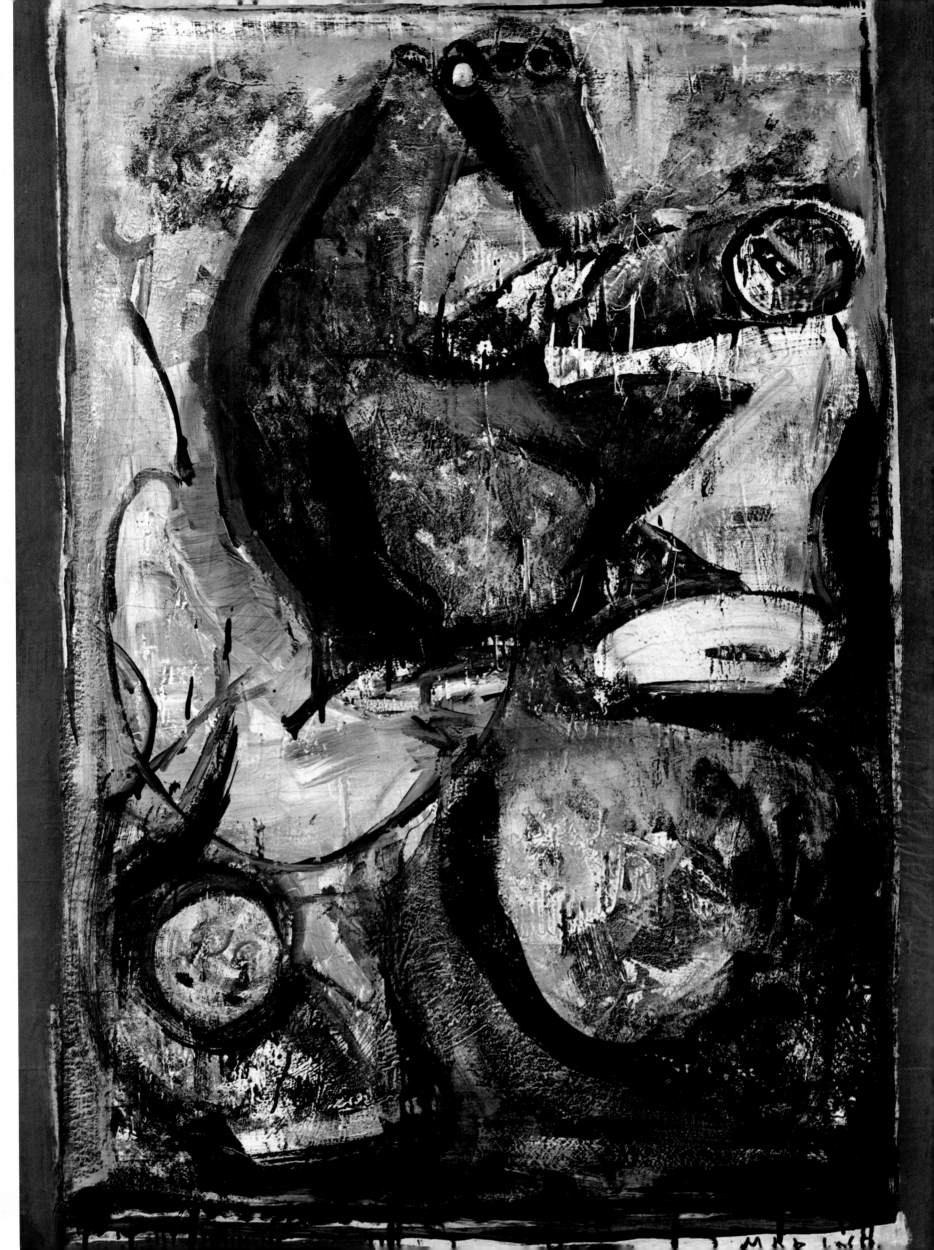

1958. *Idea for a Rider II*. Oil Paper remounted on canvas. 71×59 in: (IP. No. 272).

1950

THE PAINTER

By virtue of the considerable room it takes up in his overall achievement, Marino's painting calls for a separate discussion. While it is true, with him, that in the majority of instances painting and sculpture are interrelated, it would also appear that, chronologically, the painting tends almost always to come first. Reviewing the whole of the painted work, one notices everywhere the same cohabitation of ancient soul and modern tremor as in the sculpture, but finds a yet greater freedom of exploration. Very natural causes make for this difference. Sculpture, which is articulated in three-dimensional space, obeys laws of equilibrium which restrict forms to within certain limits. Upon a painted surface, on the other hand, there is nothing to prevent forms from breaking loose and defying any law. The primordial importance Marino awards to painting and his deep attachment to it are attested in his own words.

"For me," he has said, "to conceive of a form is to perceive a color—vision of color, ardor of

life, ardor of form. It's in colors I have looked for the point of departure for each idea which was to become a reality. Painting is to place oneself in the poetry of action; and action in coming about becomes true."

In a general way, all we have observed here with regard to Marino's sculpture, its connections with the Etruscan genius, the fusion it embodies of very ancient rhythms with an immediate feeling of the visible world, all these characteristic features of Marino's art recur in his painting, save only that the plastic imagination shows more in the forefront and more sharply here. Once again, this quickening of the dramatic which is perceptible in the painting may perhaps be ascribed to the added freedom this two-dimensional art allows. But I would rather tend to think that Marino has systematically used painting as a means for probing in new sculptural directions.

And so when one considers his most formally audacious sculptures—I have in mind the rider in the act of falling, his body leaning dangerously to the left while his right leg kicks in midair; or else the thread-like horse, held erect by its structural scheme alone— these are regularly preceded by one or several paintings in which it seems the artist has tried to evaluate the eventual risks of a sculptural transcription.

It is important to remember that Marino's first years at the Academy were devoted exclusively to painting and drawing. Hence, it is the fruit of considerable experience and of an already well advanced maturity that he puts before the public when he gives his first show of paintings. Those

222

1954. *Polychrome Trio*. Oil on canvas. 59×47¹/₄ in: (IP. No. 199).

1956. *Farce in the Theater*. Oil on canvas. 59×47¹/₄ in: (IP. No. 247).

1956. *Orpheus*. Oil on canvas. 96$^5/_8$×118 in: (IP. No. 248).

1957. *Representation in Blue*. Oil on canvas. 59×47$^1/_4$ in: (IP. No. 262)

1958. *Representation in Green*. Oil on canvas. 47$\frac{1}{4}$×39$\frac{3}{8}$ in: (IP. No. 273).

8. *Babylon.* Oil on canvas. 39³/₈×31¹/₂ in: (IP. No. 274).

1958. *Gleams of Light in the Forest.* Oil on canvas. 78⅜×71 in: (IP. No. 275).

1949

of the years 1929-1930, of a sensitive and vibrant classicism, radiate a natural charm that one is tempted to call unconscious, so much does it seem that their serene, self-assured beauty has been obtained without effort or hesitation.

The dramatizing of forms appears, however, in the couples and the trios—in for example the *Pomona* couples, after 1940—or in certain haunted, violent, impassioned compositions, such as the *Dream and Reality* of 1950. In connection with the later periods in Marino's work some have spoken of discordance and even of the decomposition of forms, pointing to the progressive shift from realistic figuration to a more abstract conception. For my part, I do not find any disparity between this or that moment in his work, which, to my eye, displays a remarkable homogeneity. And rather than abstraction, it is a stylizing of forms I notice, this stylization serving as vehicle to a new animation through which, into this hitherto calmly meditative work, Marino introduces inner restlessness and anxiety. It is to be noted, moreover, that this troubled mood is expressed in paintings well before it makes its way into the sculpture: the stricken riders were first tried out on canvas and in oils.

Like all the major sculptors, Marino is a draftsman—a draftsman even before being a painter—but what is remarkable in his case is the autonomy of the drawing and painting vis-à-vis the sculpture. Rodin, for instance, expresses himself in volumes when he draws, and it is fair to say that almost all his drawings are studies for sculptures. Marino's spontaneity, the instinctual character of his art have enabled him, to the contrary, to invest each of his means of expression with its own independent style. Thus, the drawn portraits, managed with admirable lightness of touch, stand

231

absolutely on their own and absolutely apart from the sculptured heads they pair with. Striking in these portraits of friends, of fellow-artists, of art-collectors, are the inward dimension of the likeness and, simultaneously, the keenness of the line, sure as the flight of a bird in the sky. They have that rare quality of seeming to owe nothing to technique, to skill, and this to the point where they can only be compared to poets' drawings, for example Baudelaire's of himself or else Verlaine's of Rimbaud in the streets of London.

The gift for apprehending the real is not by any means the commonest thing in today's art. It is certainly at the behest of something profound in him—at the behest, I am prepared to say, of faith—that Marino has cleaved to the figurative forms of representation. It would be absurd and highly unjust to put this down to fighting a rear-guard action, or from it to infer a refusal on his part to understand or to accept other modes of expression in art. To the contrary, Marino possesses an open-mindedness which has become rare, and it is evidenced in a statement such as this: "I make no distinction," he declares, "between abstract and figurative plastics, provided that in both cases these be authentically plastic. What counts is the quality of the work. As for me, a Mediterranean man, I cannot express myself freely otherwise than through figures. But I acknowledge and admire all other manners of self-expression." There is much modesty and nobleness in these words and they reveal at the same time Marino's acute awareness of his own situation and of the nature of his art in relation to current trends.

1941

1960. *The Fall of the Angel*. Oil on canvas. 47¹/₄ × 59 in: (IP. No. 301). *Marino Marini reworked this painting in 1967* (see p. 378).

1960. *Iberia*. Mixed media. 29$^{7}/_{8}$ × 22 in: (IP. No. 296).

1964. *Shooting.* Oil on canvas. 59×59 in: (IP. No. 309).

1963. *The Enchantment of the Dancers*. Oil on canvas. 78³/₄×71 in: (IP. No. 308).

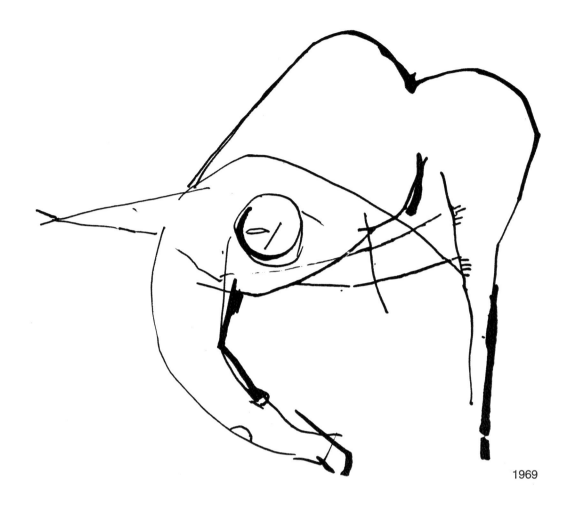

1969

THE MIRACLES

From about 1943, the title *Miracle* arose in Marino's work. But only eight years later did this idea give rise to exhilarating variations. In fact from 1956 onwards the question of continuity between the *Miracles* and the *Warriors* was not resolved: the subject is the same, it is still a question of the rider and his horse, and one may therefore wonder for what reason the artist deemed it necessary to relinquish one title for another. Their numerous similarities aside, a fundamental difference between the two sets does however exist and after a thoughtful examination of the works it may be defined. The difference lies, it seems to me, not in the forms and the structural concept, which can be clearly seen reaching back and forth between one subject and the other, but is to be looked for in the underlying nature of the inspiration. And so the very first thing would be to try to

1969

get at what Marino had in mind when, unconsciously, he developed from the *Miracle* to the *Warrior*.

I am aware here that I am venturing onto rather unsure ground and if I do, it is upon the strength of a few very sparing remarks Marino has made in connection with the *Miracles* and the meaning of that term. According to his words, which I summarize, each of the so designated works was conceived in a dazzling instant, each of them would have been, so to speak, revealed to him and would thereby have had the character of an inward and climactic *event*. Of this epiphany the ensuing sculpture may hence be considered as really nothing else than a material report.

The foregoing indicates a very special creative process, without any bearing upon the one standing back of the other works, but regarding which an initial comparison comes readily to mind. The "dazzling instant" Marino alludes to bears a striking resemblance to that "simple hallucination" Rimbaud would experience and which caused him to see "quite frankly a mosque instead of a factory, a class in drumming taught by angels; barouches rolling along skyways, a drawing room at the bottom of a lake; monsters, mysteries..." Just as for Rimbaud's vision, poetic illumination lies at the source of Marino's *Miracles*. To anyone objecting that the image Rimbaud proposes is engendered by an association—which might be qualified as convulsive—of two widely unlike realities, whereas Marino maintains the natural combination of horse and rider, it is not hard to find a reply. For indeed, the man-animal couple represented in the *Miracles* signifies not as a subject, but only as the stepping-stone to a *vision* inaccessible to any rational perception.

What I shall say about the *Warriors* and about the anxiety in which they are steeped implies a progressive intensifying of the artist's concern, a concern that heightened from one work to the next

240

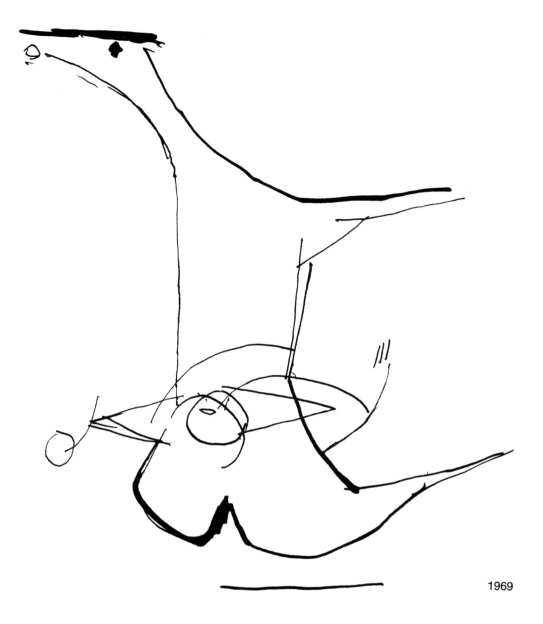

1969

and at last reached a degree of paroxysm, but which was in reaction to a pressure *coming from the outside:* it is, so he himself asserts, a conviction of impending doom, provoked by the general world situation, which had little by little unseated his riders and paralyzed his horses. With the *Miracles,* on the other hand—and once again we have his own words on the matter to go by—, it is an *inner experience,* intensely undergone, which has given rise to these images, convulsive like the others. And so my guess would be that in the Marinian "Passion" the *Warriors* and the *Miracles* correspond to two forms of inspiration, felt in opposite manners. The one, that of the *Warriors,* reflective, tends to the expression of despair, while the other, that of the *Miracles,* self-generating, fulgurant, comes under the sign of enthusiasm in the Dionysian sense of the word. Or, to frame this opposition in other terms, the *Warriors* tell of apprehension, of dread before ineluctable death: their form, their movement, their gravity suggest a sinking, a fall, a damnation; whereas the *Miracles* proclaim anguish surmounted, a joyous release, ascent.

I think Marino will forgive me if I return once again to Etruria. It seems to me that what he speaks of having experienced at the moment his *Miracles* were conceived is not without some imaginable link with certain magical enchantments the followers of Tages and of Vegoe may have known in the course of their rites. Etruscan religious practices in large measure revolved around haruspicy and "the fulgural art," that is to say divination by inspection of entrails and divination by lightning. With utmost care the officiants, haruspex or fulgurator, would, in the one case, study the structure and anomalies of the organ under examination, or, in the other, observe the lightning's path, its origin and the point where it struck; then, after these operations—which probably required certain preliminary exercises assuring the necessary state of receptiveness—there would occur the illumination enabling them to pronounce the augury. Everything in these soothsayers' practices was shaped by the expectation, the recognition and the veneration of the marvelous.

To my mind, it is his sense of the marvelous that makes Marino one of their kin, and in his *Miracles* above all. But here the phenomena are inverted: the divination takes place at the same moment the flash does, it is pronounced by the illumination through which the work is conceived, and it is finally the work itself which constitutes the marvelous. For the *Miracles* are prodigies, incontestably. They are prodigies, to begin with, because they exist, in all the *natural* strictness of their form and their growth; and also because they are *true,* as miracles ought to be.

What Franco Russoli wrote on the subject of the *Warriors* applies equally well to the *Miracles:* "...a thorough understanding and a perfect grasp of this sculpture is impossible if one disregards what is represented in this sculpture, if in appraising it one is guided alone by the pure and arid principles that are respectful of form. For example, the diagonal disposing of the bodies, the heads and limbs angling away from the fundamental directional line, these constitute a brilliant transcription, in plastic terms, of a *true* gesture; and from the keen observing of the true also derives the fantastic and expressive quality of transfiguration."

Depending upon the viewer's inspiration, this transfiguration may lead the mind's eye to see, in each *Miracle,* the most startling and wonderful apparitions. The "moving center" formed by the rider and his horse may suddenly become rocket, bird, strange denizen of the ocean's floor, fabulous prehistoric beast. (In it, I, for my part, saw the image of a forgotten god who, after a long sleep and terrible metamorphoses, rises, snorts fiercely, and demands the rendering of his due.)

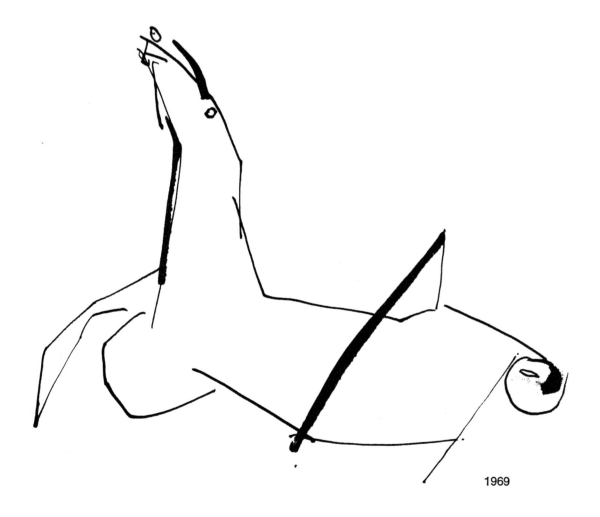

1969

242

1943. *The Miracle.* Polychrome plaster and collage. H. 27¹/₂ in: (CS. No. 161)

1951. *Little Miracle.* Bronze. 21¹/₄×27 in: (CS. No. 288).

953. *Miracle.* Bronze.
100½×31½×31½ in:
(CS. No. 313).

1954. *Miracle.* Bronze. $46^{1}/_{2} \times 64^{5}/_{2} \times 28^{3}/_{4}$ in: (CS. No. 327).

1954. *Miracle.* Idem.
(CS. No. 327a).

1953-1954. *Miracle*. Study. Bronze. 40¼×25⅝ in: (CS. No. 314).

1954. *Miracle.* Polychrome wood. 46¹/₂×67³/₄ in: (CS. No. 327b).

1957-1958. *Miracle.* Study. Bronze. H. 45¹/₄ in: (CS. No. 349)

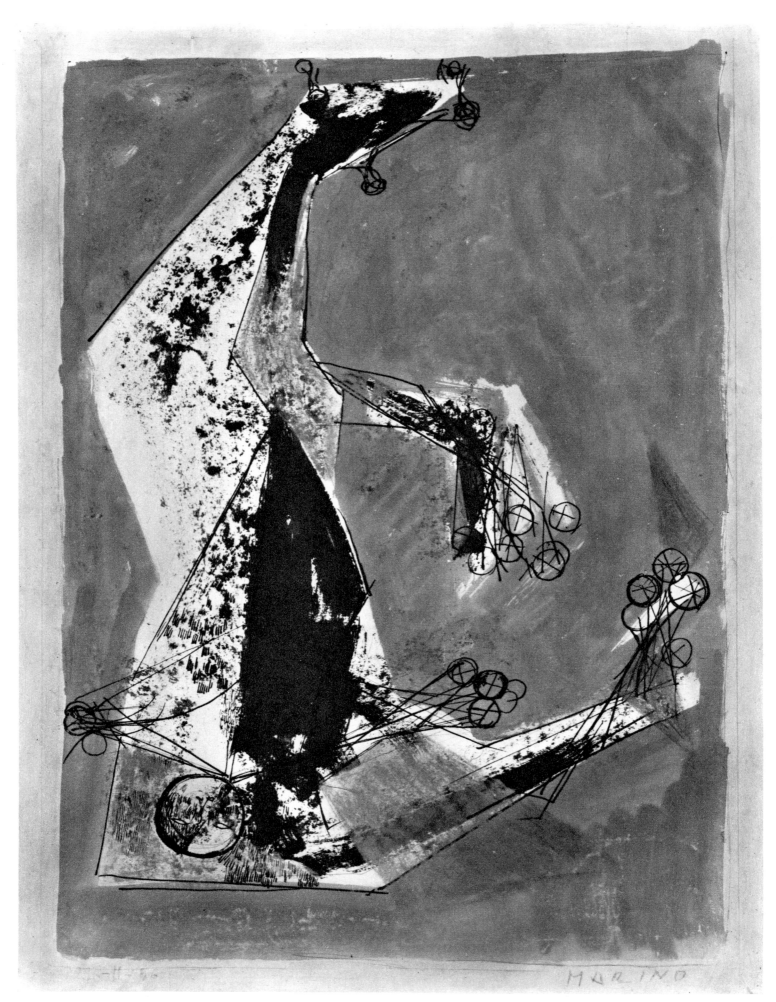

1956. *Miracle*. Tempera on paper. 32$^7/_8 \times$24$^3/_8$ in: (IP. No. 245).

1969

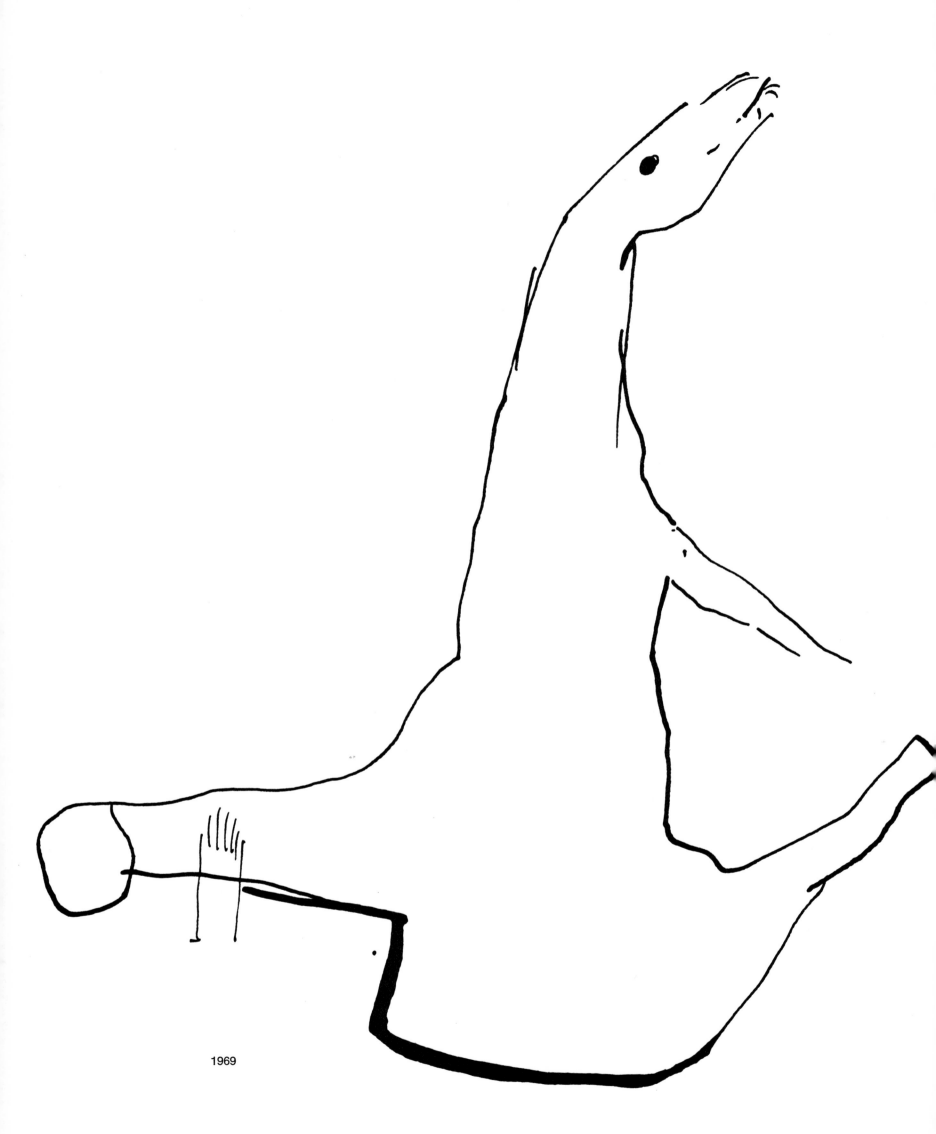

1969

1957-1958. *Miracle, Composition.* Bronze. 51³/₈×21¹/₄×22³/₄ in: (CS. No. 350)

1959-1960. *Miracle*. Bronze. 66$\frac{1}{2}$×50$\frac{3}{8}$×110$\frac{1}{4}$ in: (CS. No. 357).

1954. *Black Miracle*. Mixed media. Paper remounted on canvas. $50^3/_8 \times 33^3/_4$ in: (IP. No. 200).

1958. *Miracle*. Mixed media. Paper remounted on canvas. 52³/₄×32¹/₄ in: (IP. No. 276).

1955. *Miracle.* Study. Tempera. Paper remounted on canvas. 33×24⅝ in: (IP. No. 229).

64-1965. *The Shape of an Idea.* Bronze. H. 79$^3/_8$ in: (CS. No. 377).

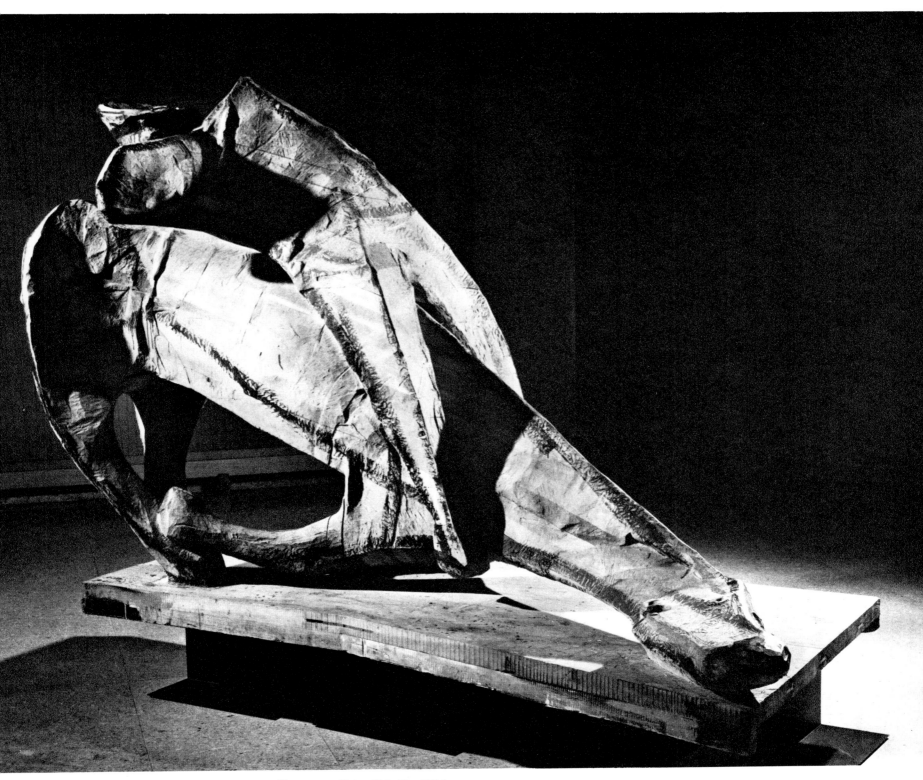

1959-1960. *Miracle.* Wood. About 70$^3/_4$×51×114$^1/_8$ in: (CS. No. 357a).

1952. *Miracle*. Bronze. H. 65 in: (CS. No. 293).

1952. *Miracle*. Detail. (CS. No. 293a).

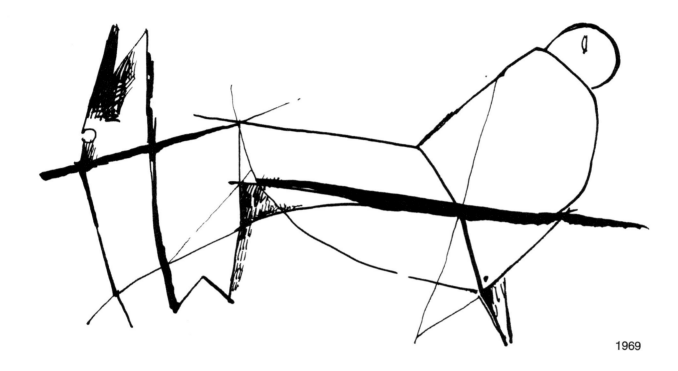

1969

THE WARRIORS

His *Warriors* come rather late in Marino's work. In them it would not be difficult to see an allegory evoking man's accumulated misfortunes and his final defeat at the hands of a society which bit by bit dismantles all his natural and instinctual foundations. However, these tormented compositions, where man and beast are reduced to convulsions and dying protest, invite not one but a variety of interpretations.

Actually, the directest approach to an understanding of the *Warriors* has been hinted at by Marino himself. Discussing the equestrian statues in the chapter before this, I cited remarks in which the artist speaks of the ever-growing distress which increasingly unsteadies the rider, robs him of the power to control his horse, which, in its turn, becomes more and more unresponsive and balky. "I believe," were Marino's words, "that we are heading toward the end of a world."

261

1969

To that declaration, he immediately appended a commentary, which I think it necessary to transcribe in full, for it sheds added light upon this new aspect of his work. "The sensation I refer to," he went on, "resembles the feelings of those Romans who, in the twilight of the Empire, were to watch a secular order collapse under the pressure of the Barbarian onslaught. My equestrian statues tell of the pangs caused by the events of my age. With each succeeding version of my horse, its restiveness increases; the rider, his strength waning further and further, has lost his dominion over the animal and the disasters he is succumbing to resemble those which laid Sodom and Pompeii low. My aim then is to render palpable the last stage in the dissolution of a myth, the myth of the heroic and victorious individual, the humanists' *uomo di virtù*. My effort of these past fourteen years has not been a striving for the heroic, it is to be understood as tragic."

These words, moving in their simplicity and conciseness, are, I think, to be taken literally. If we meditate upon the meaning of Marino's equestrian statues, and consider them all, from the first, mysteriously hieratic horses and riders down to these stricken warriors screaming in death's grip, it is a fabulous procession that takes shape before our eyes, something unmatched in the history of sculpture. From the image, wrested from the dim past, of the horseman in his mythological entity to the profound corrosion consuming this image, staggering, writhing, gasping under the assault of a world which dooms human virtues, it is the tragedy of our time that is represented.

The murals in the Tomb of the Inscriptions at Tarquinia show us a strange cavalcade. Naked

262

1968. *Theme of the Warrior.* Grey stone. 78³/₄×39²/₈ in: Detail from p. 270. (CS. No. 380a)

1956-1957. *Warrior*. Bronze. 29$^1/_8$×39$^3/_8$×27$^1/_2$ in: (CS. No. 344).

1956-1957. *Composition.* Bronze. 8¹/₄×14⁵/₈×9 in: (CS. No. 347).

1958-1959. The *Warrior*. Study. Bronze. 28×48³/₄×29¹/₈ in: (CS. No. 351).

1959-1960. *Warrior.* Bronze. 53¹/₈×66⁷/₈×44⁷/₈ in: (CS. No. 359).

1960. *Large Warrior.*
Bronze.
$173\frac{1}{8} \times 141\frac{5}{8}$ in:
(CS. No. 365).

1968. *Theme of the Warrior*. Grey stone. 78³/₄×39³/₈ in: (CS. No. 380).

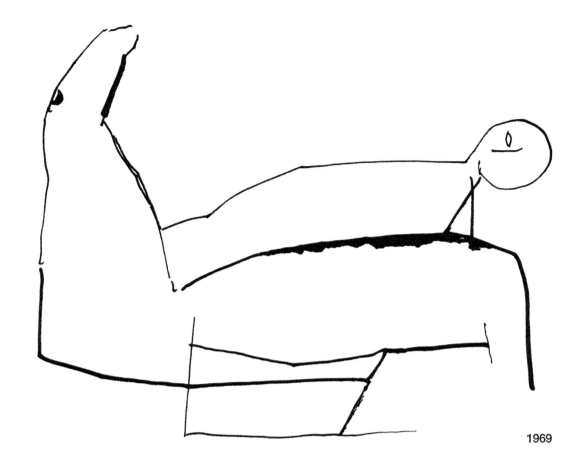

1969

upon their alternately red and black horses, the Etruscan warriors are making broad gestures. The horses' blue and white manes float over their necks arched like scimitars. This majestic procession moves trimly toward the death-door while in its train come leaping dancers, musicians and other participants in these revels. Portrayed there is a vision of life and death belonging to an age of innocence. It is Marino's also: with him, that is the spontaneous view, part of an Etruscan inheritance we have been at pains to stress. But—and it is this that gives its tragic dimension to his work— innocence is soon crossed by knowledge, whose pressure grows ever heavier and more intolerable as the pace of History quickens.

Born in 1901, Marino was witness to two world wars, not to mention countless civil and local wars of equally indescribable horror. Entering upon the peak of his life, the scene before him is more than ever that of a world ridden by conflicts, teetering on the brink of monstrous catastrophes. Added to that is man's steady asphyxiation by a machinelike society, his depersonalization through the effects of collective suggestion, the withering away of human instinct, its replacement by reflex, and the submersion of the individual by anonymous tides. Many artists—and many people whose orientation is not towards art—have been at grips, are still at grips with this feeling of despondency, of frustration which can reach the point of panic; but if one may judge from the evidence of a large part of his work, such a frame of mind does not seem to be Marino's natural one. In him the underlying thing is innocence, immediate communication with the real, the underlying drive. It is only gradually that disquiet, then anxiety slip into his work, invading it from without. Like an Aeolian harp the faintest breeze sets astir, Marino, at the outset, picked up the subtle echoes of an ancient harmony; but those melodious accents were progressively warped and then drowned out by the infernal dissonances of the present-day world. The horse, which symbolizes man's animal dimension, his virility and his capacity to create, sags little by little under the weight of its rider who reels and at last falls, becoming the wreckage of himself, a dirge pronounced by sculptured forms whose poignancy heightens all the way to the monument called *Cry* which the Berliners have judiciously —be it temporarily—set up in the heart of their city, a few steps away from a wall that is at once the source and symbol of our apprehensions.

Marino's achievement is a cycle, tantamount, if you wish, to Beethoven's, extending from the pastoral to the heroic, developing from blissful communion to tragic consciousness. In the opening pages of this book I spoke of how sorely a sense of symphony is lacking in our contemporary artists: Marino's is one of the rare works which fills this vacancy. That work is an expanse within which the mind drifts as upon the vastness of a sometimes calm, sometimes ruffling sea, able sometimes to break into sudden, unpredictable whirlpools, or to swell in towering waves run up from far below.

1969

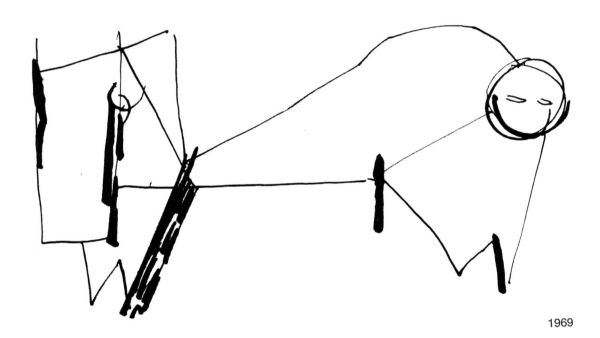

1969

1969

1959-1960. *Warrior*. Polychrome plaster. 53^1/$_8$×66^7/$_8$×44^7/$_8$ in: (CS. No. 359b).

1962. *The Warrior*. Oil. Paper remounted on canvas. 51¹/₈×59 in: (IP. No. 307).

). *Warrior*. Tempera. Paper remounted on canvas. 59×59 in: (IP. No. 297).

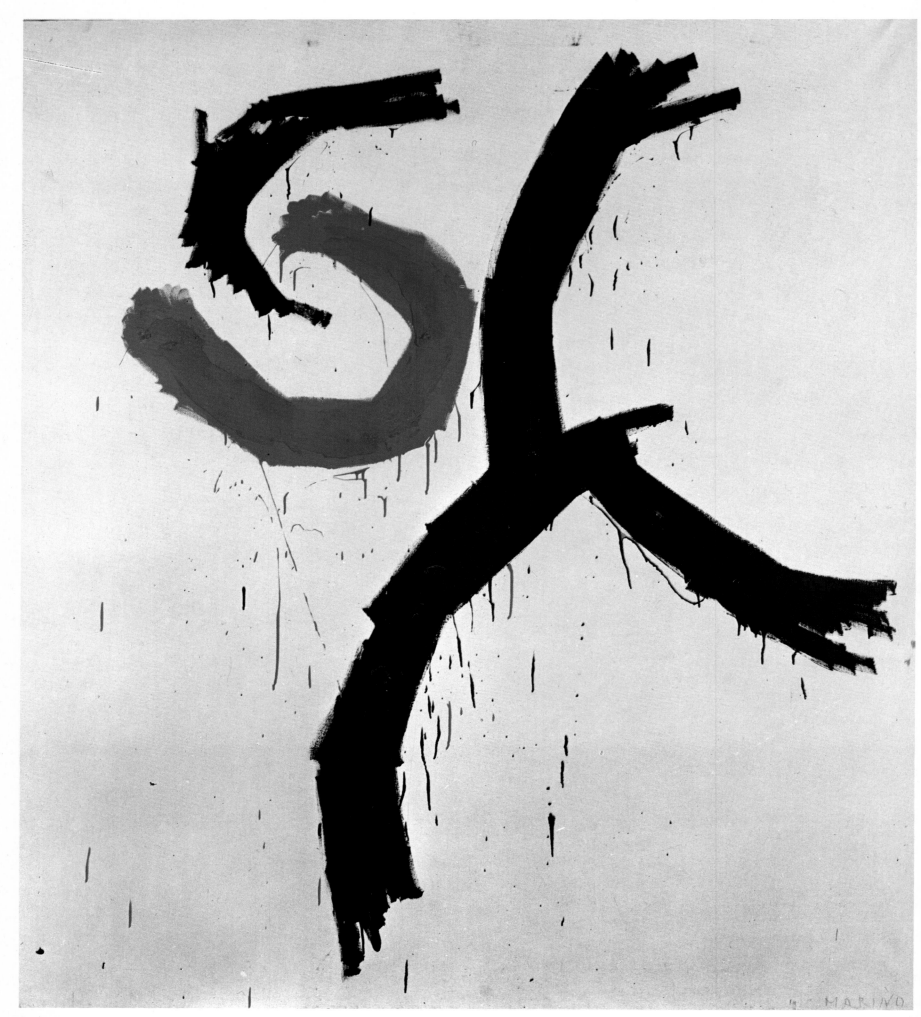

1960. *Synthesis*. Oil on canvas. 74³/₄×74³/₄ in: (IP. No. 298).

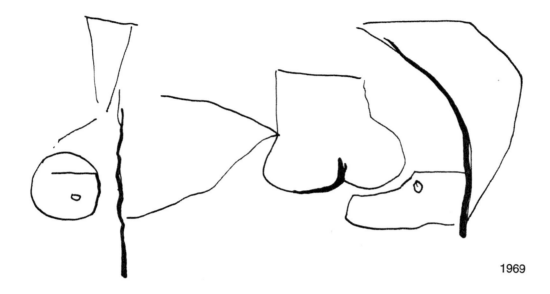

1969

BETWEEN REALITY AND MYTH

Among us all, it is, I think, the sculptor who is inhabited by the ambition that most nearly rivals the demiurge's. For his, too, is the purpose to give life, to give soul to inert matter, which beneath his hand takes shape and vibrates. It was in *The Metamorphoses* I came upon the fable which, in my view, more forcefully than any other illustrates the meaning of this creative endeavor.

Ovid relates the birth of the child-god Tages, founder of the Etruscan craft of divination, who, before the astonished gaze of a ploughman, sprang one day from a clod of earth. The peasant, says Ovid, "beheld the fate-revealing clod in the midst of the fields move at first of its own accord and no one touching it, and afterwards assume a human form, and lose that of earth, and open its new-made mouth with the decrees of future destiny."

No one, in so far as I know, has ever pointed out how well this splendid version of the myth may serve, without undue extrapolation, as an account of the origins of sculpture and of the sculptor's intent. Indeed, what does the artist actually do if not mould a shapeless lump of clay in his

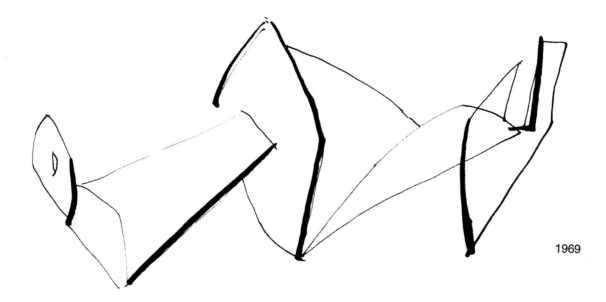

1969

hands, if not cause it to "assume a human form, and lose that of earth"? Ovid's winged language beckoning the imagination to take flight, may we not, when he speaks of "the decrees of future destiny," identify those decrees with the artist's will, that destiny with the form and life the clod takes between his fingers? And too, the human form which, no sooner born, begins to reveal fate, is this not a symbol for all sculptured form, inasmuch as every work of art worthy of the name expresses itself in terms of destiny?

It is also interesting to note that the ancient writers described Tages as having the appearance of a boy with the wisdom of an old man. Word of his coming having spread about the countryside, from all directions the population flocked to where he was. There again it is permissible to recognize the figure of the artist, in whom there must inevitably coexist, if he wishes to fulfill the role of The Maker, the child's freshness of soul and the arcana of knowledge.

Though my fondness for that author is of long standing, I am not an inveterate reader of Ovid, and I can only find it an odd coincidence that, while engaged upon the present study, I happened to reread that fifteenth book of *The Metamorphoses*, where Tages' birth is recounted. Finishing the story, I found I was already thinking of Marino, for it seemed nothing short of self-evident that this extraordinary artist was directly descended from the little Etrurian god, sorcerer and soothsayer and yet so tangible, so corporeal that one might be half inclined to try to revive his worship.

If then the encountering of Tages while I was at work upon this book enabled me to see in Marino something significant I might otherwise have missed... why, no, I do not believe it was

280

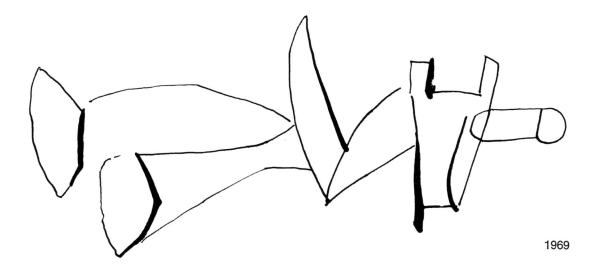

1969

merely a question of chance, in the usual sense of that word. I would rather employ another expression, one that was dear to André Breton, and call it *objective chance* which designates the fortuitous, unmotivated coming together of facts or realities beheld hitherto as foreign to one another and whose entering into contact engenders poetic truth.

Ending this book, which pretends only to survey Marino's achievement, one may gauge how much remains still to be said about it. If one considers his artist's activity as having begun in 1917, the year when he enrolled in the Florence Beaux Arts Academy, it is better than a half-century of work we see before us. Its themes and moods ranging from the peacefulness of simple physical contentment to the distress and shipwreck of the soul, we are escorted through periods that are now elegiac or playful, now disturbed or prophetic, but sustained throughout is that high sense of the world's wonder which, in every work of art, is the secret of grace. Portraits, Pomonas, Jugglers, Dancers, Pugilists, Horses and their Riders, Warriors and Miracles, we have watched them file past, an enchanted society evolving upon the frontier between reality and myth, a world of figures whose diversity and evocativeness legitimize the term I used to designate it earlier: a *Legend of Forms.* Franco Russoli has spoken well and with warmth of the *personae* that people Marino's world. "They are drawn," he has said, "from a milieu that lies outside time, or else from the most distant spheres of culture and figurative imagination, and transported into the life of today." Then, pursuing his brilliant analysis, Russoli gives us this incisive description of Marino's undertaking: "One would say that he is seeking to show the continuity of human vicissitudes, the inevitable recurrence of

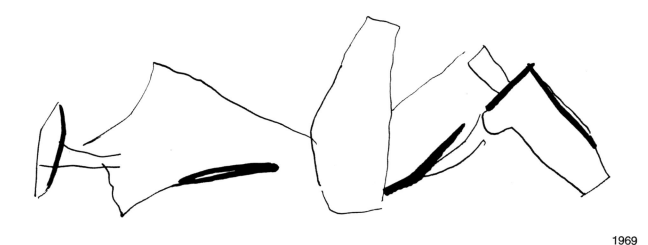

1969

events, his faith in the endeavor and dignity of man, judge of himself and of the developments which seem to threaten his annihilation, but which he is able to dominate nevertheless."

During the fifty years just past, there have been only too frequent instances of mere experiment parading as something inspired; the cards of surprise, shock, defiance and even provocation have all been played—cleverly sometimes, sometimes brilliantly—but almost always to the detriment of non-immediate ends and profound sources; quirk and manner have too often taken precedence over passion and style. All the foregoing will have enabled the reader to decide whether Marino is not today one of the handful of those who, through their work, have sought to express a totality of being. Not that this truth is necessarily visible in each separate work, looked at in isolation, but it becomes manifest once the artist's production is viewed as a whole.

Everyone knows—or should know—that the figurative art/abstract art opposition is the very epitome of the false antithesis and the false problem, kept alive by doctrinaire minds in the name of misunderstood experiments and a misleading notion of progress, completely absurd when it is a question of art. It is obvious that no art is exempt from abstraction, this, whatever else may be said, constituting one of the principal selective modes whereby the artist apprehends the visible world. It would, therefore, be in terms of nearness to, or distance from, nature that the question might be more suitably, more legitimately posed. One could probably say, simplifying somewhat, that with those known as abstract artists intellection is paramount, while with the others, it is sensory perception that comes first; but there exists no work of art in which these two operations are not combined, in however varying proportions. For that matter, as Leibnitz maintained, "There is nothing in the intelligence which the senses have not priorly contained." Hence, rather than classify a work

282

1960. *Composition.* Bronze. $6^3/_2 \times 11^3/_8 \times 5^1/_8$ in: (CS. No. 364).

1960. *Composition.* Bronze. 6³/₄×10¹/₄×4³/₈ in: (CS. No. 363).

1960. *Composition.* Tempera. Paper remounted on canvas. 49¹/₄×33 in: (IP. No. 299).

1960. *Group of Elements IV.* Mixed media. Paper remounted on canvas. 35³/₈×65 in: (IP. No. 300).

1964. *Composition.* Oil on paper. 39³/₈×59 in: (IP. No. 310).

1965. *Group of Elements I.* Mixed media. Paper remounted on canvas. 35$\frac{1}{2}$×75 in: (IP. No. 311).

1966. *Composition:* Tempera. Paper remounted on canvas. 31$\frac{1}{2}$×60$\frac{7}{8}$ in: (IP. No. 321).

1967. *Passion for the Game.* Oil on wood. 78³/₄×78³/₄ in: (IP. No. 323).

1964-1965. *Group of Elements.* Bronze. 41³/₈×112¹/₄×55¹/₈ in: (CS. No. 376).

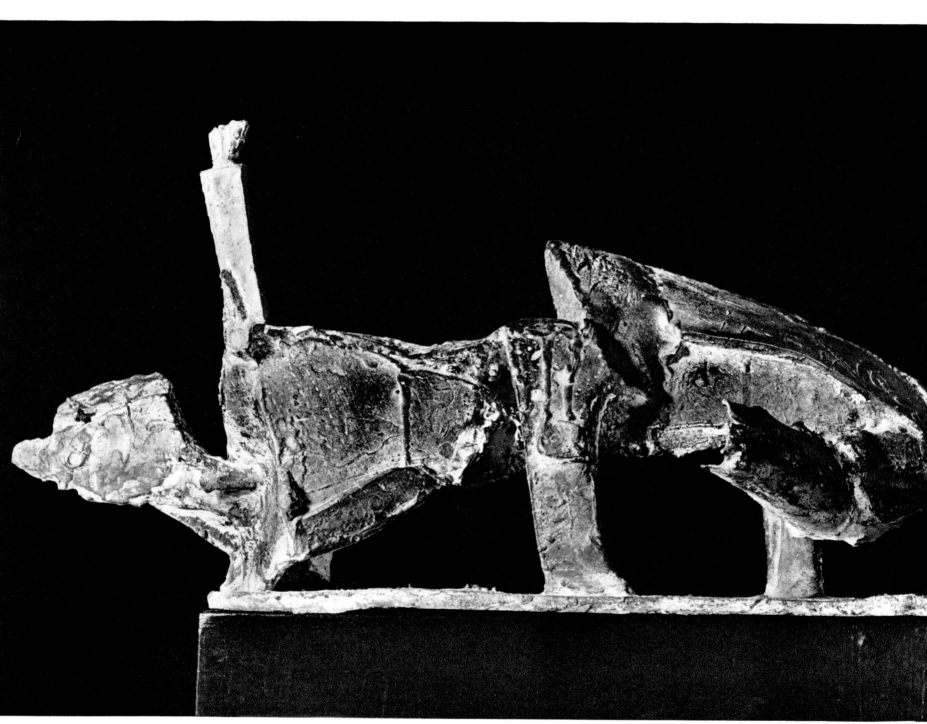

1963. *Small Cry*. Bronze. 8$\frac{1}{4}$×5$\frac{7}{8}$×11 in: (CS. No. 373).

1969

as abstract or figurative, I prefer to say that it reflects more or less of the natural. I am reminded of an anecdote concerning one of our greatest contemporary philosophers, I hope I shall be forgiven if I leave him unnamed. On the subject of Jean-Paul Sartre's *L'Etre et le néant,* he said, in the course of a conversation with a friend, "You know, he put too much nothingness in that story of his. You'll find in reality that there is a lot more being than there is nothingness." Likewise, I believe that there is a lot more *nature* in art than is customarily allowed nowadays; and, in Marino's work, that whereby we are arrested is, precisely, the generous share of nature one discovers there and, emanating from it, an impression of densely alive substance.

Marino, when moved to break his wonted silence, shows himself highly aware of these elementary truths. "It is only in appearance," says he, "that simplification leads away from nature: it leads back to nature, because it extracts the essence from nature. Dissolved, destroyed forms, overthrown bodies, horses, debris sticking to the ground, bits of flesh, are matter once again, the formless transformed. But these collapsed masses ask for re-establishing; these forms in decay long for revival as solid and whole masses." Reality, for Marino, is the form which "supports the flesh like a bone-structure. It shuns the haphazard." And by way of conclusion the author of the *Miracles* asks this question, not without a grain of wickedness: "Might one say the same thing of abstraction?"

Reviewing Marino's achievement and considering the pattern it describes as it unfolds in time, it occurs to one that this work starts, grows, extends and fills out the way a tree does, that is to say, in a natural and irresistible manner. Nurturing it, to be sure, is a fund of practical knowledge and of repeated meditations upon the particular problems of art, but these elements, as with the humus and the subsoil in the case of the tree, are transmuted into sap. Once, when we were talking about

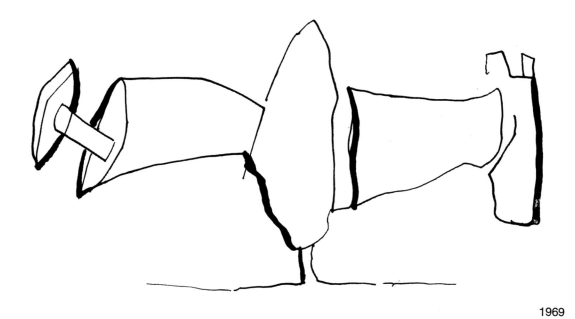

1969

Marino a very long time ago, I heard Giacometti say how much he admired this instinctive growth, this ease. I remember that he employed the word exuberance, contrasting it with what he called his own constrictedness. Now, antinomic though they are, these two artists are comparable in their mutual fascination before the real and through their common design to give a face to human destiny. Giacometti attacks the real by intense concentration upon a single point, penetrating it like a drill, seeking the particles at its secret and trembling core; whereas Marino's gaze is one that encompasses, embracing, along with the object, all the planes and horizons which condition it. And so it is that each of Marino's works looks like a sampling of reality, a piece of reality that has been lived through, experienced, and on the basis of which it is possible to reconstruct the whole. In Giacometti's work there is an oscillation between two poles, chaos and, to borrow Jacques Dupin's phrase, an "agonizing lucidity"; and from this permanent tension arises the existential *angoisse* that from the outset stamps each of his gestures. But it is mistakenly that certain commentators have qualified as existential the distress expressed notably in the *Warriors* or in a monument like *Cry.* For existential distress, as we know, is never provoked by a determined or determinable existent, it is, according to Sartre's own terms, "distress in the face of oneself." No such state was present in Marino at the start; distress infiltrated his work gradually, imposed from without by mounting external pressures, and ended at last by giving his work its ultimately tragic expression. At a period when, precociously obsessed by death, Giacometti, with parsimony, was shutting up skeletons inside cages or else throwing to the ground the shattered pieces of a *Woman with her throat cut*, Marino's work, to the contrary, was thriving and in it he was meaning to register the intimate rhythms of movement and measure which are, said Valéry, "what is real inside reality." From the first little

292

1969

terracotta nudes to the first horses and the polychrome rider, Marino is above all minded to give us the plastic effigy of the movement which quickens in the soul and makes it thrill in harmony with the forces animating all the world. Through his figures he restores to man a majesty which lay obscurely within us all. He knows that only a dancer, a rider and his horse moving in faultless step can give us the true feeling of immobility: of an immobility which is neither abandon nor repose, but rather expectation before what is to come to be. Next, guised as horsemen of the apocalypse, death makes its entrance upon Marino's chessboard. As so well described by Franco Russoli, it is "the desolate chant of living debris cindered into structures by a thunderbolt, but that once upon a time had a human figure and which the Poet is able to see and recreate in a new, fiercely *beautiful* architecture..."

Among all the interpretations of the Etruscan spirit poets have provided us, the most radically divergent are those of Gabriele D'Annunzio and D. H. Lawrence. In the view of the author of *Forse che sì, forse che no,* the mysterious people slumbering in the tombs of Cerveteri, Tarquinia, Volterra and other Tuscan sanctuaries seem to have been the prey of an inexorable and tragic fate. "For," he wrote, "Melancholy is the Etruscan muse. 'Tis she who in his wanderings in exile and in hell accompanies a great Tuscan steeped in atrabile..." But for Lawrence it is contact between persons, communion in sensuality and joy that are exhaled by this art in which he discerns "the natural flowering of life." "To the Etruscans," he goes on, "all was alive; the whole universe lived; and the business of man was himself to live amid it all. He had to draw life into himself, out of the wandering huge vitalities of the world. The cosmos was alive, like a vast creature. The whole thing breathed and stirred."

Those are, in fact, two sides to the same coin—and they are the same two sides we find in Marino's work, in its earlier phase containing all of Lawrence's generous outpouring, and in more recent years all of D'Annunzio's moral affliction. But the melancholy that Marino expresses, poignant as it is, never takes the shape of despair. Beset though he may be by gloom, the Etruscan in him is too firmly pledged to daylight for him ever to foresake its promise.

Etruscan mythology included a demon of death named Charun. His appearance was that of a monster with the beak of a bird of prey, the ears of a horse, and the great bared fangs of a carnivore about to devour its victims. Franz de Ruyt, at the conclusion of his book on Charun, wrote these lines: "The nature of man does not vary over the course of the ages; neither do his psychological reactions, only their outward manifestations, determined by the contingencies of the moment and the evolution of ideas. Charun, Etruscan demon of death, is an aspect, *hic et nunc,* of human reactions before the troubling mystery which inevitably engulfs this treasure, no less strange, no less elusive: life."

If I close with these lines, which for me possess nobleness and profundity, it is because they enable me to summarize the nature of the power exerted by Marino's art. His entire achievement expresses the permanence of the human spirit and its surge towards the universal, but expresses it in a language that is ours. As a vision of death, his stricken horseman is less vivid than Charun, the threatful demon, but it is more appropriate to men in our plight. As for his images of life, from the reveries of plenitude to the Mozartian divertimento, they restore in us an awareness of calls sounding from afar and convey us to those shores where transfigured reality gathers and trembles, like a tear in the eye of a nymph on the threshold of the sacred wood.

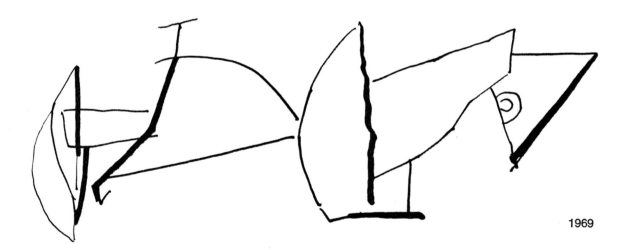

1969

953. *Juggler*. Oil on cardboard. Approximately $39^{3}/_{8} \times 23^{5}/_{8}$ in: (IP. No. 170).

967. *The Cry.* Study. Tempera on paper. 25⁵/₈×36¹/₄ in: (IP. No. 324).

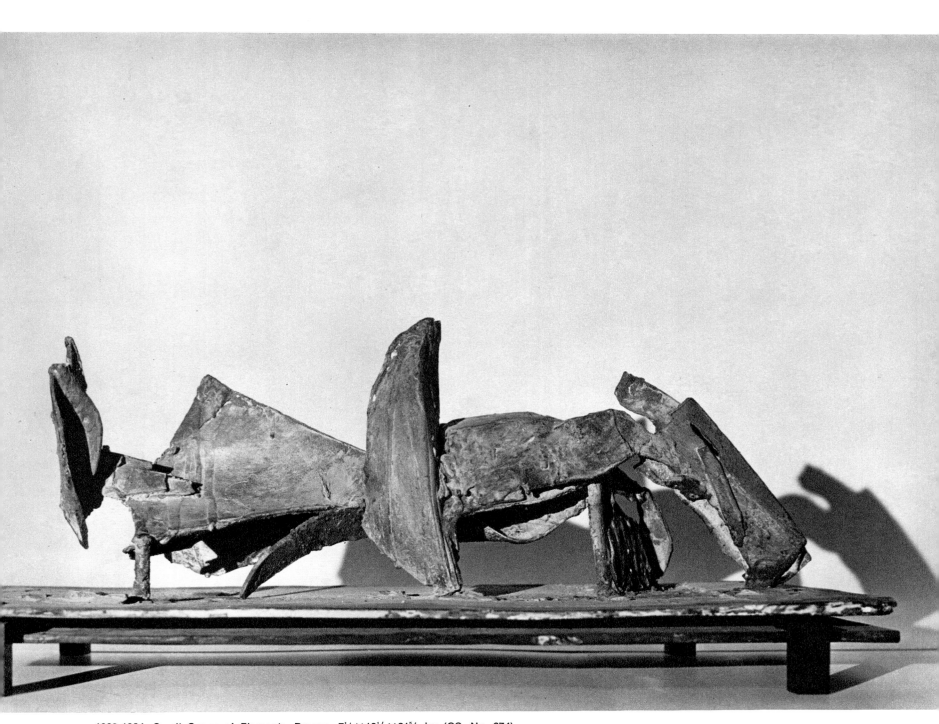

1963-1964. *Small Group of Elements.* Bronze. 7¹/₂×10¹/₈×21⁵/₈ in: (CS. No. 374).

967. *The Cry.* Study. Tempera on paper. 25¹/₈×35⁷/₈ in: (IP. No. 325).
From a sketch done in 1960.

1962. *Large Cry.* Detail from p. 298-299. (CS. No. 370a).

1967. *Mobile-Immobile.* Tempera. Paper remounted on canvas. 53⅝×76 in: (IP. No. 326).

1967. *Intensity.* Tempera. Paper remounted on canvas. 35⅜×70½ in: (IP. No. 327).

1968. *Vivacity*. Tempera. Paper remounted on canvas. 32⅝×70½ in: (IP. No. 333).

1968. *Energy*. Tempera. Paper remounted on canvas. 33¾×70½ in: (IP. No. 334).

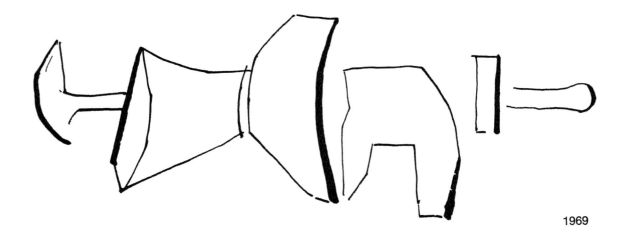

1969

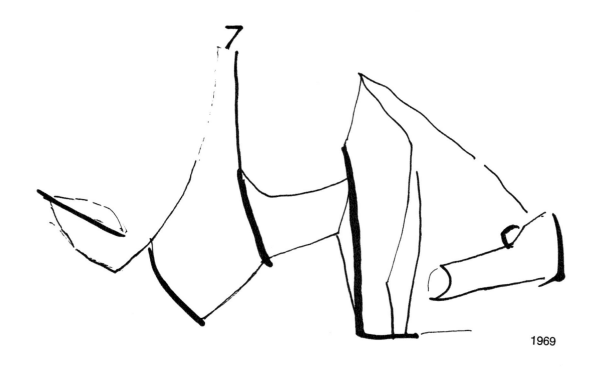

1969

G. DI SAN LAZZARO

GENERAL
CATALOGUE
OF MARINO MARINI'S WORK

SCULPTURE
PAINTINGS
LITHOGRAPHS
ENGRAVINGS

1938

INTRODUCTION
TO GENERAL CATALOGUE
OF SCULPTURE

1945

Genius—said Marcel Proust—is instinct. If this is so, must one have an instinct for genius? Not that of the social life of bees, ants or beavers, but like some insects such as certain species of spiders, wasps, etc., that terrifying instinct which urges them to paralyze the female, without killing her, in order to facilitate the reproductive act. The instinct of genius, as Proust understood it, was, in a way, the sublimation of the sexual instinct.

Is this definition fitting for the author of A la Recherche du Temps Perdu? I don't know and, furthermore, this is not my field. On the other hand, it seems to me to be perfect for two of the century's greatest European artists, Pablo Picasso and Marino Marini, whom this same Proust would probably not have understood (neither Picasso, nor Braque, nor Matisse is ever mentioned by the author although he was a great admirer of the Russian Ballet).

And yet, could one better define the genius of a Picasso or a Marino Marini? In a world where the combined efforts of science and technique are working towards self-destruction, Picasso and Marino Marini appear to us to be the only two artists whose instinct—genius—plunges its roots into a world such as we knew it before the atomic age.

Of course, other forms of genius exist to which it would be absurd to apply Proust's definition. One can even maintain, with Dubuffet, that genius is innate in man: education—that is, culture such as it has been (falsely) idealized since Plato—has sacrificed it to the taboos of society.

Man can expect nothing from this so-called conquest of space, anymore than he can expect something for art in some fields of modern research. These problems of technique pure and simple, certainly very curious and interesting in themselves, find no resonance in the domain of the spirit. The latter, in truth, is not a problem of technical or even scientific orientation. The spirit is the vox clamantis in deserto, *the voice crying in the wilderness, the refusal—since the world has existed— to accept a society such as the police and clerks have fashioned it.* The spirit is the indefinable cry of that human consciousness for which even the greatest philosophers have not yet been able to give an acceptable explanation.

However, let us return to Proust's definition: genius is instinct. We know that instinct is not a blind force, quite to the contrary. Instinct, we could say, is the impulsion of total identification. Just as the ant or bee identifies only with itself—by a motivation which forbids any ambiguity, any alienation—the work of a Picasso or a Marino Marini is a world closed to all uncertainty. Even though one can sometimes think that this world was engendered by doubt, this cannot touch their work. As in Dante's Inferno, one can go in but never come out. The identification of the two artists with their work is absolute.

One can create a Braque or a Matisse as one does a tapestry—and even marvelous tapestries— all day long, or by looking heavenward admire a Velasquez or a Tintoretto, but the world of Picasso, like that of Marino Marini, though nurtured by other worlds, belongs only to them.

1944

1952

We do not say that it is in their own image—as man was created in the image of God—it is the indestructible identification of themselves. Like Picasso, Marini's whole being is found in his work; he is identified with it by a „true, effective fusion'', by that phenomenon known as „reciprocal fusion''.

We will leave Picasso now to his exegetes and take into consideration only the art of Marino Marini whose complete works we wanted to compile in this book, complete at least until today: a few hundred sculptures and paintings, one hundred engravings and as many lithographs.

Marino Marini does not offer us a „representation'' of a human figure or situation. He identifies himself completely with that form or that situation. It is enough to compare his world with that of another great sculptor, Maillol, who drew his own plastic universe from antique statuary with great virtuosity and not without technical daring; we are witness to a representative world, nostalgic, cultural but not instinctive. Maillol could have found his inspiration in Mayan or Gothic art: his work would not have suffered. Marini, on the contrary, is one with a world which is his and that of his ancestors. His force of identification is as powerful as Rodin's in „L'homme qui marche'', or in „Saint John the Baptist''. Those who have some knowledge of modern sculpture know that there is no one between Rodin, who died in 1917, and the revelation of Marino Marini around 1940.

Naturally, there have been artists who, with talent and sensitivity, have created masterpieces out of marble, bronze, wood or iron. But is it sculpture? Marvelous, living architecture, yes, and often forms of stupefying purity. But sculpture such as we understand it—and which is not modelling either although it is easily confused with it—is something else altogether. If Picasso, in modern terms, has become synonymous with „strange'', Marino Marini is, on the contrary, synonymous with sculpture. The remarkable works of Brancusi, Gonzalez, Moore and even Laurens are only songs, poems transcribed in diverse materials. Sculpture, for the last quarter of a century, has had only one name: Marino Marini.

Just what do we mean by sculpture, we who refuse to give that name to works which are,

310

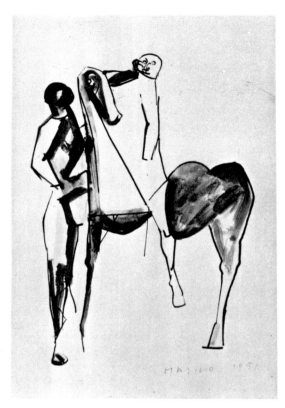

1951

nonetheless, songs—and perhaps even eternal songs—created in marble, bronze, iron (and also in other metals and plastics)? „In every instant," wrote Marcel Proust, „the artist must listen to his instinct, which is what makes art the truest of all, the most austere school of life and the true last judgment", (we have chosen to underline the last).

A last judgment is exactly what Marino Marini has given us in his work, sculptured and painted as well as drawn and engraved. It is also a last judgment that Proust left us, but an author can only judge a segment of society and the creatures that compose it; one cannot expect more from the author of Le Temps Retrouvé. The plastic arts, on the contrary, can give us much more: the last judgment of man. It is through sculpture that Marino Marini has been able to pass such a judgment and, in saying this, we are not thinking only of his remarkable portraits. Sculpture is not a regional art, it is the eternal expression of the human ephemera (and we could not say it more aptly than Patrick Waldberg's marvelous text); it cannot limit itself to a game of full and empty spaces, of curves and straight lines, or offer a sample of magic silhouettes cut out of space. It cannot cheat with reality for it is itself, far more than literature, absolute reality. It is born as much from instinct, from the artist's genius, as from his ardent, craftsman's hands. A sculpture in which one does not sense the force of the creative instinct and the warmth of the hands which gave it birth is only an object. Form is not the outcome of sculpture, it is its point of departure.

However, since the object has become the symbol of our society of faceless larvae, it must be said that the art of Marino Marini carries, even in his latest decompositions which he calls „compositions of elements", that last judgment, that fascination which are the true goal of art, and only sculpture can achieve it. Through the ancient themes of the Pomonas, the Dance, the horse and horseman, War, the artist has expressed and weighed the anguish of our era. These portraits, these horsemen and their horses, these strong, earthy girls look at us as Paul Klee's pictures look at us. Are we still assassins? Impostors and fanatics? This is, perhaps, the last time that a great artist, through the eyes of his works, will look at us and judge us. All those more or less kinetic objects which are wrongly called sculpture demand, just to the contrary, to be looked at; they make us spectators and, occasionally, Peeping Toms.

Marini wrote that his first vision is a vision of color (as it is for Chagall). By starting from color he reaches form: thus, sculpture is the outcome of his inner emotion.

Starting from color and life, he finds himself by identifying with form which becomes sculpture. And yet his paintings, not to speak of his drawings—and he is truly as great a draughtsman as Picasso or Chagall—are admirable and we have reproduced in this work about one hundred incontestable masterpieces. But this age is rich in painters with genius whereas it is poor in sculptors—we are speaking of his age; that is, the first two-thirds of the twentieth century—and it is understandable that his unique gift as a sculptor has been praised especially.

We must also point out that Marino Marini is the only great italian artist whose fame comes only from the power of his art, whereas others owe a good half of their popularity to their allegiance to a great political party or to the propaganda of official organizations. These are considerations which may seem out of place in this book and yet they bring to light the direct contact —without outside intervention—between Marino Marini's art and the crowd of his admirers the world over. Even the critics could not but follow such enthusiasm, the mute and passionate dialogue between man and the work of art. It is a unique case in the history of contemporary art and it seemed important to mention it.

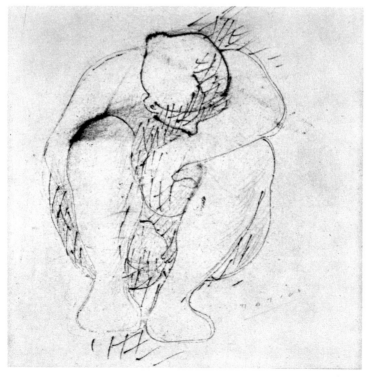

1938

3

4

1926

n° 1. *Bather.* Terracotta. Height: 29$\frac{1}{8}$ in: Galleria d'Arte Moderna, Milan. (p. 19).

n° 2. *Small Figure.* Bronze. Height: 17$\frac{1}{8}$ in: Unique copy: Private Coll., Rome. (p. 18).

One or two false copies of this work probably exist.

n° 2 a. *Small Figure.* Idem. (p. 18).

1927

n° 3. *"Mosca" Montale.* Terracotta. Height: about 11$\frac{3}{4}$ in: Private Coll., Florence.

The model for the sculpture was "Mosca," the close friend of the famous Italian poet Eugenio Montale.

n° 4. *Portrait of Paola Ojetti.* Bronze. Height: about 9$\frac{7}{8}$ in: Ojetti Coll., Florence.

Paola Ojetti is the daughter of the writer Ugo Ojetti, who died in 1946.

n° 5. *Priest.* Wax. Height: about 27$\frac{1}{2}$ in: Galleria d'Arte Moderna, Rome.

n° 6. *Portrait of the Painter Sensani.* Wax. Height: 16$\frac{1}{2}$ in: (Destroyed).

5

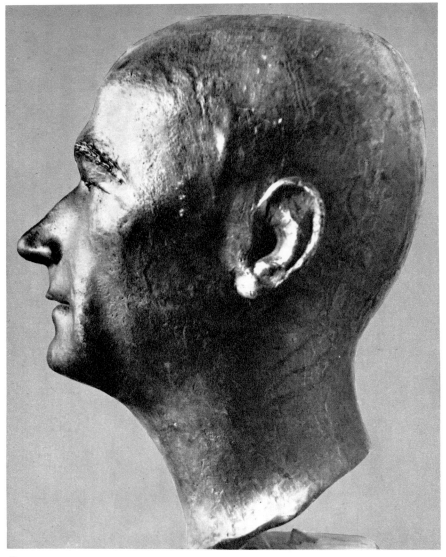

6

7

9

12

10

11

315

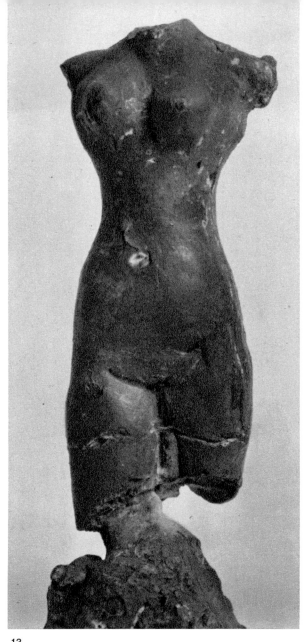

13

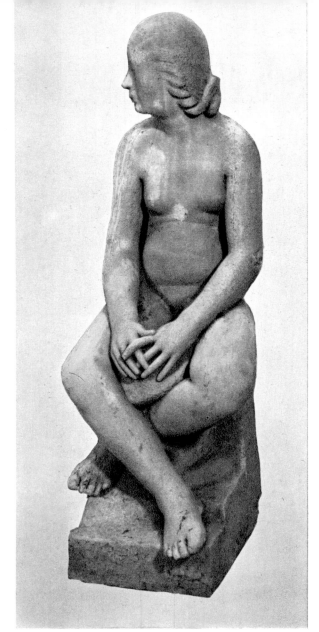

14

15

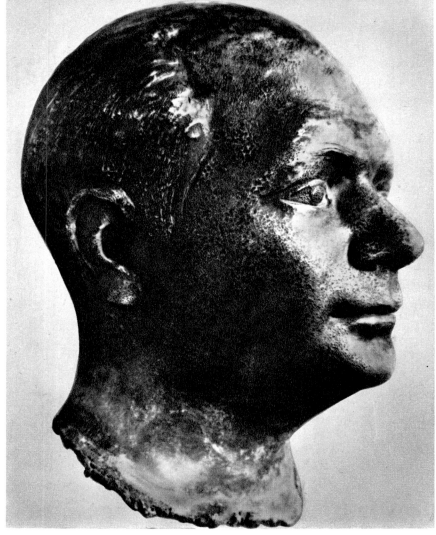

17

19

18

1929

n° 13. *Small Nude.* Height: 8⁵/ₓ in:
Bronze: Property of the artist (3 copies).
Polychrome plaster: Marina Marini Coll., Milan.
This torso, despite its classic appearance, was modeled from a young girl whom the artist knew at this period.

n° 14. *Young Girl.* Stone.
Height: about 51¹/₄ in:
Mondadori Coll., Pieve di Camaiore.
This work was commissioned by the Senator Bastianelli and was intended as an ornament for a garden. It was carved in Florence and is now slightly damaged.

n° 15. *Nude Woman.* Terracotta. Height:
about 55¹/ₓ in: Galleria d'Arte Moderna, Rome.
Marino Marini in his youth was equally responsive to his surroundings and to the great works of art of the past. It was as if he had wanted to work directly from life like Poussin, unconsciously following the example of Cézanne. The nude, to which he has restored so much sensuality in this work, was modeled on the wife of a well-known painter in Florence.

n° 16. *People.* Terracotta.
26 x 42⁷/ₓ x 17¹/₂ in:
Unique copy: property of the artist. (p. 22).

n° 16 a. *People.* Detail. (p. 22).

n° 16 b. *People.* Detail. (p. 22).

n° 17. *Portrait of the Painter Alberto Magnelli.* Bronze. Height: about 12⁵/ₓ in:
Property of the artist.
The painter Alberto Magnelli was one of the first of Marino Marini's friends in Florence.

n° 18. *The Blind Man.* Bronze.
Height: about 21¹/₂ in:
Galleria d'Arte Moderna, Florence.
The influence of the Florentine artistic world can be seen in this work. The climate of realism was at this period in Florence sustained by the painter and writer Ardengo Soffici.

n° 19. *The Bourgeoise.* Polychrome terracotta. Height: 14⁵/ₓ in: Property of the artist.
This formed part of the Series on "The People" — of which "The couple" (p. 22) was the major work.

317

20

22

n° 20. *Self-portrait.* Polychrome plaster.
Height: about 13³/₄ in:
Galleria d'Arte Moderna, Rome.
This was the artist's first self-portrait.

n° 21. *Study.* Polychrome terracotta.
Height: 7⁷/₈ in: Property of the artist.

n° 22. *Small Venus* (1929-1930).
Height: about 5 in:
Bronze:
1. Dominion Gallery, Montreal.
2. and 3. Property of the artist.
Terracotta: Property of the artist.
A young French girl, a close friend of the artist, inspired this unquestionably classic work.

n° 23. *Sleeping Woman* (1929-1930). Terracotta. Length: 63³/₄ in:
Galleria Nazionale d'Arte Moderna, Rome.
(p. 21).

n° 24. *Female Form.* Terracotta.
Length: 43¹/₂ in:
Galleria Nazionale d'Arte Moderna, Rome.
(p. 21).

n° 25. *Siren.* Terracotta. Height: 8⁵/₈ in:
Riccardo Jucker Coll., Milan.

n° 26. *Young Girl Seated* (1929-1930).
Height: 55¹/₈ in:
Bronze: Gianni Agnelli Coll., Turin.
Terracotta: J. Nehmad Coll., Milan
Property of the artist.

318

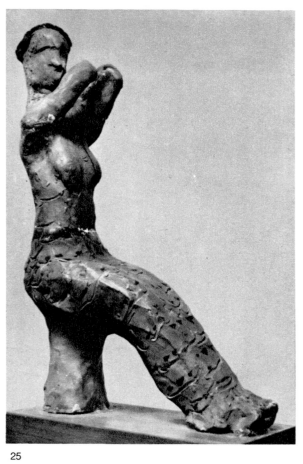

25

21

27

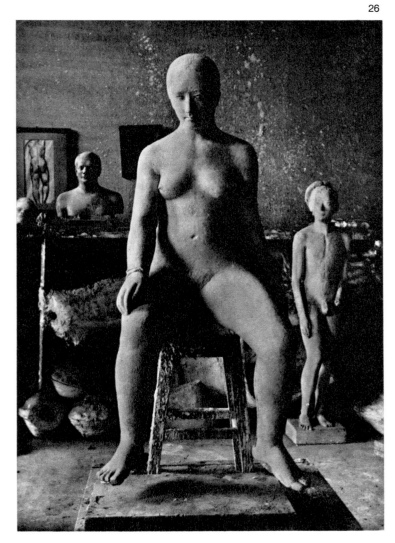

26

29

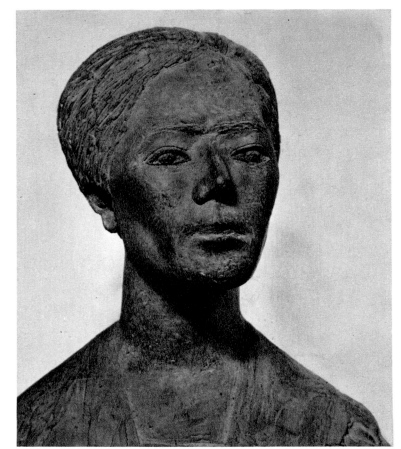

29 a

28

1930

n° 27. *Portrait of a Woman.* Terracotta.
Height: about 13³/₄ in:
Lorenzo Papi Coll., Florence.

n° 28. *Madonna and Child.*
Polychrome plaster. Height: about 25¹/₂ in:
Willy Bagnoli Coll., Milan.

n° 29. *Portrait of Gaby.* Stone.
Height: about 19⁵/₈ in:
G. Blair Laing Coll., Toronto.

n° 29 a. *Portrait of Gaby* (1932). Terracotta.
Height: 19⁵/₈ in:
Musée National d'Art Moderne, Paris.

1931

n° 30. *Reclining Woman.* Terracotta.
15³/₈ x 5¹/₂ in: Riccardo Jucker Coll., Milan.

n° 31. *Ersilia.* Polychrome wood.
57³/₄ x 17¹/₂ x 26³/₄ in:
Kunsthaus, Zurich. Reworked in 1949. (p. 23).

1932

n° 32. *Nude.* Plaster. Height: 57 in:
Property of the artist. A copy in terracotta
also exists.

n° 33. *Small Angel.* Study. Plaster. Height:
about 11³/₄ in: (Lost). Stone. Height: 78³/₄ in:
Property of the City of Milan.
*A photograph of the model, a large sculpture
in stone, which the artist had executed when
he was a teacher at the Academy in Monza
and which has recently been found in a
municipal refuse dump in a suburb of Milan,
is reproduced here.*

n° 34. *Seated Woman.* Terracotta.
9 x 11³/₄ in: Riccardo Jucker Coll., Milan.

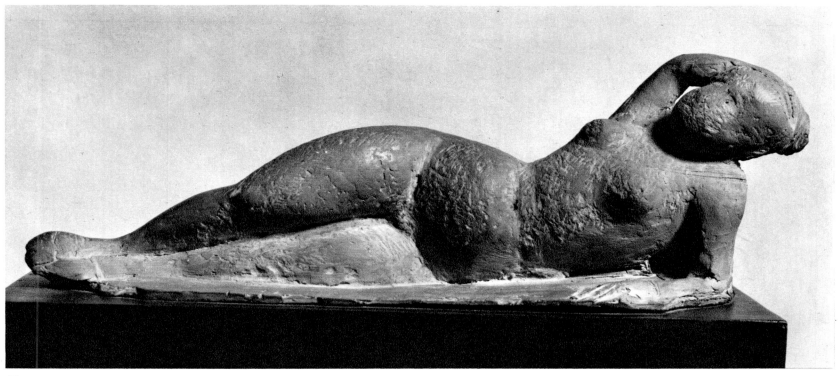

30

38

37

32

39

43

43 a

43 b

n° 35. *Swimmer*. Wood. 45⅝ x 19⅝ in:
Emilio Jesi Coll., Milan. (p. 26).

n° 35 a. *Swimmer*. Idem. (p. 27).

n° 36. *Juggler*. Bronze: 11 x 3¼ x 3¼ in:
1. Dominion Gallery, Montreal.
2. Property of the artist. (p. 28).

n° 37. *Portrait of a Young Girl*. Terracotta.
Height: 12¾ in: Private Coll.

n° 38. *Portrait of a Young Girl*. Plaster.
Height: about 13¾ in: Property of the artist.

n° 39. *Bas-relief*. Bronze: 28⅜ x 24¾ in:
1. Maurice Goldman Coll., London.
2. Emilio Jesi Coll., Milan.
3. Hanover Gallery, London.
4. Kunsthalle, Mannheim, Federal Republic
of Germany.
5. Kunstkabinett, Frankfurt.
Et al. Property of the artist.

1933

n° 40. *Boxer*. Bronze. 32¼ x 19⅝ in:
Former Cardazzo Coll. (p. 25).

n° 41. *Icarus*. Wood. Height: 69¾ in:
Battiato Coll., Milan (p. 28).

n° 42. *Juggler*. Terracotta. Height: 47¼ in:
Alessandro Avetta Coll., Alassio, Italy. (p. 31).

n° 43. *The New Queen*. Detail. Plaster.
78¾ x 11¾ in: Triennale, Milan. (Destroyed).
*This large bas-relief intended for the Milan
Triennale, was rejected by the Fascist Govern-
ment.*

n° 43 a. *The New Queen*. Detail.

n° 43 b. *The New Queen*. Detail.

n° 44. *Portrait*. Bronze.
Height: about 11¾ in: Private Coll.

44

1934

n° 45. *Boxer*. Bronze. Height: 47¹/₄ in: Galleria Civica d'Arte Moderna, Turin. (p. 29).

n° 46. *Bather*. Stone from Vicenza. Length: about 59 in: Private Coll. (p. 19).
This was one of the first sculptures which the artist carved in stone.

n° 47. *Portrait of the Painter Pompeo Borra.* Plaster. Height: about 16⁷/₈ in: Private Coll., Milan.

n° 48. *Portrait of the Lawyer Vecchi.* Polychrome terracotta. Height: 13³/₄ in: Private Coll., Milan.

1935

n° 49. *Seated Bather*. Plaster. Length: about 47¹/₄ in: Property of the artist.
This large plaster work has never been cast in bronze.

n° 50. *Pomona*. Bronze. 30³/₄ x 13³/₄ x 43¹/₄ in: 1. and 2. Pierre Matisse Gallery, New York. 3. Emilio Jesi Coll., Milan.

n° 51. *Boxer*. Wood. Height: about 64⁷/₈ in: Musée du Jeu de Paume, Paris. (Lost).
The Musée du Jeu de Paume bought this work, the finest example in wood in the series on Athletes, in 1936. It was left in the cellars of the museum during the German occupation of Paris and has never been found since.

n° 52. *Self-portrait*. Bronze. Height: 10¹/₄ in: Emilio Jesi Coll., Milan. (p. 17).

47

48

50

57
51

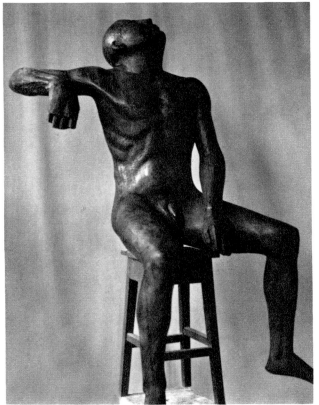

n° 53. *Little Boxer*. Bronze.
8¹/₄ x 3¹/₈ x 5¹/₈ in:
1. John Butler Coll., New York.
2. R. D. S. May Coll., London.
3. Mr. and Mrs. Richard Davis Coll.,
New York.
4. Alfred Westholm Coll., Gothenburg.
5. Marina Marini Coll., Milan. (p. 32).

n° 54. *Seated Boxer*. Bronze. Height:
about 26³/₈ in:
1. Mr. and Mrs. Perry T. Rathbone Coll., Cambridge, Mass. on loan to the Museum of Fine
Arts, Boston, Mass.
2. Property of the artist. (p. 30).

n° 55. *Small Rider*. Plaster. Height:
about 17³/₄ in: Private Coll. (p. 24).

n° 56. *Small Figure*. Bronze. Height: 9 in:
1. Charles Grace Coll., Philadelphia.
2. Louis E. Stern Coll., in the Philadelphia
Museum of Art, Philadelphia.
3. Christian Faerber Coll., Gothenburg.
4. Mrs. Steinmann Coll., New York.
5. Eric Estorick Coll., London.
6. Pierre Matisse Gallery, New York.
7. Galerie Rosengart, Lucerne. (p. 24).

n° 57. *Portrait of a Child*. Height: 9 in:
Stone: Formenti Peroni Coll., Milan.
Wax: Michelangelo Masciotta Coll., Florence.

49

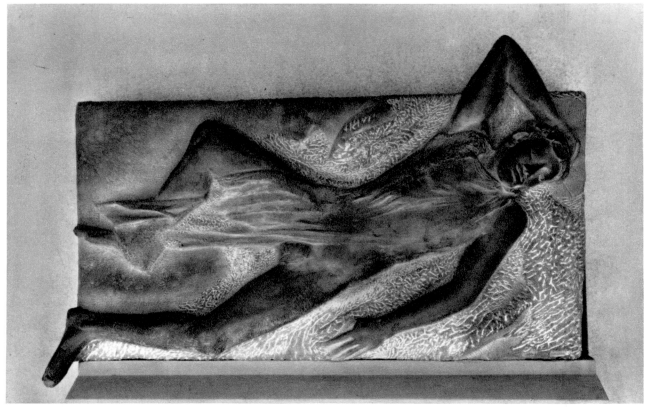

61

n° 58. *Portrait of Hélène Worms*. Bronze. Height: about 13³/₄ in: Private Coll., Paris.

n° 59. *Portrait of Marina Torlonia*. Wax. Height: about 13³/₄ in: Private Coll.

Marino Marini has executed only a few works in wax, including the portrait of Marina Torlonia, a young girl belonging to an aristocratic Roman family.

n° 60. *Portrait of Lucosius*. Terracotta. Height: 14¹/₄ in:
1. Property of the artist.
2. Galleria d'Arte Moderna, Rome.

The model was one of the artist's students at the Academy in Monza.

n° 61. *Bacchus*. Stone.
10⁵/₈ x 65³/₈ x 43³/₄ in: Kunsthaus, Zurich.

This work was originally commissioned by an

American collector, but was bought by the Kunsthaus, Zurich, where it had been exhibited.

1936

n° 62. *Small Nude*. Height: 9⁷/₈ in:
Terracotta: Property of the artist.
Bronze: Prof. Walter Hallstein Coll., Brussels, Dominion Gallery, Montreal. (p. 24).

n° 63. *Young Boxer*. Bronze.
25¹/₄ x 11³/₄ x 11³/₄ in:
Della Ragione Coll., Genoa.

n° 64. *Rider*. Bronze. 63 x 80³/₄ in:
Emilio Jesi Coll., Milan. (p. 205).

n° 64 a. *Rider* (1936-1937). Polychrome wood. 63 x 80³/₄ in: Battiato Coll., Milan.

n° 65. *Prize-fighter. Study*. Plaster. Height: 13³/₈ in: Unique copy: private Coll.

n° 66. *Crucifix*. Bronze. Height: 8⁵/₈ in:
1. J. B. Whelan Coll., London.
2. Battiato Coll., Milan.
3. Riccardo Jucker Coll., Milan.
4. Enrico Franzoni Coll., Locarno.
5. Gippo Toninelli Coll., Milan.
6. Alberta Carnacini Coll., Bologna.
Et al. Property of the artist.

A sculpture in plaster of another crucifix belongs to the collector Tosi in Milan.

n° 67. *Portrait of a Woman*. Wax. Height: 11³/₄ in: Galleria la Tavolozza, Palermo.

n° 68. *Portrait of Bebe Baslini*. Polychrome plaster. Height: about 13³/₄ in:
Baslini Soro Coll., Rome.

59

58

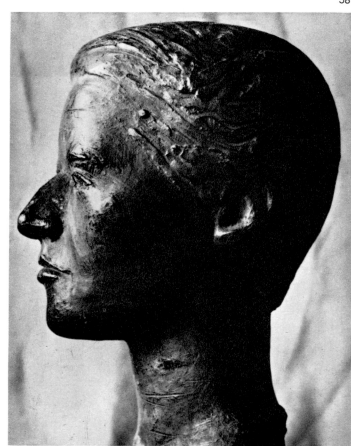

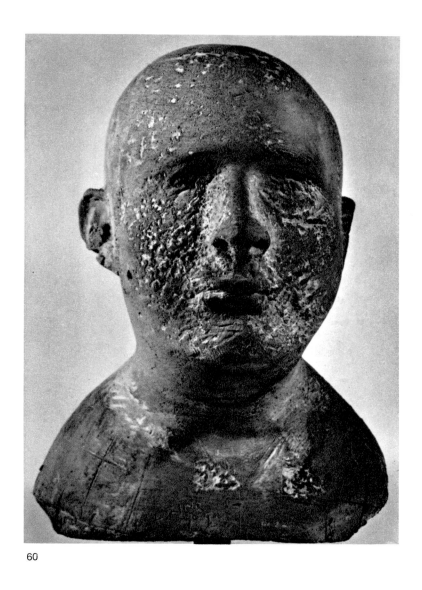

60

69

67

68

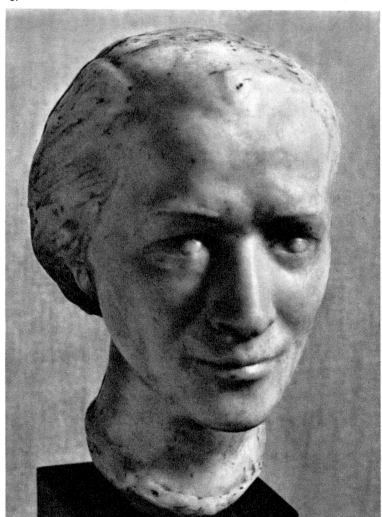

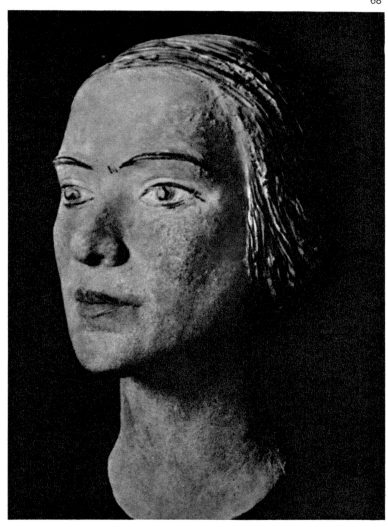

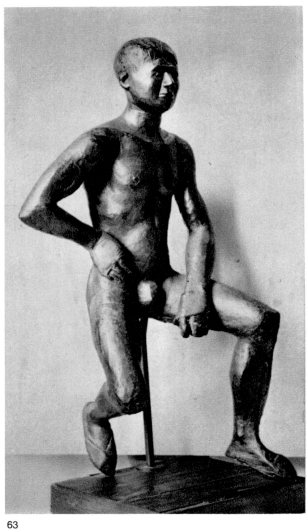

63

66

n° 69. *Portrait of a Pupil*. Terracotta. Height: about 13³/₄ in: Property of the artist.

n° 70. *Portrait of Baronessa Trêves*. Plaster. Height: 11 in: Property of the artist.

n° 71. *Portrait of Baronessa Trêves* (with a hat). Terracotta. Height: 11 in: Property of the artist.

1937

n° 72. *Imaginary Portrait*. Terracotta. Height: about 9⁷/₈ in: Property of the artist. (p. 89).

n° 73. *Portrait of Signora Verga*. Polychrome terracotta. Height: 9 in: Emilio Jesi Coll., Milan. (p. 82).

n° 73 a. *Portrait of Signora Verga*. Terracotta. 10⁵/₈ x 10⁵/₈ in: Della Ragione Coll., Genoa.

n° 74. *Portrait of the Sculptor Fausto Melotti*. Wax. Height: about 14⁵/₈ in: Emilio Jesi Coll., Milan.

A bronze of this portrait probably exists.

n° 74 a. *Portrait of the Sculptor Fausto Melotti*. Bronze. Height: about 11³/₄ in: Property of the artist. (p. 70).

n° 75. *Head*. Polychrome terracotta. Height: 15 in: Private Coll., Milan.

n° 76. *Portrait of the Painter Funi*. Polychrome plaster. Height: 11³/₄ in: Funi Coll., Milan.

n° 78. *Horse*. Bronze. 60³/₈ x 59³/₄ in: Base: 39³/₄ x 12³/₈ in: Unique copy: Della Ragione Coll., Genoa.

n° 79. *Gentleman on Horseback*. Study. Terracotta and bronze. Height: about 22¹/₂ in: Property of the artist.

65

70

71

79

n° 80. *Gentleman on Horseback.* Bronze.
Height: 61⁹/₈ in:
1. Folksam Fack Coll., Stockholm.
2. A/S. Selnaagbygg, Vinderen, Oslo.
3. The National Gallery of Canada, Ottawa.
Et al. Camera dei Deputati, Rome. (p. 192).

n° 80 X. *Portrait of a Woman.*
Height: 10⁵/₈ in: Bronze: Mottola Coll., Milan.
Polychrome terracotta: E. Jesi Coll., Milan.
(p. 90).

*This is a portrait of the model who sat for
the series " Young Girl " (n° 82, 83, 90) and
" The Friends " (n° 128).*

75

73 a

74

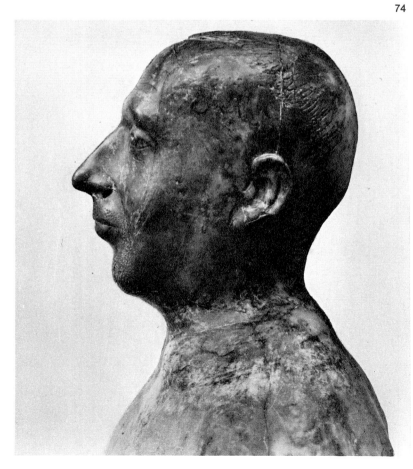

76

64 a

83

78

1938

n° 81. *Bather*. Height: 32$^{5}/_{8}$ in: Stone:
Galleria Nazionale d'Arte Moderna, Rome.
Bronze:
1. Galleria Toninelli, Milan.
2. Property of the artist. (p. 35).

330

84

n° 82. *Young Girl.* Plaster. Height: 61 in: Unique copy: Zoia Coll., Milan. (p. 36).

The same model sat for the series of "Young Girls" comprising three large sculptures (n° 82, 83, 90).

n° 82 a. *Young Girl.* Idem. (p. 36).

n° 82 b. *Young Girl.* Idem. (p. 36).

n° 83. *Young Girl.* Height: 59⁷/₈ in: Terracotta: Emilio Jesi Coll., Milan. Bronze:
1. Private Coll., New York.
2. Property of the artist.

n° 83 a. *Young Girl.* Detail. (p. 37).

n° 84. *Portrait of America Vitali.* Stone. 19⁵/₈ x 7⁷/₈ in: Della Ragione Coll., Genoa.

86

88

n° 85. *Portrait of a Woman.* Wax. Height: 7⁷/₈ in:
1. Private Coll., Genoa.
2. Property of the artist.

n° 86. *Portrait of America Vitali.* Height: about 12⁵/₈ in: Bronze: Vitali Coll., Milan. Plaster: Property of the artist.

n° 87. *Portrait of a Woman.* Polychrome plaster. Height: 17³/₄ in: Property of the artist.

n° 88. *Portrait of Raffaele Carrieri.* Bronze. 8⁷/₈ x 9¹/₂ in: Raffaele Carrieri Coll., Milan.

85

87

89

n° 89. *Bas-relief*. Plaster. 47$\frac{1}{4}$ x 47$\frac{1}{4}$ in:
Battiato Coll., Milan.

n° 89 a, b, c, d, e, f, g, h, i, j, k. *Bas-reliefs*.
Plaster. 10$\frac{1}{4}$ x 10$\frac{1}{4}$ in: (Destroyed).

89 a

89 h

89 b

89 e

89 i

89 c
89 d

89 f
89 g

89 j
89 k

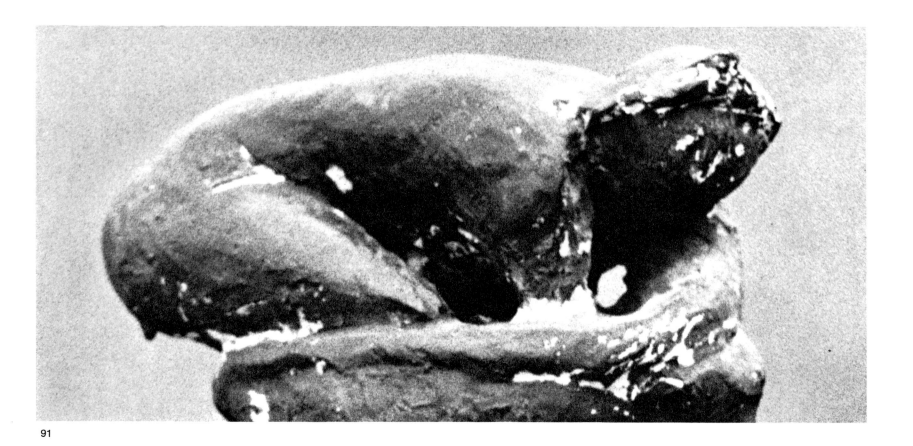

91

92 93

1939

n° 90. *Young Girl.* Bronze. Height: 45¹/₄ in:
Unique copy: Emilio Jesi Coll., Milan. (p. 38).

n° 91. *Small Nude.* Height: 7⁷/₈ in:
Bronze:
1. Pierre Matisse Gallery, New York.
2. Mr. and Mrs. David Finn Coll.,
New Rochelle, New York.
Terracotta: Marina Marini Coll., Milan.

n° 92. *Pomona* (1939-1940). Terracotta.
Height: 63 in:
Galleria d'Arte del Cavallino, Venice.

n° 92 a. *Pomona.* Detail. (p. 111).

n° 93. *Juggler.* Height: 67¹/₄ in:
Bronze:
1. Margaret Josten Coll., New York.
2. Landesgalerie, Hanover.
3. Hanover Gallery, London.
Polychrome bronze: et al. Property of the artist.
Terracotta: Marelli Coll., Milan.

99

95

98

96

100

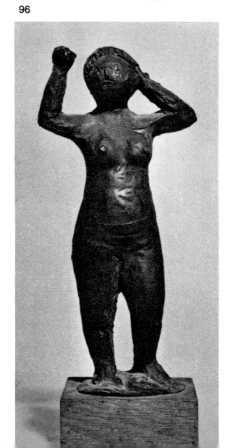

97

101

107

n° 95. *Little Horse.* Bronze. Height: 6⅜ in:
1. Della Ragione Coll., Genoa.
2. Formenti Peroni Coll., Milan.

n° 96. *Pomona.* Bronze. Height: 7½ in:
Della Ragione Coll., Genoa.
*This sculpture, generally regarded as a 1940
work, probably dates from 1935.*

n° 97. *Head.* Wax. Height: 4¾ in:
Formenti Peroni Coll., Milan.

n° 98. *Horse.* Bronze. Length: 23⅝ in:
Property of the artist.

n° 99. *Horse.* Bronze: 49¼ x 13⅞ x 29⅛ in:
1. W. and N. Bär Coll., Zurich.
2. Gianni Mattioli Coll., Milan.
3. H. de Sola y hijos Coll., San Salvador.
4. Hanover Gallery, London.
Et al. Property of the artist.

n° 100. *Horse.* 46½ x 61 in: Bronze:
Unique copy: Emilio Jesi Coll., Milan.
Terracotta: W. Bagnoli Coll., Milan.

n° 101. *The Pilgrim.* Bronze.
68⅛ x 16½ x 48¾ in:
Unique copy: Emilio Jesi Coll., Milan.

1940

n° 102. *Pomona.* Bronze. Height: 68⅞ in:
Unique copy: Emilio Jesi Coll., Milan. (p. 113).

n° 102 a. *Pomona.* Back view. (p. 112).

n° 103. *Small Juggler.*
Bronze: Height: 11 in:
Property of the artist (2 copies).
Plaster: Property of the artist. (p. 151).

n° 104. *Juggler.* Bronze. 26 x 16⅛ x 31⅛ in:
1. Musées Royaux des Beaux-Arts, Brussels.
2. Pierre Matisse Gallery, New York.
3. Private Coll., Zurich.
Et al. Property of the artist. (p. 152).

n° 104 a. *Juggler.* Idem. (p. 153).

n° 105. *Little Rider.* Height: 9½ in:
Terracotta: Property of the artist.
Ceramic: Galleria Toninelli, Milan.

105

108

111

112

113

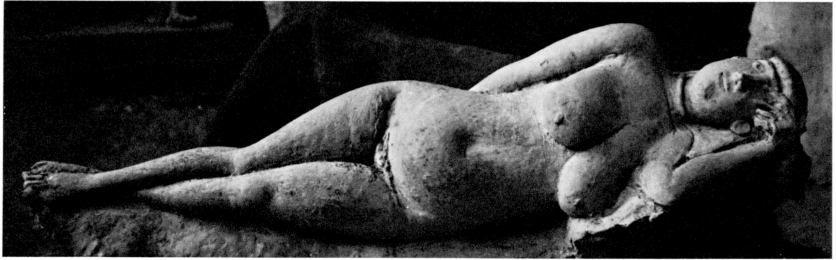

114

115

116

1941

n° 106. *Donatella*. Terracotta. Height:
about 15 in: Property of the artist. (p. 69).

n° 107. *Rider*. Terracotta.
Height: about 19¹/₂ in: Private Coll., Locarno.

n° 108. *Donatella*. Terracotta.
Height: about 9 in: Property of the artist.
*In spite of the realism of this figure, it is
actually a portrait drawn from the imagination.*

n° 109. *Portrait of the Painter Filippo De
Pisis*. Bronze. Height: 13³/₄ in:
1. Private Coll., Stockholm.
2. Property of the artist. (p. 72).

n° 110. *Pomona*. Bronze. Height: 63 in:
1. Musées Royaux des Beaux-Arts, Brussels.
2. Marina Marini Coll., Milan.
3. Property of the artist. (p. 114).

1942

n° 111. *The Dream of Venus*. Plaster.
Length: about 43¹/₄ in: (Destroyed).

n° 112. *Nude*. Terracotta. 15³/₄ x 7¹/₂ in:
Property of the artist.

n° 113. *The Dream of Venus*. Plaster.
Length: about 43¹/₄ in: (Destroyed).

n° 114. *Head.* Bronze. Height: 13³/₄ in:
Property of the artist.

n° 115. *Small Figure*. Bronze.
13³/₈ x 4⁵/₈ x 5¹/₈ in: Property of the artist.

n° 116. *Venus*. Bronze. Height: 43¹/₄ in:
1. Robert H. Tannahill Coll., Detroit.
2. Conrad Furrer Coll., Zurich.
3. Pierre Matisse Gallery, New York.

n° 117. *Portrait of Regina Conti*. Terracotta.
Height: 7⁷/₈ in: Enrico Conti Coll., Lugano.

117

118

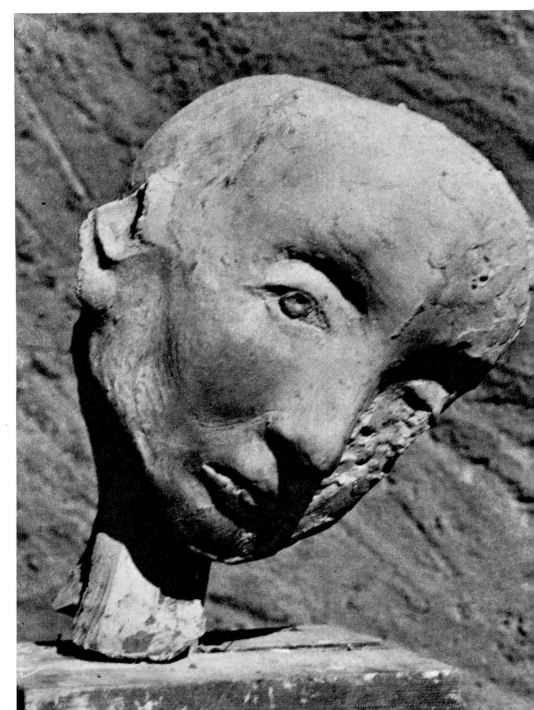

120

121

119

n° 118. *Portrait of Massimo Campigli.*
Height: 15 in:
Bronze: H. Throne Holst Coll., Stockholm.
Property of the artist.
Plaster: Campigli Coll., Rome.

n° 118 a. *Portrait of Massimo Campigli.*
Detail. (p. 80).

n° 119. *Portrait of the Painter Arturo Tosi.*
Bronze. Height: 9⁷/₈ in: Vismara Coll., Milan.

n° 119 a. *Portrait of the Painter Arturo Tosi.*
Polychrome plaster. Height: 9⁷/₈ in:
Emilio Jesi Coll., Milan. (p. 71).

n° 120. *The Hanged Man.* Plaster.
Height: about 9⁷/₈ in: Private Coll., Lugano.

n° 121. *Portrait of Paolo Pedrazzini.* Bronze.
Height: about 15³/₄ in:
1. Pedrazzini Coll., Locarno.
2. Property of the artist.

n° 122. *Little Rider.* Study. Terracotta.
12⁵/₈ x 11 in:
Unique copy: Marina Marini Coll., Milan.

n° 123. *Horse.* Bronze. Height: 29¹/₂ in:
1. Curt Valentin Gallery, New York.
2. Laing Galleries, Toronto.
3. Modern Art Gallery, Basle.

123

125

124
122

126

n° 124. *Small Horse*. Bronze.
21⁵/₈ x 4³/₄ x 4⁸/₄ in:
1. Macchiati Coll., Milan.
2. Sergio Grandini Coll., Lugano.
3. Property of the artist.

n° 125. *Quadriga*. 20¹/₈ x 20¹/₂ in:
Bronze:
1. Curt Valentin Gallery, New York.
2. Eric Estorick Coll., London.
3. Galerie d'Art Moderne, Basle.
Property of the artist (2 copies).
Terracotta: Property of the artist.

n° 126. *Bas-relief*. Plaster.
Property of the artist.

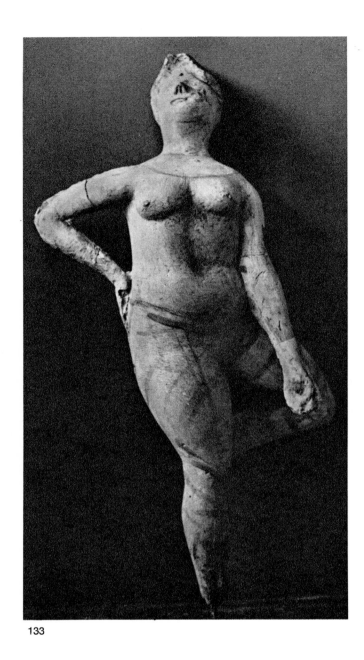

133

138

135

134

132

340

139

142

137

n° 127. *Pomona*. Polychrome plaster.
Height: 27¹/₂ in: Property of the artist.
(p. 115).

n° 128. *The Friends*. Terracotta.
24³/₄ x 4³/₈ x 10¹/₄ in:
Unique copy: Scamperle Coll., Rome. (p. 39).

n° 129. *Bather*. Height: 23¹/₄ in:
Bronze: City Art Museum of St. Louis.
Plaster: Property of the artist. (p. 41).

n° 130. *Small Boxer*. Plaster.
12⁵/₈ x 17³/₈ in: Property of the artist. (p. 40).

n° 131. *Self-portrait*. Polychrome plaster.
Height: 16¹/₈ in: Property of the artist. (p. 377).

n° 131 a. *Self-portrait*. Detail. (p. 68).

1943

n° 132. *The Dream of Venus*. Plaster.
Length: about 47¹/₄ in: (Destroyed).

n° 133. *Dancer*. Polychrome plaster.
Height: about 43¹/₄ in: Property of the artist.

n° 134. *Small Pomona*. Bronze.
Height: 16⁵/₈ in:
1. Joseph Hirshhorn Coll., Greenwich.
2. Justin W. Smith Coll., Minneapolis.
Et al. Marina Marini Coll., Milan.

n° 135. *Small Pomona*. Bronze.
Height: 16⁷/₈ in:
1. Frank Perls Gallery, Beverly Hills.
2. Curt Valentin Gallery, New York.
3. Galerie Gérald Cramer, Geneva.
4. Marina Marini Coll., Milan.

n° 136. *Small Nude*. Height: about 17³/₄ in:
Bronze: Private Coll., Zurich.
Property of the artist (2 copies).
Plaster: Property of the artist. (p. 62).

n° 136 a. *Small Nude*. Idem. (p. 63).

n° 137. *Bather*. Bronze. Height: 51¹/₈ in:
Laing Galleries, Toronto.

n° 138. *Little Angel*. Terracotta.
9⁷/₈ x 7⁷/₈ in: Former G. Zanini Coll., Milan.

n° 139. *Pregnant Woman*. Plaster.
Height: about 13³/₄ in: Galleria Toninelli, Milan.

n° 140. *Small Pomona*. Bronze.
Height: 16⁷/₈ in:
1. Alex L. Hillman Coll., New York.
2. Private Coll., New York.
3. Yale University, New Haven.
4. George Heard Hamilton Coll., New Haven.
5. Marina Marini Coll., Milan. (p. 116).

n° 141. *Composition*. Bas-relief. Bronze.
16⁷/₈ x 16⁷/₈ in:
1. Private Coll., New York.
2. Property of the artist. (p. 42).

n° 142. *Full-length Portrait*. Polychrome
plaster. Height: 55¹/₈ in: Property of the artist.

n° 142 a. *Full-length Portrait*. Detail. (p. 49).

341

152

154 x
155

n° 143. *The Prisoner.* Bronze.
Length: 42$^1/_8$ in: Property of the artist. (p. 48).

n° 144. *Arcangelo* (*Archangel*). Polychrome
plaster. Height: 51$^3/_4$ in: Christoph Bernoulli
Coll., on loan to Basle Museum. (p. 74).

n° 144 a. *Arcangelo* (*Archangel*). Detail.
(p. 77).

n° 145. *Suzanne.* Bronze. Height: 26$^3/_8$ in:
1. Joseph Hirshhorn Coll., Greenwich.
2. Dr. H. Phihl Coll., Gothenburg. (p. 47).

n° 146. *Small Nude.* Length: 15$^3/_4$ in:
Bronze:
1. Galerie Rosengart, Lucerne.
2. Modern Art Gallery, Basle.
3. Marina Marini Coll., Milan.
4. Dominion Gallery, Montreal.
Terracotta: Property of the artist. (p. 50).

n° 147. *Small Nude.* Bronze. 12$^5/_8$ x 7$^1/_8$ in:
Property of the artist. (p. 51).

n° 148. *Young Woman.* Bronze.
Height: 52$^3/_8$ in:
1. Alma Morgenthau Coll., New York.
2. Valli Coll., Florence.
3. Mr. and Mrs. Jack Rosenberg Coll.,
New York.
4. W. and N. Bär Coll., Zurich. (p. 52).

153

154

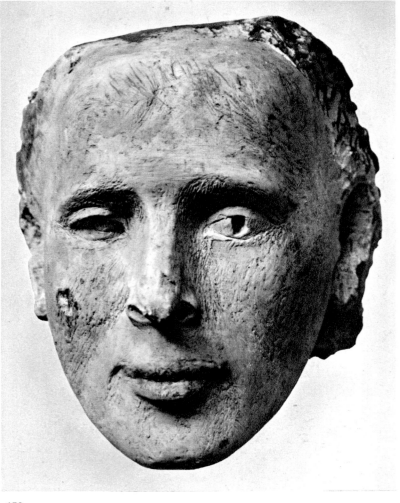

156

n° 149. *Arcangela* (*Archangel*). Bronze. Height: 49¹/₈ in: Atheneum Art Museum, Helsinki. (p. 79).

n° 150. *Portrait of Marina Marini*. Bronze. Height: 11³/₄ in:
1. Mrs. Dorothy Norman Coll., New York.
2. Christian Faerber Coll., Gothenburg.
3. Property of the artist. (p. 83).

n° 151. *Portrait of Ginevra*. Plaster. Height: about 23⁵/₈ in: Property of the artist. (p. 92).

n° 152. *Female Head*. Plaster. Height: 5⁷/₈ in:

n° 153. *Arcangela* (*Archangel*). Bronze. Height: 51¹/₈ in: Property of the artist.

n° 154. *Portrait of Maria Pedrazzini*. Polychrome plaster. Height: about 13³/₄ in: Property of the artist.

n° 154 x *Portrait of Maria Pedrazzini*. Plaster. Height: 7⁷/₈ in: M. Pedrazzini Coll., Locarno.

n° 155. *Portrait of Madame Melms*. Bronze. Height: 52 in: Property of the artist.

n° 156. *Portrait of Giuditta Campigli*. Plaster. Height: 12⁵/₈ in: Property of the artist.

n° 157. *Portrait of Doctor Werner Amsler*. Height: 13³/₄ in: Bronze: Kunstmuseum, Winterthur, Switzerland. Polychrome plaster: Property of the artist.

n° 158. *Portrait of Marie-Claude*. Cement. Height: about 10⁵/₈ in: Mme Adrienne Pedotti Coll., Lugano.

n° 159. *Portrait of Anita*. Terracotta. Height: 9⁷/₈ in: Property of the artist.

159

158

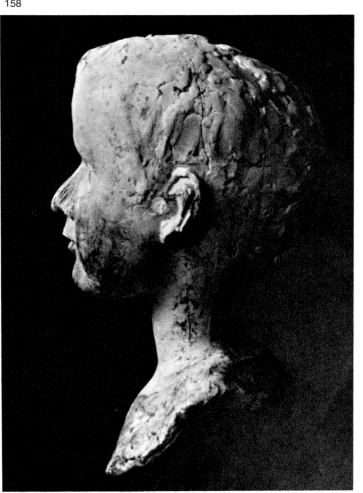

157

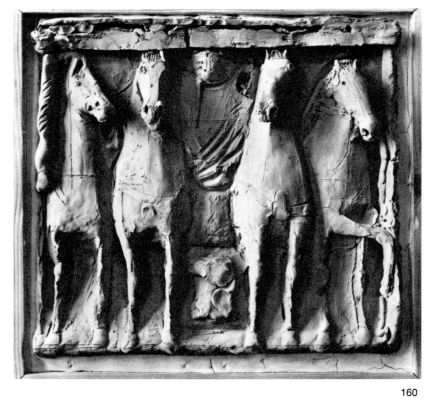

160

163

n° 160. *Quadriga.* Terracotta.
13¹/₄ x 13¹/₄ in:
Kunstmuseum, Basle. (Gift of the artist).

n° 161. *The Miracle.* Polychrome plaster and collage. Height: 27¹/₂ in: Unique copy: Emilio Jesi Coll., Milan. (p. 243).

"The Miracle", Marino Marini wrote to a friend, "may be meant in a realist sense. It may be interpreted in an inspired and abstract form, such as those of the Riders, which I have called Miracle when it fulfills this ideal." The spiritual impulse of the Miracles corresponds to the aspect of creation opposite to

162

166

167

*the powerful eroticism of the early Riders,
but is it possible to say, as one of his
critics has affirmed, that Marino Marini's
sculpture is not erotic? Like his paintings, it
is both erotic and spiritual, but his eroticism
is no less sacred (in the way in which Mircea
Eliade understands the word) than its spiri-
tuality; in short, this is the "orientalism" of
Marino Marini.*

n° 162. *The Three Graces.* Bronze.
17³/₄ x 16¹/₈ in:
1. Private Coll., New York.
2. Curt Valentin Gallery, New York.

n° 163. *The Three Graces.* Bronze.
21⁵/₈ x 21⁷/₈ in: Private Coll., New York.

n° 164. *Rider.* Bas-relief. Bronze.
16⁷/₈ x 16⁷/₈ in:
1. Curt Valentin Gallery, New York.
2. Property of the artist.

n° 165. *Little Horse.* Terracotta.
15 x 10¹/₄ in: Property of the artist.

n° 166. *Horse.* Polychrome plaster.
Height: 27¹/₂ in:
Unique copy: Von Schumacher Coll., Zurich.

n° 167. *Portrait of Gianni Pedrazzini.*
Plaster. Height: about 12⁵/₈ in:
Maria Pedrazzini Coll., Locarno.

164

165

177

169
171

172

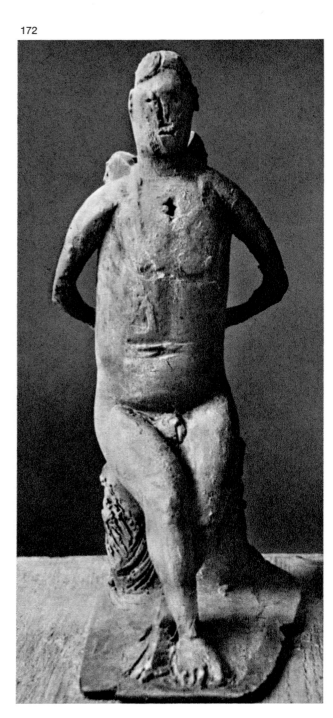

346

1944

n° 168. *Small Dancer.* Bronze.
Height: 23⁵/₈ in:
1. Michael Behrens Coll., London.
2. Leopoldo Zorzi Coll., Bari, Italy.
3. Property of the artist.

n° 169. *Small Pomona.* Bronze.
18⁷/₈ x 3¹/₄ x 5⁷/₈ in: Property of the artist.

n° 170. *Small Nude.* Terracotta. Height:
about 15 in: Property of the artist.

n° 171. *Seated Figure.* Plaster.
Height: 15³/₄ in: (Destroyed).

n° 172. *Relic.* Terracotta.
Height: about 15³/₄ in: Property of the artist.

n° 173. *Seated Figure.* Bronze.
Height: 27¹/₂ in:
1. Wadsworth Atheneum, Hartford.
2. Private Coll., Dusseldorf. (p. 61).

n° 173 a. *Seated Figure.* Detail. (p. 60).

n° 174. *Juggler.* Polychrome bronze.
Height: 36³/₈ in:
1. Mrs. Nancy Grace Coll., Philadelphia.
2. Rollier Coll., Milan.
3. Property of the artist. (p. 136).

n° 175. *Small Pomona.* Polychrome plaster.
Height: 23⁵/₈ in:
Property of the artist. (p. 121).

n° 176. *Portrait of Karl Von Schumacher.*
Polychrome plaster. Height: about 11³/₄ in:
Dr. Pierre Von Schumacher Coll., Schloss
Mauensee, Zurich.
*Any existing copy in bronze of this work is
false.*

n° 177. *Portrait of Madame Baumann.*
Terracotta. Height: about 9⁷/₈ in:
Property of the artist.

176

170

168

179

180

n° 178. *Portrait of Maria Pedrazzini.*
Bronze. Height: 15³/₄ in:
Property of the artist.

n° 179. *Portrait of Contessa Carolina Maraini.*
Height: about 11³/₄ in:
Polychrome plaster:
A. and. H. Orsola Greco Soldati Coll., Lugano.
Plaster: Property of the artist.

n° 180. *Portrait of Noemi Bolla.*
Polychrome plaster. Height: 13³/₄ in:
Augusta Bolla Coll., Lugano.

n° 181. *Portrait of Hedy Hahnloser.* Plaster.
13³/₈ x 7¹/₈ x 9⁷/₄ in:
Prof. Hahnloser Coll., Berne. 2 Bronzes. (p. 85).

n° 182. *Portrait of Noemi Bolla.* Terracotta.
Height: 8⁵/₈ in: Property of the artist.

n° 183. *Portrait of Gianni Pedrazzini.*
Plaster. Height: 13³/₄ in:
Property of the artist. Two versions exists.

n° 184. *Portrait of Remo Rossi.* Plaster.
Height: 11³/₄ in: Property of the artist.

178

182

185

n° 185. *Small Rider.* Terracotta. Height:
9⁷/₈ in: Former Raffaele Carrieri Coll., Milan.

n° 186. *Small Rider.* Height: 13³/₈ in:
Bronze:
1. Edwin H. Morris Coll., New York.
2. Hanover Gallery, London.
3. W. and N. Bär Coll., Zurich.
4. Hanover Gallery, London.
5. Louis D. Cohen Coll., Great Neck,
New York.
6. Property of the artist.
Ceramic: Property of the artist.

183

184

186

187

189
197

188

350

200

1945

n° 190. *Small Nude.* Bronze. Height: 16⁵/₈ in:
1. Cincinnati Art Museum, Cincinnati.
2. D. Westman Coll., Stockholm.
3. Galerie d'Art Moderne, Basle.
4. Laing Galleries, Toronto.
Property of the artist. (2 copies). (p. 59).

n° 191. *Nude.* Bronze. Height: 45¹/₄ in:
1. Ennio Morlotti Coll., Milan.
2. Landesmuseum, Hanover.
3. Mr. and Mrs. David Finn Coll., New York.
(p. 58).

n° 191 a. *Nude.* Idem. (p. 58).

n° 192. *Seated Woman.* Bronze.
Height: 18¹/₈ in:
Riccardo Jucker Coll., Milan. (p. 57).

n° 193. *Small Nude.* Bronze.
Height: 10³/₄ in:
1. Baron Ph. de Rothschild Coll., Pouillac, France.
2. Mr. and Mrs. S. H. Stead Ellis Coll., London.
3. R. D. S. May Coll., London.
4. Pierre Matisse Gallery, New York.
Property of the artist. (2 copies). (p. 48).

n° 194. *Dancer.* Height: about 57 in:
Bronze:
1. Angelo Tanzi Coll., Milan.
2. Ayala and Sam Zachs Coll., Toronto.
Terracotta: Private Coll., Milan. (p. 141).

n° 195. *Venus.* Height: 43¹/₄ in:
Terracotta: Gianni Mattioli Coll., Milan.
Bronze: Nasjonalgalleriet, Oslo. (p. 53).

n° 196. *Judith.* Bronze.
53¹/₈ x 20¹/₈ x 25⁵/₈ in: Unique copy:
Middelheim Park Museum, Antwerp. (p. 54).

199

n° 187. *Small Rider.* 14⁵/₈ x 16¹/₈ in:
Bronze:
1. Louis D. Cohen Coll., Great Neck,
New York.
2. Jeffrey H. Loria Coll., New York.
3. Property of the artist.
Ceramic: Property of the artist.

n° 188. *Small Rider.* Height: about 11³/₄ in:
Bronze:
1. Hanover Gallery, London.
2. 3. 4. Galerie Gérald Cramer, Geneva.
5. 6. et al. Laing Galleries, Toronto.
Terracotta: Property of the artist.

n° 189. *Rider* Bas-relief. Bronze.
About 16⁷/₈ x 16⁷/₈ in: Private Coll., Zurich.

205

n° 197. *Pomona.* Stone. Height: 68⅞ in: W. and N. Bär Coll., Zurich.

n° 197 a. *Pomona.* Detail. (p. 118).

n° 198. *Pomona.* Bronze.
63 x 20⅛ x 20½ in:
1. Hanover Gallery, London.
2. Bochum Museum, Bochum, Federal Republic of Germany.
3. Pietro Campilli Coll., Rome.
Et al. Property of the artist (p. 117).

n° 199. *Small Bather.* Bronze. 9 x 11⅜ in:
1. Riccardo Jucker Coll., Milan.
2. J. Nehmad Coll., Milan.

n° 200. *Portrait of Manuel Gasser.*
Height: 11¾ in:
Polychrome terracotta:
Manuel Gasser Coll., Zurich.
Plaster: Property of the artist.

n° 201. *Portrait of Madame Étienne Grandjean.* Polychrome plaster. Height: 13¾ in: Grandjean Coll., Zurich. (p. 87).

n° 202. *Portrait of Germaine Richier.*
Bronze.
Height: 13 in: Property of the artist. (p. 95).
A head with bust also exists: Height: 22⅞ in:
Property of the artist.
Marino Marini met Germaine Richier in Zurich in 1941.

n° 203. *Portrait of Georg Schmidt.*
Height: 14¼ in:
Polychrome plaster:
Kunstmuseum, Basle. (Gift of the artist).
Bronze: Private Coll., Copenhagen. (p. 84).

n° 204. *Portrait of Johann Ulrich Gasser.*
Polychrome terracotta. Height: 9⅞ in:
Manuel Gasser Coll., Zurich. (p. 78).

n° 205. *Romantic Portrait.* Plaster.
Height: about 15 in:
Galleria d'Arte Moderna, Milan.
Variation: Property of the artist.

207

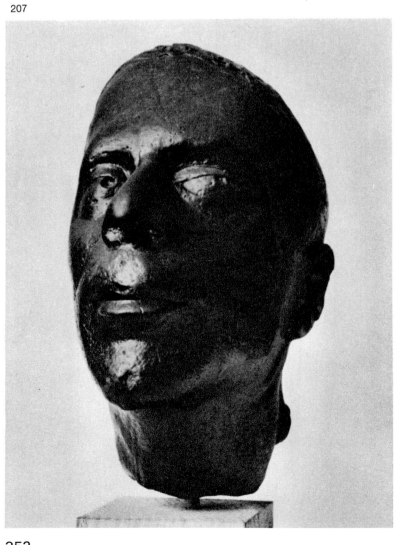

206

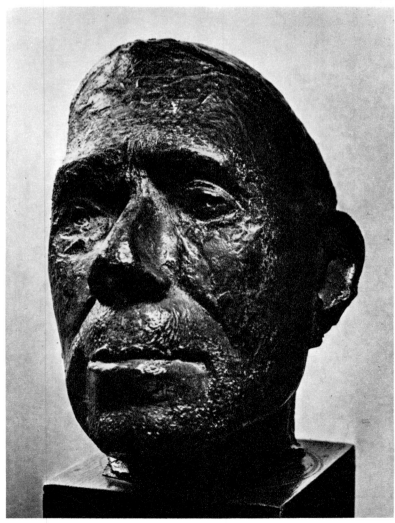

212

211

210

n° 206. *Portrait of Lamberto Vitali.*
$10^5/_8$ x $5^1/_2$ in:
Bronze:
Museum of Modern Art, New York.
Samuel A. Lewisohn Coll., New York.
Lead: Emilio Jesi Coll., Milan.
Stone: Lamberto Vitali Coll., Milan.

n° 207. *Portrait of Lamberto Vitali.* Wax.
$10^5/_8$ x $5^1/_2$ in: Lamberto Vitali Coll., Milan.

n° 208. *Horse.* $18^1/_8$ x $11^3/_4$ in:
Plaster: Property of the artist.
Bronze: Property of the artist (2 copies).
(p. 194).

n° 209. *Rider.* Polychrome bronze. Height:
$40^5/_8$ in:
1. Konstmuseet, Gothenburg.
2. Mrs. Edward Hilton Coll., London.
3. Mr. and Mrs. E. Mendoza Coll., Caracas.
(p. 193).

n° 210. *Little Horse.* $14^1/_4$ x 11 in:
Bronze:
1. Curt Valentin Gallery, New York.
2. Pierre Matisse Gallery, New York.
3. and 4. Laing Galleries, Toronto.
5. Property of the artist.
Terracotta: Property of the artist.

n° 211. *Little Horse.* Bronze: $13^7/_8$ x $11^3/_4$ in:
Mabel Garrison Siemonn Coll., Baltimore Museum of Art, Baltimore.

n° 212. *Horse.* Bronze. Height: $30^1/_2$ in:
1. Mme. Lucy Rudolph Coll., Zurich.
2. National Gallery of Canada, Ottawa.
3. Hanover Gallery, London.
Et al. Dominion Gallery, Montreal.
Property of the artist.

1946

n° 213. *Small Seated Pomona.* Bronze.
Height: $17^3/_8$ in:
1. Emilio Jesi Coll., Milan.
2. Macchiati Coll., Milan.
3. Property of the artist. (p. 123).

n° 214. *Juggler.* Bronze. Height: 72 in:
1. Galleria d'Arte Moderna, Rome.
2. Pierre Matisse Gallery, New York.
3. Kunsthaus, Zurich. (Gift of W. and N. Bär).
et al. Property of the artist. (p. 160).
A few copies were carved by the artist after the casting in bronze. This endows the sculpture with a certain oriental over-refiniment.

353

215

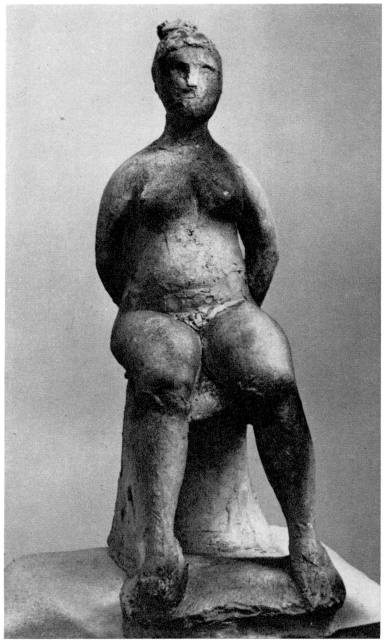

217

221

222

223
224

n° 214 a. *Juggler.* Polychrome plaster.
Height: 72 in: Property of the artist. (p. 161).

n° 215. *Small Rider.* 20¹/₈ x 11 x 8⁵/₈ in:
Bronze:
1. Lawrence J. Heller Coll., Bethesda.
2. Carlo Frua di Angeli Coll., Milan.
3. Roth Coll., Zurich.
4. Raffaele Carrieri Coll., Milan.
5. Hanover Gallery, London.
6. Galleria d'Arte Moderna, Rome.
7. H. E. Smeets Coll., Weert, Holland.
8. Museum of Modern Art, Kyoto.
Polychrome plaster: Marina Marini Coll., Milan.

n° 216. *Portrait of the Painter Carlo Carrà.*
Height: 9¹/₂ in: Lead: Emilio Jesi Coll., Milan.
Bronze:
1. Mr. and Mrs. Robert Osborn Coll., Salisbury.
2. Museo Rivoltella, Trieste.
Plaster: Property of the artist. (p. 93).

n° 216 a. *Portrait of the Painter Carlo Carrà.*
Plaster. · Variation. Height: 9¹/₂ in:
Property of the artist.

n° 217. *Little Judith.* Bronze.
Height: 27¹/₂ in:
1. J. Hirshhorn Coll., Greenwich.
2. Pierre Matisse Gallery, New York.

n° 218. *Portrait of Marina Marini.*
Polychrome plaster. Height: 12¹/₄ in: Property
of the artist. (p. 88).

1947

n° 219. *Portrait of Emma Jeker.*
Height: 13³/₄ in: Plaster: Property of the artist.
Lead: Jeker Coll., Milan. (p. 97).

n° 220. *Pomona.* Bronze.
65³/₄ x 17³/₄ x 20¹/₂ in:
Unique copy: Emilio Jesi Coll., Milan. (p. 124).

n° 220 a. *Pomona.* Detail. (p. 125).

n° 221. *Nude.* Bronze. 31¹/₂ x 6⁵/₈ x 7¹/₈ in:
1. Adrian Ryan Coll., London.
2. Mr. and Mrs. Louis N. Cohen Coll., Chicago.
3. Mr. and Mrs. Malcolm Coll., Brusch.
4. Private Coll., Gothenburg.
5. Property of the artist.

n° 222. *Portrait of a Woman.* Polychrome
plaster. Height: 12⁵/₈ in: Property of the artist.

229 b

232

233

n° 223. *Portrait of Mrs. Fischer*. Bronze.
Height: 15³/₄ in:
Mr. and Mrs. E. Fischer Coll. New York.

n° 224. *Portrait of a Woman*.
Height: about 15³/₄ in:
Bronze: Pizzocaro Coll., Milan.
Plaster: Property of the artist.

n° 225. *Portrait of Emilio Jesi*. Bronze.
Height: 9¹/₂ in:
Unique copy: Emilio Jesi Coll., Milan. (p. 73).

Emilio Jesi is the greatest collector of Marino Marini's sculptures and paintings in Italy.

n° 226. *Portrait of Carlo Cardazzo*.
Height: 12¹/₄ in:
Polychrome plaster:
Property of the artist.
Lead: Private Coll., Copenhagen. (p. 94).

Carlo Cardazzo, primarily a collector, was one of the most important promoters of modern art in Italy until his death in 1963. He created the Galleria del Cavallino in Venice and the Galleria del Naviglio in Milan.

n° 228. Horse. Bronze.
Height: about 39³/₈ in:
1. Mr. and Mrs. Ralph F. Colin Coll., New York.
2. Mr. and Mrs. Walter A. Haas Coll., San Francisco.
3. Galleria Ghiringhelli, Milan.
4. Campanini Coll., Milan.
5. Dr. H. Phihl Coll., Gothenburg. (p. 195).

n° 229. *Rider*. Wood. Height: 63³/₄ in:
Gianni Agnelli Coll., Turin. (p. 196).

n° 229 a. *Rider*. Detail. (p. 197).

n° 229 b. *Rider*. Bronze. Height: 63³/₄ in:
1. Private Coll., New York.
2. Henry Hope Coll., Bloomington.
3. Tate Gallery, London.
Et al. Museum Boymans van Beuningen, Rotterdam.

n° 229 c. *Head of a Horse*. Detail in cement.
Length: 19³/₄ in: Property of the artist. (p. 183).

n° 230. *Rider*. Bronze. 40⁵/₈ x 24³/₄ in:
Base: 17³/₄ x 9⁷/₈ in:
1. Riccardo Jucker Coll., Milan.
2. Blanden Memorial Art Gallery, Fort Dodge, Iowa.
3. Richard Avedon Coll., New York.
4. Robert Strauss Coll., Houston.
5. Pierre Matisse Gallery, New York.
6. Laing Galleries, Toronto.
Et al. P. Campilli Coll., Rome.
Property of the artist. (p. 198).

n° 231. *Rider*. Detail. Height: 40¹/₈ in:
Polychrome plaster: Property of the artist.
Bronze:

1. Museum of Modern Art, New York.
2. Samuel Marx Coll., Chicago.
3. Kölnisches Stadtmuseum, Cologne.
4. Stedelijk Museum, Amsterdam. (p. 202).

n° 232. *Rider*. Bronze: 35³/₈ x 8³/₈ x 11³/₄ in:
1. James T. Soby Coll., New Canaan.
2. Portland Art Museum, Portland.
3. Prof. E. Grandjean Coll., Zurich.
4. Lee Ault Coll., New Canaan.
5. John Butler Coll., New York.
6. Pierre Matisse Gallery, New York.
Et al. Property of the artist.

356

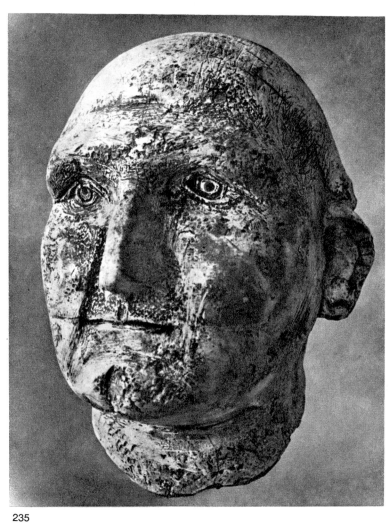

235

234

236

237

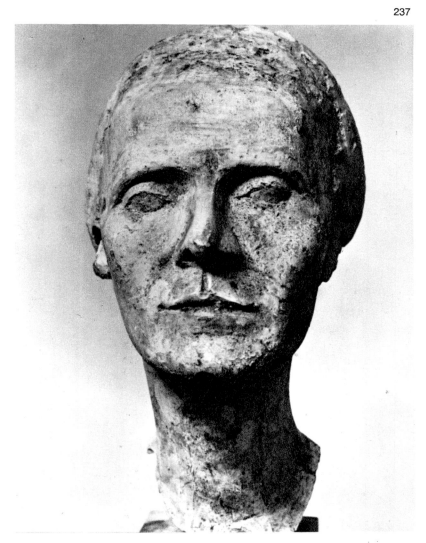

n° 233. *Small rider.* Bronze.
Height: 13³/₄ in:
1. Louis Stern Coll., Philadelphia Museum of Art, Philadelphia.
2. University of Nebraska Art Gallery, Lincoln.
3. Tosi Coll., Milan.
4. Galerie Rosengart, Lucerne.
5. Walter Carsen Coll., Toronto.
6. Property of the artist.

1948

n° 234. *Portrait of Nelly.* Bronze.
Height: 11³/₄ in:
Mr. and Mrs. John L. Bunce Coll., Hartford.

n° 235. *Portrait of M. Lampugnani.* Bronze.
Height: 11³/₄ in: Lampugnani Coll., Milan.

n° 236. *Portrait of Fernande Wittgens.*
Bronze. Height: 18¹/₈ in:
Unique copy: G. Mattioli Coll., Milan.
Modified copy: Property of the artist.

n° 237. *Portrait of Signora Scalini.* Terracotta. Height: 15³/₄ in: Scalini Coll., Milan.

n° 238. *Rider.* Bronze. 44⁷/₈ x 48³/₄ in:
Unique copy: Emilio Jesi Coll., Milan. (p. 201).

n° 239. *Small Rider.* Bronze.
Height: 21³/₄ in:
1. James Schramm Coll., Burlington.
2. Frank Perls Gallery, Beverly Hills.
3. Paul Zimmerman Coll., Hartford.
4. Mr. Lionni Coll., Philadelphia.

n° 240. *Small Rider.* Height: about 16¹/₂ in:
Bronze: Louis Le Brocquy Coll., London.
Ceramic:
Mr. and Mrs. Schnelling Coll., London.

239
240

242 a

358

n° 241. *Nude.* Bronze. Height: 19¹/₄ in:
1. Samuel A. Lewisohn Coll., New York.
2. Modern Art Gallery, Basle.
3. Mautner Markhof Coll., Vienna.
4. Dr. Friederick von Celsing Coll., Stockholm.
5. Riccardo Jucker Coll., Milan.
6. Sergio Grandini Coll., Lugano.
Et al. Property of the artist. (p. 64).

n. 242. *Dancer.* Polychrome plaster.
Height: 69¹/₄ in: Property of the artist. (p. 135).

n° 242 a. *Dancer.* Height: 69¹/₄ in:
Bronze:
1. James T. Soby Coll., New Canaan.
2. Curt Valentin Gallery, New York.
Polychrome bronze: Wilhelm Lehmbruck Museum, Duisburg, Federal Republic of Germany.

n° 243. *Dancer.* Bronze. Height: 46 in:
1. Galleria d'Arte Moderna, Milan.
2. W. and N. Bär Coll., Zurich.
3. Hanover Gallery, London. (p. 143).

n° 244. *Portrait of Ambassador Dunn.*
Height: 11³/₈ in: Bronze: Dunn Coll., Rome.
Plaster: Property of the artist.

n° 244 a. *Portrait of Ambassador Dunn.*
Detail. (p. 81).

n° 245. *Portrait of the Sculptor Hermann Haller.* Polychrome plaster. Height: 13³/₄ in: Kunsthaus, Zurich. (p. 96).

Marino Marini made many sculptures of Swiss personalities, including the sculptor Haller, in the course of frequent visits to Switzerland during and after the war.

251

244

n° 246. *Portrait of Samuel Barber.* Bronze.
11 x 8⁵/₈ in: Sam Barber Coll., Mount Kisco, New York (p. 91).

n° 247. *Pomona.* Bronze. Height: 66¹/₈ in:
1. Lady Hay Coll., on loan to the Scottish National Gallery of Modern Art, Edinburgh.
2. Statens Museum for Kunst, Copenhagen.
3. Municipal Museum, The Hague. (p. 126).

n° 247 a. *Pomona.* Idem. (p. 127).

n° 248. *Small Pomona.* Study. Bronze.
Height: 18⁷/₈ in: Property of the artist. (p. 128).

n° 249. *Rider* (1949-1951). Polychrome wood. 42⁷/₈ x 70³/₄ in:
Kunstverein, Dusseldorf. (p. 190).

n° 249 a. *Rider.* Detail. Bronze.
42⁷/₈ x 70³/₄ in:
1. Sturgis Ingersoll Coll., Philadelphia.
2. Walker Art Center, Minneapolis.
3. City Art Museum, St. Louis. (p. 191).

n° 250. *Rider (The Town's Guardian Angel).*
Polychrome wood. Height: 70³/₄ in:
Prof. H. Krayenbühl Coll., Zurich. (p. 209).

n° 250 a. *The Town's Guardian Angel.*
Bronze. Height: 70³/₄ in:
1. Peggy Guggenheim Coll., Venice.
2. Edgar Kaufmann Coll., Pittsburgh.
3. C. J. Engels Coll., Curaçao. (p. 208).

n° 251. *Rider.* Ceramic. 13³/₄ x 15⁹/₄ in:
Lorenzo Papi Coll., Florence.
Variation: Attilio Bacci Coll., Milan.

254

251 a

252

253

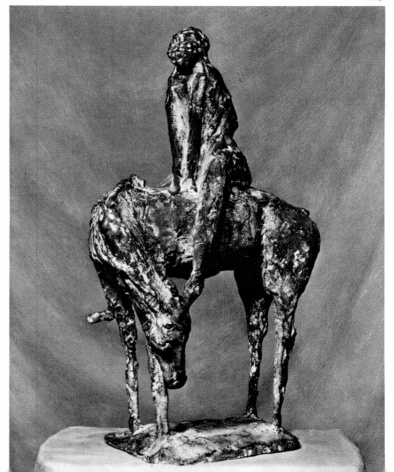

360

269

258

255

n° 251 a. *Rider.* Bronze. $13^3/_4$ x $15^3/_4$ in:
1. Peter Watson Coll., London.
2. Arthur Jeffress Coll., London.
3. Mr. and Mrs. A. Körner Coll., London.
4. Mr. Gösta Olson Coll., Stockholm.
5. Baronne Lambert Coll., Brussels.
6. Private Coll., Zurich.

n° 252. *Composition.* Plaster. Height: 27 in:
Property of the artist.

n° 253. *Small Rider.* Bronze.
Height: $16^1/_2$ in:
1. John S. Newberry Coll., Detroit.
2. Mrs. B. P. Watson Coll., New York.
3. Mr. and Mrs. Ralph F. Colin Coll.,
New York.
4. Mrs. Robert von Hirsch Coll., Basle.
5. Mrs. Eleonora Saidenberg Coll., New York.
6. Leight B. Block Coll., Chicago.

n° 254. *Small Rider.* Polychrome bronze.
$17^3/_8$ x $7^1/_8$ x $9^1/_2$ in:
1. Joseph Hirshhorn Coll., Greenwich.
2. Curt Valentin Gallery, New York.
3. D. Hutchinson Coll., East Bengholt,
England.
4. Adrian Ryan, Coll., London.
5. Ch. Faerber Coll., Gothenburg.
6. Marina Marini Coll., Milan.

1950

n° 255. *Small Figure.* Study. Bronze.
Height: about $7^1/_8$ in: including base.
Unique copy: Ella Winter Coll., London.

n° 256. *Small Pomona.* Bronze.
Height: $5^1/_2$ in: Property of the artist. (p. 129).

n° 258. *Portrait of Monique.* Height: $12^5/_8$ in:
Bronze: Benjamin Watson Coll., Danbury.
Polychrome plaster: Property of the artist.

361

260

259

262

n° 259. *Portrait of Nelson Rockefeller.*
Height: about 11³/₄ in:
Bronze: Private Coll., New York.
Plaster: Property of the artist.

n° 260. *Portrait of the Architect Wallace Harrison.* Bronze. Height: 11³/₄ in:
Private Coll., New York.

n° 261. *Portrait of Riccardo Jucker.*
Height: 14¹/₄ in:
Bronze: R. Jucker Coll., Milan.
Plaster: Property of the artist. (p. 99).
Riccardo Jucker is considered as one of the greatest Italian collectors of modern art.

n° 262. *Portrait of H. Gates Lloyd.* Bronze.
Height: 11³/₄ in:
H. Gates Lloyd Coll., Haverford.

n° 263. *Portrait of Igor Stravinsky.*
1st version. Bronze. Height: about 11³/₄ in:
1. Richard Zeisler Coll., New York.
2. San Francisco Museum of Art, San Francisco.
3. Curt Valentin Gallery, New York. (p. 102).
This portrait of Stravinsky was modeled in the United States and cast in bronze in Milan.

n° 264. *Small Horse.* Bronze.
Height: 20⁷/₈ in:
1. Mrs. McFadden Harrison Coll., New York.
2. W. A. Bechtler Coll., Zurich.
3. John Temple Coll., Chicago.
4. Kölnisches Stadtmuseum, Cologne.
5. Franck Stanton Coll., New York.
6. Pierre Matisse Gallery, New York.

n° 265. *Small Rider.* Bronze.
Height: 11³/₄ in:
1. Mrs. Gertrude Mellon Coll., Greenwich.
2. Lyonel Feininger Coll., New York.
3. Wright Ludington Coll., Santa Barbara.
4. John Cowles Coll., Minneapolis.
5. Miss Ann Smeltzer Coll., New York.
6. Mme. Robert von Hirsch Coll., Basle.

268

n° 266. *Small Horse.* Bronze. 21⁵/₈ x 18⁷/₈ in:
1. Hanover Gallery, London.
2. Eric Estorick Coll., London.
3. Frank Perls Gallery, Beverly Hills.
4. Dr. H. Phihl Coll., Gothenburg.
5. Christoph Bernoulli Coll., Basle.
6. Wadsworth Atheneum, Hartford.

n° 267. *Small Rider.* Bronze. 11 x 16¹/₂ in:
1. Baronne Lambert Coll., Brussels.
2. Sven Ericson Coll., Stockholm.
3. Mrs. H. Heinz Coll., Pennsylvania.
4. Mrs. Werner Josten Coll., New York.
5. Galerie Vömel, Dusseldorf. (p. 204).

n° 268. *Small Rider.* Bronze. Height: 4 in:
Theodor Ahrenberg Coll., Chexbres, Switzerland.

n° 269. *Horse.* Bronze. Height: 46 in:
1. Edgar Kaufmann Coll., Bear Run, Penn.
2. Hamburger Kunsthalle, Hamburg.
3. H. C. Bechtler Coll., Zurich.
4. Toledo Museum of Art, Toledo, Ohio.
5. Max Fischer Coll., Stuttgart. (p. 361).

264

271

273

1951

n° 270. *Juggler.* Bronze. Height: 63 in:
1. Richard Avedon Coll., New York.
2. Curt Valentin Gallery, New York.
3. Chase Manhattan Bank, New York. (p. 154).

n° 271. *Seated Figure.* Terracotta.
Height: about 13³/₄ in: Property of the artist.

n° 272. *Head.* Stone. Height: about 11³/₄ in:
Emilio Jesi Coll., Milan.

272

n° 273. *Portrait of the Architect Antonio Car-minati.* Polychrome plaster. Height: 11³/₄ in:
Property of the artist.

n° 274. *Small Filiform Horse.* Bronze.
Height: 15 in:
1. Dr. Sven Paulsson Coll., Stockholm.
2. Frua de Angeli Coll., Milan.
3. Dr. Schliom Coll., Zurich.
4. Vömel Gallery, Dusseldorf.
5. Symon Goldberg Coll., Amsterdam.
6. Mr. Gabriele H. Grunebaum Coll.,
Scarsdale, New York.

n° 275. *Small Filiform Horse.* Bronze.
10⁵/₈ x 6⁵/₈ x 1¹/₂ in: Property of the artist.

n° 276. *Small Horse.* Bronze.
Height: about 11³/₄ in:
Lady Norton Coll., London.

n° 277. *Portrait of Igor Stravinsky.*
2nd version. Height: 12⁵/₈ in:
Bronze:
1. Claes Philip Coll., Stockholm.
2. Smith College Museum of Art, Northampton.
3. Minneapolis Institute of Art.
4. Kunstmuseum, Essen, Federal Republic of
Germany.
5. Galleria d'Arte Moderna, Milan.
6. Property of the artist.
Plaster: Property of the artist. (p. 103).

n° 278. *Horse.* Study. Bronze.
Height: 12³/₄ in:
1. Riccardo Jucker Coll., Milan.
2. D'Arquian Coll., Brussels.
3. Dr. Rusche Coll., Cologne.
4. Landesgalerie, Hanover.
5. Ralph Lamberson Coll., New York.
6. Marina Marini Coll., Milan. (p. 214).

n° 279. *Small Rider.* Height: 12³/₈ in:
Bronze:
1. Mrs. Betty Maclean Coll., Dallas.
2. Mr. and Mrs. J. Z. Steinberg Coll., Chicago.
3. Mr. Arnold Maremont Coll., Winnetka.
4. Frank Perls Gallery, Beverly Hills.
5. Mees Sikkens Lakfabricken Coll., Sassein-heim, Holland.
6. Mr. and Mrs. Samuel Maslon Coll., Min-neapolis.
Polychrome plaster: Galerie Rosengart, Lu-cerne.

274

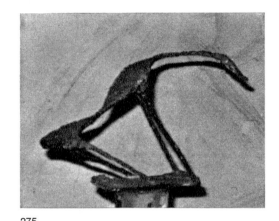

275

281

279

280

276

n° 280. *Rider.* Bronze.
Height: about 15³/₄ in:
1. Ted Weiner Coll., Fort Worth.
2. Mrs. Hans Arnhold Coll., New York.
3. Galerie Berggruen, Paris.
4. Galerie Gérald Cramer, Geneva.
Variations:
1. Modern Art Gallery, Basle.
2. Mr. Maurice Goldman Coll., London.
3. Leopoldo Zorzi Coll., Bari, Italy.
4. Western Australian Art Gallery, Perth.

n° 281. *Rider.* Bronze. Height: 21⁵/₈ in:
1. Joseph Hirshhorn Coll., Greenwich.
2. Galerie Rosengart, Lucerne.
3. Ch. Faerber Coll., Gothenburg.
4. Modern Art Gallery, Basle.
5. and 6. Galerie Berggruen, Paris.

283

289

284

n° 282. *Horse.* Bronze. 90¹/₂ x 82⁵/₈ in:
1. Private Coll., New York.
2. J. Throne Holst Coll., Stockholm.
3. Museum of Contemporary Art, University of São Paulo (p. 211).

n° 283. *Rider.* 35³/₈ x 29¹/₂ in: Polychrome plaster: David Thompson Coll., Pittsburgh.
Bronze:
1. Baronne Lambert Coll., Brussels.
2. Alfred Jaretzki Coll., New York.
3. Eric Estorick Coll., London.
4. Andrew Biberg Coll., Gothenburg.

n° 284. *Horse.* Bronze. Height: 23¹/₈ in:
1. Frua de Angeli Coll., Milan.
2. José Luis and Beatriz Plaza Coll., Caracas.
3. Private Coll., Stockholm.
4. Modern Art Gallery, Basle. (2 copies).
5. Mrs. Margaret Josten Coll., New York.

286

285

n° 285. *Little bull.* Bronze. Height: 13 in:
1. and 2. Hanover Gallery, London.
3. Saidenberg Gallery, New York.
4. Galerie Gérald Cramer, Geneva.
5. Hanover Gallery, London.
6. Walter Carsen Coll., Toronto.

n° 286. *Rider.* Study. Bronze.
10¹/₄ x 7¹/₂ x 11³/₄ in:
1. Frank Perls Gallery, Beverly Hills.
2. Mr. and Mrs. Heyward Cutting Coll., Chicago.
3. Miss I. Coca Coll., New York.
4. Prof. Sanders Coll., Schiedam, Rotterdam.
5. Bo Boustedt Coll., Kungälv, Sweden.
6. Private Coll., Dusseldorf.
Et al. Property of the artist.
Galerie Rosengart, Lucerne.

n° 287. *Rider.* Bronze.
Height: about 45¹/₄ in:
1. Mrs. Lillian Florsheim Coll., Chicago.
2. Hanover Gallery, London.
3. Union of Industrial Workers, Stockholm.
4. Ragnar Moltzau Coll., Oslo.
5. Manufacturers' Trust Company, New York.
(p. 206).

n° 287 a. *Rider*. Detail. (p. 207).

n° 288. *Little Miracle*. Bronze. 21¹/₄ x 27 in:
1. Chrysler Art Museum of Provincetown.
2. Pierre Matisse Gallery, New York.
3. Ch. Kasher Coll., New York.
4. Mrs. P. Gratsos Coll., London.
5. Galerie Gérald Cramer, Geneva.
6. Private Coll., Zurich.
Et al. Property of the artist. (p. 244).

1952

n° 289. *Horse*. Polychrome bronze.
18¹/₈ x 12⁵/₈ x 5 ¹/₈ in:
1. Theodor Ahrenberg Coll., Chexbres, Switzerland.
2. Mrs. S. W. Marsch Coll., New York.
3. Eunice Johnson and Associates Coll., Chicago.
4. G. Grunebaum Coll., Scarsdale, New York.
5. Mr. H. Oldquist Coll., Stockholm.
6. Property of the artist.

n° 290. *Portrait of Christian Faerber*.
Height: 15¹/₈ in:
Bronze:
Statens Museum for Kunst, Copenhagen
Plaster: Property of the artist.

n° 291. *Portrait of Curt Valentin*.
1st version. Bronze. Height: 11³/₈ in:
Property of the artist.
Curt Valentin, an American of German birth, was the well-known art dealer who organized Marino Marini's exibitions in both the United States and Europe.

n° 292. *"Gertrude," the Little Horse*.
Bronze. Height: 9³/₄ in:
1. Hollis Baker Coll., Grand Rapids.
2. Mrs. Gertrude Bernoudy Coll., St. Louis.
3. Alex Hillman Coll., New York.
4. Modern Art Gallery, Basle.
5. Rudolph B. Schulhof Coll., King's Point, New York. (p. 215).

n° 293. *Miracle*. Bronze.
Height: 65 in:
1. Olsen Foundation, Guilford, Conn.
2. Nathan Cummings Coll., Chicago.
3. Middelheim Park Museum, Antwerp.
Et al. Property of the artist. (p. 260).

n° 293 a. *Miracle*. Detail. (p. 260).

291

n° 294. *Small Rider*. Bronze.
22⁷/₈ x 15³/₄ x 9³/₈ in:
1. Galerie Gérald Cramer, Geneva.
2. Laing Galleries, Toronto.
3. and 5. Pierre Matisse Gallery, New York.
4. Modern Art Gallery, Basle.
6. Galerie Rosengart, Lucerne.
7. Mrs. Helen Serger Coll., New York.
8. Bridgestone Museum, Tokyo.
Et al. Property of the artist.

n° 295. *Small Rider*. Bronze.
Height: about 13³/₄ in: Property of the artist.
(3 copies).

n° 296. *Rider*. Bronze. 43⁵/₈ x 35³/₈ x 35³/₈ in:
1. Windfohr Coll., Ft Worth, Texas.
2. and 4. Hanover Gallery, London.
3. Gustav Stein Coll., Cologne.
5. Mr. and Mrs. Richard Hodgson Coll., New Canaan.
6. A. Saltzman Coll., New York.
Et al. Property of the artist.

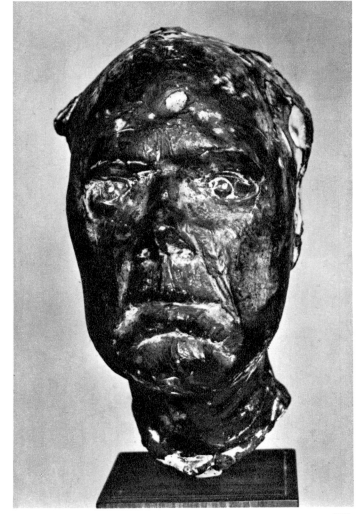

290

1952 - 1953

n° 297. *Dancer*. Bronze. Height: 61 in:
1. Baron Lambert Coll., Brussels.
2. Arthur Lang Coll., New York.
3. Koninklijk Museum, Antwerp.
4. Munson Williams Proctor Institute, Utica, New York. (p. 144).

After Marino Marini had made several journeys and fairly long visits to the United States, his female forms became noticeably slimmer.

n° 297 a. *Dancer*. Idem. (p. 145).

1953

n° 298. *Dancer*. 61 x 12⁵/₈ x 13³/₄ in:
Bronze:
1. Albright Knox Art Gallery, Buffalo.
2. Walter Bechtler Coll., Zurich.
Lead: Emilio Jesi Coll., Milan. (p. 148).

296

294

n° 298 a. *Dancer.* Polychrome plaster.
61 x 12⁵/₈ x 13³/₄ in:
Property of the artist. (p. 149).

n° 300. *Small Juggler in Polychrome.*
Bronze. Height: 18⁷/₈ in:
1. Mrs. Gertrude Lenart Coll., New York.
2. Hanover Gallery, London.
3. Galerie Gérald Cramer, Geneva.
4. Pierre Matisse Gallery, New York.
5. Galerie Rosengart, Lucerne.
6. Missing.
Et al. Marina Marini Coll., Milan.
One copy was sold to the Staatliche Museum, Berlin. (p. 157).
These statuettes, which can be seen on the mantlepiece of the artist's drawing-room in Milan (p. 156), were designed as theater characters.

n° 301. *Large Rider.* Polychrome plaster.
83³/₄ x 81⁵/₈ in: Property of the artist. (p. 189).

n° 301 a. *Large Rider.* 83³/₄ x 81⁵/₈ in:
Polychrome wood: Rijksmuseum Kröller-Müller, Otterlo, Holland.
Bronze:
1. J. Hirshhorn Coll., Greenwich.
2. Grether Coll., Basle.
3. Neubauleitung für das Landtagsgebäude, Stuttgart.
Et al. W. and N. Bär Coll., Zurich. (p. 203).

n° 302. *Dancer.* Height: 70 in:
Bronze:
1. Sam Zachs Coll., Toronto.
2. Walter Carsen Coll., Toronto.
3. Pierre Matisse Gallery, New York.
4. Prof. H. Krayenbühl Coll., Zurich.
Lead: Riccardo Jucker Coll., Milan.

n° 302 a. *Dancer.* Detail. Front view.
(p. 146).

n° 302 b. *Dancer.* Detail. Back view.
(p. 147).

n° 302 c. *Dancer.* Polychrome plaster.
Height: 70 in: Property of the artist. (p. 138).

295

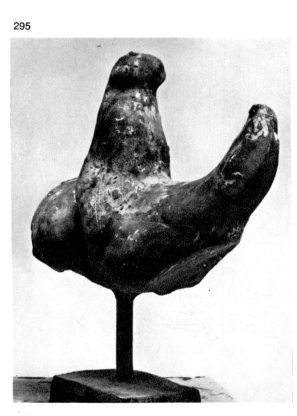

303

304

305

311   302

n° 303. *Small Juggler.* Bronze.
Height: 18¹/₂ in:
1. Hanover Gallery, London.
2. Pierre Matisse Gallery, New York.
3. Galerie Rosengart, Lucerne.
4. Private Coll., London.
5. Property of the artist.

n° 304. *Small Dancer.* Bronze.
Height: 18¹/₈ in:
1. Mrs. Michael Erlanger Coll., New York.
2. Galerie Rosengart, Lucerne.
3. Hanover Gallery, London.
4. Galerie Gérald Cramer, Geneva.
5. Pierre Matisse Gallery, New York.
6. W. and N. Bär Coll., Zurich.
Et al. Marina Marini Coll., Milan.

n° 305. *Juggler.* Polychrome bronze and
bronze. Height: 20¹/₂ in:
1. Galerie Rosengart, Lucerne.
2. Conger Goodyear Coll., New York.
3. Mrs. Alma Morgenthau Coll., New York.
4. Curt Valentin Gallery, New York.
5. Pierre Matisse Gallery, New York.
6. Vömel Gallery, Dusseldorf.
Et al. Marina Marini Coll., Milan.

n° 306. *Small Juggler.* Bronze.
Height: 18⁷/₈ in:
1. Heyward Cutting Coll., Chicago.
2. Galerie Gérald Cramer, Geneva.
3. Pierre Matisse Gallery, New York.
4. and 5. Galerie Rosengart, Lucerne.
6. Pierre Matisse Gallery, New York.
Et al. Marina Marini Coll., Milan.

n° 307. *Jugglers.* Bronze. Height: 18¹/₈ in:
1. Galerie Gérald Cramer, Geneva.

2. Pierre Matisse Gallery, New York.
3. Saidenberg Gallery, New York.
4. Pierre Matisse Gallery, New York.
5. Galerie Gérald Cramer, Geneva.
Et al. Marina Marini Coll., Milan.

n° 308. *Small Juggler.* Bronze.
Height: 18 in:
1. Mr. and Mrs. Hans Moller Coll., New York.
2. Galerie Gérald Cramer, Geneva.
3. Pierre Matisse Gallery, New York.
4. Marina Marini Coll., Milan.

n° 309. *Small Juggler.* Bronze.
Height 19³/₄ in:
1. Galerie Rosengart, Lucerne.
2. Mr. and Mrs. Heyward Cutting Coll., Chicago.
3. Eric Estorick Coll., London.
4. and 5. Pierre Matisse Gallery, New York.
6. Prof. H. Krayenbühl Coll., Zurich.
Et al. Marina Marini Coll., Milan.

n° 310. *Portrait of Manfred V. Mautner
Markhof.* Height: 15³/₄ in:
Bronze: Manfred V. Mautner Markhof Coll.,
Vienna.
Polychrome plaster: Property of the artist.
(p. 86).
The sitter was a Viennese industrialist.

n° 311. *Large Bull.* Bronze.
Height: about 43³/₈ in:
1. Curt Valentin Gallery, New York.
2. Museu de Arte Moderna, Rio de Janeiro.
3. Pierre Matisse Gallery, New York.
4. Laing Galleries, Toronto.
5. Hanover Gallery, London.

306   307   308   309

312

n° 312. *Small Miracle*. Bronze.
Height: 17³/₄ in:
1. R. J. Schoelkopf Coll., New York.
2. Curt Valentin Gallery, New York.
3. Galerie Rosengart, Lucerne.
4. Pierre Matisse Gallery, New York.
5. Galerie Berggruen, Paris.
6. J. Hirshhorn Coll., Greenwich.
Et al. Prof. Sanders Coll., Schiedam,
Rotterdam.
Dominion Gallery, Montreal.

n° 313. *Miracle*. 100¹/₂ x 31¹/₂ x 31¹/₂ in:
Bronze:
1. Stadtische Kunsthalle, Mannheim, Federal
Republic of Germany.
2. Rotterdam-Zuid (Monument to victims of
the war).
3. Museum of Modern Art, New York.
Et al. Property of the artist. (p. 245).

n° 314. *Miracle* (1953-1954). Study. Bronze.
40¹/₄ x 25⁵/₈ in:
1. Max Wasserman Coll., New York.
2. Emilio Jesi Coll., Milan.
3. Kunstmuseum, Winterthur, Switzerland.
Et al. Property of the artist. (p. 247).

n° 315. *Rider*. Bronze.
Height: about 68³/₄ in:
1. Curt Valentin Gallery, New York.
2. Instituto Torcuato di Tella, Buenos Aires.
3. Modern Art Gallery, Basle.
Variation: Joseph Strick Coll., Los Angeles.

1954

n° 316. *Two Small Studies*. Bronzes. On
the left: Height: 4¹/₈ in: On the right: Height:
4³/₈ in: Marina Marini Coll., Milan.

n° 318. *Juggler*. Bronze. Height: 66¹/₈ in:
1. J. Hirshhorn Coll., Greenwich.
2. Martha Jackson Gallery, New York.
3. Pierre Matisse Gallery, New York.
Et al. Property of the artist. (p. 158).

n° 318 a. *Juggler*. Polychrome plaster.
66¹/₈ x 16⁵/₈ x 16 ⁵/₈ in:
Property of the artist. (p. 159).

n° 319. *Acrobats*. Bronze. Height: 21³/₄ in:
1. Mr. Stephen Hahn Coll., New York.
2. A. Hollaender Coll., Washington.
3. Hanover Gallery, London.
4. Galerie Gérald Cramer, Geneva.

n° 320. *Small Juggler*. Bronze.
Height: 18³/₄ in:
1. Galerie Berggruen, Paris.
2. J. Hirshhorn Coll., Greenwich.
3. Baronne Lambert Coll., Brussels.
4. Hanover Gallery, London.
5. Max Stern Coll., New York.
6. Pierre Matisse Gallery, New York.
Et al. Marina Marini Coll., Milan.

315
316

319

320

321

322

328

n° 321. *Small Juggler*. Bronze.
Height: 19³/₄ in:
1. and 2. Galerie Gérald Cramer, Geneva.
3. Laing Galleries, Toronto.
4. Property of the artist.
Variation: Property of the artist.

n° 322. *Dancer*. Bronze. Height: 55⁷/₈ in:
1. Hanover Gallery, London.
2. David Pincus Coll., Philadelphia.
3. Modern Art Gallery, Basle.

n° 322 a. *Dancer*. Polychrome plaster.
Height: 55⁷/₈ in: Property of the artist. (p. 137).

n° 323. *Three Small Studies*. From left to
right: Height: 3³/₄ in, 4 in, 3¹/₈ in:
Marina Marini Coll., Milan.

n° 324. *Portrait of Lucy Lambert*.
Height: 15³/₄ in:
Lead: Baronne Lambert Coll., Brussels.
Bronze: Property of the artist. (p. 98).

n° 325. *Portrait of Curt Valentin*.
2nd version. Bronze. Height: 9¹/₄ in:
1. Museum of Modern Art, New York, (gift of
the artist).
2. Kunsthalle, Hamburg, (gift of the artist).
3. Property of the artist. (p. 100).

n° 327. *Miracle*. Bronze.
46¹/₂ x 64⁵/₂ x 28³/₄ in:
1. Kunsthistorisches Museum, Vienna.
2. Palais des Beaux-Arts, Charleroi, Belgium.
3. Private Coll., Milan.
Et al. Museum of Art, Baltimore. (p. 246).

n° 327 a. *Miracle*. Idem. (p. 246).

n° 327 b. *Miracle*. Polychrome wood.
46¹/₂ x 67³/₄ in: Kunstmuseum, Basle. (p. 248).

n° 328. *Small Rider*. Bronze.
Height: about 13³/₄ in:
1. Vömel Gallery, Dusseldorf.
2., 3. and 4. Klipstein and Kornfeld, Berne.
5. Mr. and Mrs. David Finn Coll., New
Rochelle, New York.

1955

n° 329. *Figure*. Bronze. Height: 16⁷/₈ in:
Property of the artist.

n° 330. *Portrait of the Countess Gabrielle
Seefried*. Height: about 15³/₄ in:
Bronze: Lilly von Schnitzler Coll., Frankfurt.
Lead: Property of the artist.

323

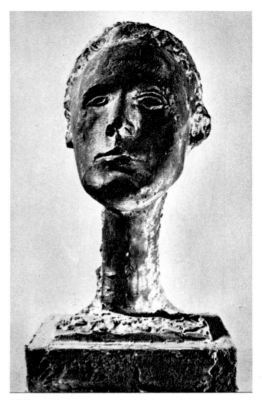

329

n° 338. *Composition.* Bronze.
$16^1/_8$ x $11^3/_4$ x $8^3/_8$ in:
1. and 2. Galerie Gérald Cramer, Geneva.
3. Private Coll., New York.
4. and 5. Property of the artist.

n° 339. *Miracle.* Study. Bronze.
Height: $17^3/_4$ in:
1. Philip Gersh Coll., New York.
2. Pierre Matisse Gallery, New York.
3. Museum of Modern Art, New York.
Property of the artist. (4 copies).

n° 340. *Small Composition.* Bronze.
Height: $6^3/_4$ in: Property of the artist.

n° 341. *Small Juggler.* Bronze.
Height: $19^3/_8$ in:
1. Gutekunst and Klipstein, Berne.
2. Galerie Gérald Cramer, Geneva.
3. Modern Art Gallery, Basle.
4. Gutekunst and Klipstein, Berne.
5. Hanover Gallery, London.
6. Symon Goldberg Coll., Amsterdam.
Et al. Marina Marini Coll., Milan.

n° 342. *Composition.* Bronze.
15 x $15^3/_4$ x $5^1/_8$ in:
1. Private Coll., New York.
2. Modern Art Gallery, Basle.
3. Pierre Matisse Gallery, New York.
4. Property of the artist.

n° 343. *Composition.* Bronze.
$7^1/_2$ x $3^7/_8$ x $12^9/_8$ in:
1. Laing Galleries, Toronto.
2. Dominion Gallery, Montreal.
3. Property of the artist.

330

331

n° 331. *Small Miracle.* Bronze.
$8^1/_4$ x $9^1/_2$ in:
1. and 2. Galerie Gérald Cramer, Geneva.
3. Galerie Rosengart, Lucerne.
4. Bo Boustedt Coll., Kungälv, Sweden.
5. Galerie Rosengart, Lucerne.
Et al. Vömel Gallery, Dusseldorf.
Property of the artist.

n° 332. *Idea for the Rider.*
$77^3/_4$ x $36^1/_8$ x $55^3/_4$ in:
Bronze:
San Diego Museum, San Diego, California.
Pierre Matisse Gallery, New York. (2 copies).
Property of the artist.
Polychrome wood: Weintraub Gallery,
New York. (p. 185).
*The sculpture in wood dates from 1956; the
bronze was cast in 1955.*

n° 333. *Small Miracle.* Bronze.
$15^9/_8$ x $17^7/_8$ in:
1. Pierre Matisse Gallery, New York.
2. Galerie Rosengart, Lucerne.
3. Private Coll., Stockholm.
4. Marina Marini Coll., Milan.

n° 334. *Small Horse.* $4^3/_4$ x $4^3/_4$ in:
Bronze: Unique copy: Private Coll., Paris.
Gold: 1968.
6 copies numbered from 1 to 6.
3 copies by the artist numbered from 0
to 000:
Private Colls.

n° 335. *Idea for the Rider.* Study. Bronze.
$22^3/_8$ x $9^1/_2$ x $13^3/_4$ in:
Hanover Gallery, London. (2 copies).
Galerie Berggruen, Paris.
Pierre Matisse Gallery, New York. (3 copies).
Jeffrey H. Loria Coll., New York.
Property of the artist. (2 copies).

n° 336. *Composition.* Bronze.
$23^1/_4$ x $15^3/_8$ x $12^9/_8$ in:
1. and 2. Pierre Matisse Gallery, New York.
3. Galerie Rosengart, Lucerne.
4. Modern Art Gallery, Basle.
5. Galerie Berggruen, Paris.
6. Prof. H. Krayenbühl Coll., Zurich.
Et al. Chrysler Art Museum of Provincetown.
Property of the artist.

1956

n° 337. *Composition.* Study. Bronze.
$51^1/_2$ x $7^7/_8$ in:
1. Marina Marini Coll., Milan.
2. Gertrude Schweitzer Coll., New York.
3. W. and N. Bär Coll., Zurich.
4. and 5. Galerie Rosengart, Lucerne.
6. Dominion Gallery, Montreal.

372

333

334

335

336

1956 - 1957

n° 344. *Warrior*. Bronze.
29¹/₈ x 39³/₈ x 27¹/₂ in:
1. and 2. Pierre Matisse Gallery, New York.
3. Dr. Max Fischer Coll., Stuttgart.
4. Property of the artist. (p. 264).

n° 345. *Rider*. 114¹/₈ x 70³/₄ in:
Bronze:
1. Shell Building, South Bank, London.
2. Paolo Marinotti Coll., Milan.
3. Bechtler Coll., Zurich.
Variation: Property of the artist.
Polychrome plaster: Property of the artist.
(p. 216).

n° 346. *Composition*. Bronze. 29⁷/₈ x 50³/₄ in:
1. Mrs. D. Steward Coll., London.
2. Pierre Matisse Gallery, New York.
3. Modern Art Gallery, Basle.
4. Bo Boustedt Coll., Kungälv, Sweden.
5. Jeffrey H. Loria Coll., New York.
6. Property of the artist. (p. 217).

373

337

340

n° 357. *Miracle.* Bronze.
66¹/₂ x 50³/₈ x 110¹/₄ in:
1. Kunsthaus, Zurich.
2. Bayerische Staatsgemäldesammlungen,
Munich.
3. Emilio Jesi Coll., Milan. (p. 254).

n° 357 a. *Miracle.* Wood.
About 70³/₄ x 51 x 114¹/₈ in:
Galleria Civica d'Arte Moderna, Turin. (p. 259).

n° 359. *Warrior.* Bronze.
53¹/₈ x 66⁷/₈ x 44 ⁷/₈ in:
1. Riccardo Jucker Coll., Milan.
2. Bo Boustedt Coll., Kungälv, Sweden.
3. Mr. and Mrs. David Finn Coll., New Rochelle, New York.
Et al. Germanisches Nationalmuseum, Nuremberg. (p. 266).

n° 359 a. *Warrior.* Detail. (p. 267).

n° 359 b. *Warrior.* Polychrome plaster.
53¹/₈ x 66⁷/₈ x 44 ⁷/₈ in:
Property of the artist. (p. 275).

n° 360. *Warrior.* Bronze. 45¹/₄ x 27¹/₂ in:
1. Manfred Behr Coll., Stuttgart.
Et al. Property of the artist.

n° 347. *Composition.* Bronze.
8¹/₄ x 14⁵/₈ x 9 in:
1. Bo Boustedt Coll., Kungälv, Sweden.
2. Hanover Gallery, London.
3. Galerie Rosengart, Lucerne.
4. Jeffrey H. Loria Coll., New York. (p. 265).

1957 - 1958

n° 348. *Equestrian Composition.* Bronze.
Height: 236 in:
Monument at The Hague. (p. 212).
*This is the largest bronze work carried out
by Marino Marini. The artist has engraved on
the base of this monument the following
inscription: "Si construì, si distrusse e un can-
to desolato restò sul mondo". (People build,
people destroy; and only a sad song remains
in the world).*

n° 348 a. *Equestrian Composition.* Detail.
(p. 213).

n° 349. *Miracle.* Study. Bronze.
Height: 45¹/₄ in:
1. Modern Art Gallery, Basle.
2. Pierre Matisse Gallery, New York.
3. Modern Art Gallery, Basle.
Et al. Property of the artist. (p. 249).

n° 350. *Miracle, Composition.* Bronze.
51³/₈ x 21¹/₄ x 22³/₄ in:
1. Pierre Matisse Gallery, New York.
2. Bo Boustedt Coll., Kungälv, Sweden.
3. Mr. and Mrs. Alex Kasser Coll., Montclair,
New York. (p. 253).

1958 - 1959

n° 351. *The Warrior.* Study. Bronze.
28 x 48³/₄ x 29¹/₈ in:
1. Pierre Matisse Gallery, New York.
2. Galerie Rosengart, Lucerne.
3. Property of the artist. (p. 265).

1959

n° 352. *Small Juggler.* Bronze.
Height: 23⁵/₈ in:
1. Galerie Rosengart, Lucerne.
2. Macchiati Coll., Milan.
3. Property of the artist. (p. 157).

n° 353. *The Warrior.* Bronze. 21⁵/₈ x 13³/₄ in:
1. Pierre Matisse Gallery, New York.
2. Bo Boustedt Coll., Kungälv, Sweden.
3. Property of the artist.

n° 354. *Small Warrior.* Bronze. 9 x 12⁵/₈ in:
1. Pierre Matisse Gallery, New York.
2. and 3. Galerie Rosengart, Lucerne.
4. Documenta, Kassel. (Gift of the artist).
5. Marina Marini Coll., Milan.
6. Property of the artist.

1959 - 1960

n° 355. *Composition.* Bronze.
11 x 14¹/₄ x 7¹/₈ in:
Jeffrey H. Loria Coll., New York.

n° 356. *Portrait of Leopoldo Zorzi.* Bronze.
Height: about 11³/₄ in:
Leopoldo Zorzi Coll., Bari, Italy.

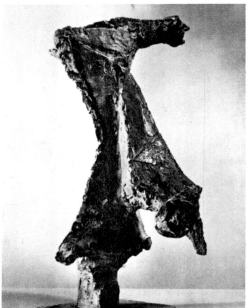

339

338

1960

n° 361. *Portrait of Siegfried Rosengart.*
Bronze. Height: 11³/₄ in:
S. Rosengart Coll.., Lucerne.
Property of the artist.

n° 362. *Portrait of Samuel Maslon.*
Height: 10⁵/₈ in:
Bronze: Maslon Coll., Minneapolis.
Polychrome plaster: Property of the artist.

n° 363. *Composition.* Bronze.
6³/₄ x 10¹/₄ x 4³/₄ in:
Property of the artist. (p. 284).
*The constructive elements of these works
(363, 364) were perhaps inspired by the large
sculpture Marino Marini did for the monument at the Hague. (p. 212).*

n° 364. *Composition.* Bronze.
6³/₂ x 11³/₈ x 5¹/₄ in:
Property of the artist. (p. 283).

n° 365. *Large Warrior.* Bronze.
173¹/₈ x 141⁵/₈ in:
1. Ted. Wiener Coll., Fort Worth.
2. Giuseppe Brion Coll., Milan. (p. 268-269).

341

374

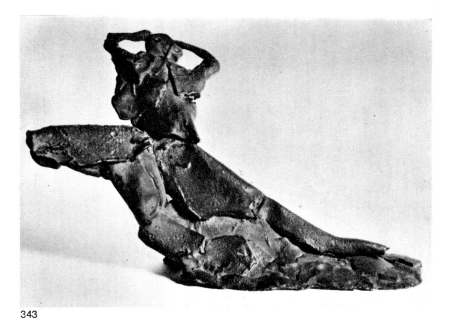

343

342

1961

n° 366. *Portrait of Henry Miller.*
Height: 10¹/₈ in:
Bronze: Springer Gallery, Berlin. (6 copies).
Plaster: Property of the artist. (p. 104).
One of the six copies in bronze has been
bought by National Gallery, Washington.
*The sculptor carried out this work during a
visit of the well-known writer Henry Miller to
his home in Forte dei Marmi.*

1962

n° 367. *Portrait of Professor Carl Georg
Heise.* Height: about 12 in:
Bronze: Hamburger Kunsthalle, Hamburg.
Polychrome plaster: Property of the artist.

n° 368. *Portrait of Henry Moore.*
Height: 14¹/₄ in:
Polychrome plaster: Property of the artist.
Bronze:
1. Bo Boustedt Coll., Kungälv, Sweden.
2. Joseph Hirshhorn Coll., Greenwich.
3. National Portrait Gallery, London. (p. 107).
*The portrait of Henry Moore, like that of Henry
Miller, was carried out at Forte dei Marmi.*

360

353

355

354

356

362

367

376

n° 369. *Portrait of Marc Chagall.*
Height: 11³/₈ in:
Bronze:
Kunsthaus, Zurich. (Gift W. and N. Bär).
Polychrome plaster:
Property of the artist. (p. 108).
In order to execute this sculpture, the artist went specially to Vence in the South of France where Chagall was then living in the house which he had purchased from the heirs of Edouard Bourdet, and in which Paul Valéry had made various engravings.

n° 370. *Large Cry.* Bronze. 66⁷/₈ x 114¹/₈ in:
Nationalgalerie, Berlin.
Property of the artist. (p. 298-299).

n° 370 a. *Large Cry.* Detail. (p. 300).

1963

n° 371. *Portrait of Jean Arp.* Bronze.
Height: 12⁷/₈ in:
Niedersächsische Landesgalerie, Hanover.
This portrait was done in Jean Arp's workshop in Soldano, Lugano.

n° 372. *Portrait of Joseph H. Hirshhorn.*
Height: 13³/₄ in:
Bronze: Joseph Hirshhorn Coll., Greenwich.
Plaster: Property of the artist. (p. 101).
The portrait of Mr. Hirshhorn was made in Zurich.

n° 373. *Small Cry.* Bronze. 8¹/₄ x 5⁷/₈ x 11 in:
1. Dominion Gallery, Toronto.
2. Bo Boustedt Coll., Kungälv, Sweden.
3. Giovanni Carandente Coll., Rome.
4. 5. 6. Property of the artist. (p. 290).

1963 - 1954

n° 374. *Small Group of Elements.* Bronze.
7¹/₂ x 10¹/₈ x 21⁵/₈ in:
1. Bo Boustedt Coll., Kungälv, Sweden.
2. 3. Property of the artist. (p. 297).

1964

n° 375. *Portrait of Hans C. Bechtler.*
Bronze. Height: 13³/₈ in:
Bechtler Coll., Zurich.

1964 - 1965

n° 376. *Group of Elements.* Bronze.
41³/₈ x 112¹/₄ x 55¹/₈ in:
1. Mr. and Mrs. R. B. Schulhof Coll., King's Point, New York.
2. Property of the artist. (p. 289).

n° 377. *The Shape of an Idea.* Bronze.
Height: 79³/₈ in: Property of the artist. (p. 258).

1967

n° 378. *Portrait of Mies Van Der Rohe.*
Final version. Bronze. Height: 13 in:
Nationalgalerie, Berlin. (p. 106).
Marino Marini made a special journey to Berlin, where the famous architect was supervising the building of the new Nationalgalerie, in order to carry out this sculpture.

n° 379. *Portrait of Gottfried B. Fischer.*
Bronze. Height: 13³/₄ in: Fischer Coll., Pieve di Camaiore, Italy. (p. 105).
Gottfried B. Fischer is the German publisher who ordered the portrait of Thomas Mann for the complete edition of the famous writer's works.

1968

n° 380. *Theme of the Warrior.* Grey stone.
78³/₄ x 39³/₈ in:
Mr. and Mrs. Alex Kasser Coll., Montclair, New York. (p. 270).

n° 380 a. *Theme of the Warrior.* Detail.
(p. 263).

N.B.: The names of the original purchasers are generally given as those of the collectors. It is clear that the sculptures bought by various Galleries have later changed hands. Several works belonging to Mr. Bär were, in January, 1969, bequeathed to the Kunsthaus, Zurich.

The missing numbers (77, 94, 227, 257, 299, 317, 326, 358) correspond to reproductions which have been omitted because they were merely photographic variations of works already reproduced in the catalogue.

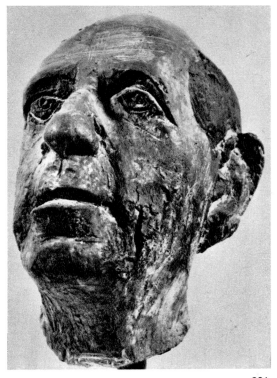

361

371

375

1942. *Self-portrait.* Polychrome plaster. H. 16¹/₈ in: (CS. No. 131).

1967. *The Fall of the Angel.* Oil on canvas. 47¹/₄×59 in: (IP. No. 301).

1966. *Group of Elements.* Tempera. Paper remounted on canvas. 35³/₈×67 in: (IP. No. 322).

1947

INTRODUCTION
TO GENERAL INDEX
OF PAINTINGS

1949

It has not been possible for us to draw up a complete list of Marino Marini's paintings as for his sculptures and engravings. Too many of his pictures, apart from his gouaches, water-colors, and paintings in mixed media, are now dispersed around the world, giving pleasure and pride to unknown, often modest, collectors who would be afraid to entrust their treasure to a photographer. As for the paintings belonging to the artist himself—of which a considerable number have been reproduced both in the first part of this work and in this catalogue—several are only provisionally finished. The artist likes to take them up from time to time; sometimes it pleases him to retouch them slightly without changing their general appearance; on other occasions, he does not hesitate to use his paint-brush like a surgeon's lancet, cutting and shaping in order to expose hidden aspects—obviously to the benefit of the work to which he thus gives a new dimension (see, for

1949

example, ,,The Fall of the Angel," p. 235, and its new version, p. 378). A work of art is only finished when it has been torn from its creator.

Like many of his fellow artists, Marini wielded a paintbrush before a chisel. Even if at the beginning of his career as a sculptor he turned towards the past, it appears to us that, right from his first paintings, he was, on the contrary, as a painter, more influenced by the research of contemporary artists. It is true that at this time sculpture had to be created out of nothing, whereas painting had received such an impulse from the Impressionists that it was enough in a sense to be carried away, to ride on the crest of the wave!

If, therefore, his talent as a sculptor stood alone, we can see that as a painter he utilized the experience of his elders, particularly that of Picasso and of Chagal—the Mediterranean occidentalism of the

381

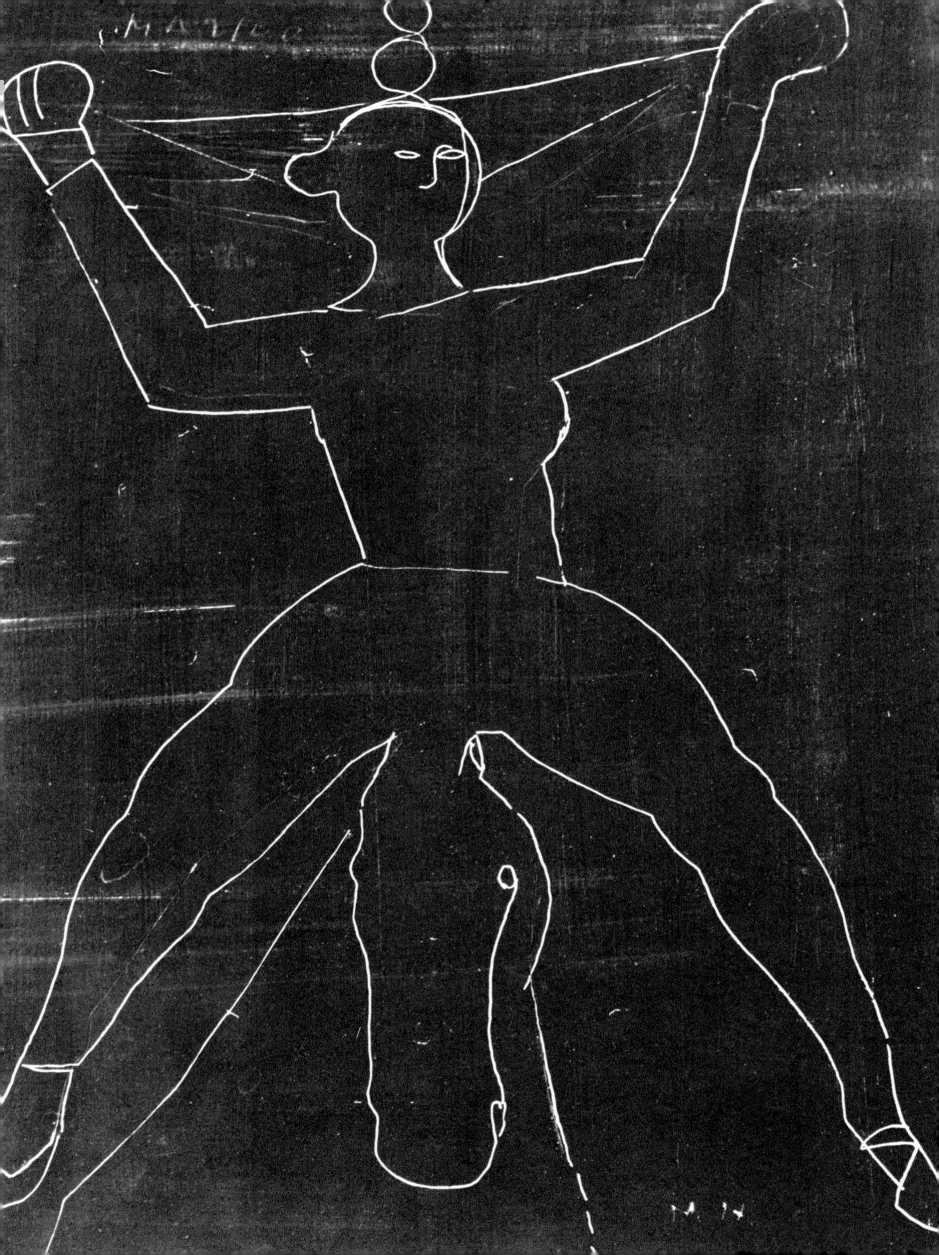

1953

former and the Byzantine orientalism of the latter — in order to create his own style. Under the opposing signs of Apollo and Bacchus, his style of painting was no less personal than that of his sculpture: sometimes they ran parallel and sometimes cut across one another. In both cases eroticism remained the driving force. Can we not see in front of the painter seated at his easel a model taking off her blouse? and this simple gesture, one of the most beautiful which a woman can perform, enables us to be present at the birth of a painting which rises from the brushes as they embellish the white canvas. The rosy flesh of a young girl soon blooms, filling the space, perhaps as light and trembling as a leaf, or perhaps as heavy and juicy as a bunch of grapes. Whether these figures are painted from top to bottom or vice versa, they fall like branches laden with fruit or blossom like wild flowers. The colors are spread in wide, smooth, transparent flat surfaces

384

◁ 1949

1959

like layers of air or of sea-water. They often owe something to the primitive preciosity of enamel or to the jeweled light of stained glass. Red, yellow, blue and green dominate, but a masterpiece can also arise from more delicate tones or even, on the contrary, from very dark colors. Although not everything is yet „Luxury, Color and Voluptuousness" in this enchanting painting, we do not yet feel the apocalypse of the 1960's.

Riders and horses succeed Pomonas, girls, jugglers; people from the theater succeed riders; warriors are finally succeeded by girls. Suddenly, however, in this world of festival, suffering utters its mournful cry; nothingness destroys being; and what has been one of the most beautiful façades of the world, the marvelous stained-glass window which the paintings of Marino Marini presented, is crushed at our feet: but we remain fascinated by the sparkling of a thousand precious fragments which are gradually going to reconstruct a new world—no longer in the image of man, but in the image of his tragedy. For if death is the supreme issue of life, it is no less certainly its origin—as the Etruscans, of whom Marino Marini is the last representative, taught us—Etruscans whom we see half-lying on their sarcophagi, lovingly and vigorously embracing the bare shoulders of their wives.

Marino Marini has painted few landscapes and, moreover, they were all executed when he was young. Indeed, it is especially the problem of being which haunts the artist—and that was true long before Existentialism was discovered by fine ladies! This world which has so patiently, even heroically, resisted external attacks, is in the process of perishing from inside itself, opening in our hands like a fruit alive with maggots. Youth is no longer desirous, as the prophets proclaim, of liberty, but of power and privileges. A new world is being born but it is already as ill as that which is the drama of its internal laceration which finishes in the terrifying scream of the Last Judgment. This is not a philosopher's essay but an artist's intuition. Will this scream of terror also be a vox clamantis in deserto? Who can suppose to have heard it sounding inside himself like a funeral toll? Whatever it may be, this new world of Marino Marini even if it does not dazzle us like his former world, fascinates us just as much. When we scrutinize it deeply, we notice with a certain relief that it is still, like that which has preceded it, an ethical erotic world (using the adjective „ethical" in its double meaning) of homo-sapiens, our world of yesterday and doubtlessly a world which would not be unpleasing to the young revolutionaries of the secondary schools and nursery schools of tomorrow.

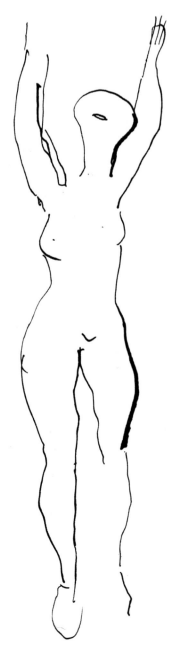

386

1969

1949. *Rider.* Pastel and ink. 25⁵/₈×19⁵/₈ in: (IP. No. 54).

1953. *Horse*. Oil. 17×24³/₄ in: (IP. No. 172).

1952. *Horse and Nude*. Gouache. 13³/₄×9⁷/₈ in: (IP. No. 132).

1950. *Rider*. Gouache. 15³/₄×11⁷/₈ in: (IP. No. 89).

2

1

1923

n° 1. *Gisella* (*L'apparita*). Oil on panel.
24³/₄ x 19⁵/₈ in: Property of the artist. (p. 389).

1926

n° 2. *Self-portrait with a Mask.* Oil on panel.
18¹/₈ x 13³/₄ in: Property of the artist. (p. 389).

n° 3. *Young Girl with a Flower.* Oil on panel.
31¹/₂ x 23⁵/₈ in: Property of the artist. (p. 389).

1927

n° 4. *Little Dancer with a Parasol.* Oil on panel. 23⁵/₈ x 15³/₄ in:
Property of the artist. (p. 389).

n° 5. *Flute Player.* Oil on panel.
24³/₈ x 18⁷/₈ in: Property of the artist. (p. 389).

n° 6. *Algerian Girl.* Oil on panel.
49¹/₄ x 29¹/₂ in: Property of the artist. (p. 391).

1928

n° 7. *Juggler.* Oil on panel. 31¹/₂ x 23⁵/₈ in:
Property of the artist. (p. 390).

n° 8. *Violetta.* Oil on panel. 32¹/₄ x 23⁵/₈ in:
Property of the artist. (p. 391).

1929

n° 9. *Juggler.* Oil on panel. 31¹/₂ x 23⁵/₈ in:
Property of the artist. (p. 390).

3

4

5

7

14

n° 10. *Pink Nude.* Oil on panel.
28³/₈ x 44¹/₈ in: Property of the artist. (p. 390).

n° 11. *Breton Landscape.* Oil on cardboard.
9 x 13 in: Property of the artist. (p. 392).

1930

n° 12. *Study for a Portrait.* Tempera.
15³/₄ x 13³/₈ in: Property of the artist. (p. 390).

1935

n° 13. *View of Athens.* Water-color.
11 x 13³/₈ in: Lamberto Vitali Coll., Milan.
(p. 392).

n° 14. *Juggler.* Tempera on panel.
31¹/₂ x 23⁵/₈ in: Property of the artist. (p. 390).

9

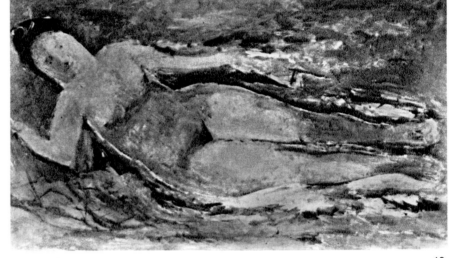

10

12

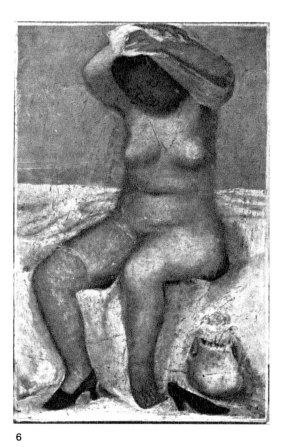

6

21

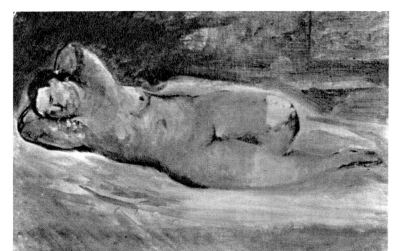

24
15

1937

n° 15. *Head of a Man.* Pastel.
$12^1/_8$ x $7^7/_8$ in: Private Coll. (p. 391).

n° 16. *Composition.* Tempera on paper.
$8^5/_8$ x $6^1/_4$ in: Emilio Jesi Coll., Milan. (p. 392).

1938

n° 17. *Gentleman on Horseback.* Tempera.
Paper remounted on canvas. 51 x $38^1/_8$ in:
Property of the artist. (p. 392).

n° 18. *Potrait.* Water-color and ink.
11 x $8^5/_8$ in: Private Coll., New York. (p. 393).

n° 19. *Rider.* Tempera on paper.
$13^3/_4$ x $8^5/_8$ in:
M. Herbert Hemphill Coll., New York. (p. 393).

8

1939

n° 20. *Portrait.* Tempera and ink.
11⁷/₈ x 8⁵/₈ in:
Former Buchholz Gallery Coll., New York.
(p. 393).

1940

n° 21. *Model in the Studio.* Oil on cardboard. 18¹/₈ x 14⁵/₂ in:
Property of the artist. (p. 391).

1941

n° 22. *Study.* Tempera.
Paper remounted on canvas. 13⁹/₈ x 10⁵/₈ in:
U. Tognazzi Coll., Rome. (p. 393).

n° 23. *Nude.* Tempera on paper.
14¹/₈ x 10¹/₈ in:
W. and N. Bär Coll., Zurich. (p. 394).

1942

n° 24. *The Awakening.* Oil on cardboard.
13⁹/₄ x 19⁹/₈ in: Private Coll., Milan. (p. 391).

11

16

13

17

25

22

20

19

18

26

393

23

27

28

32

33

394

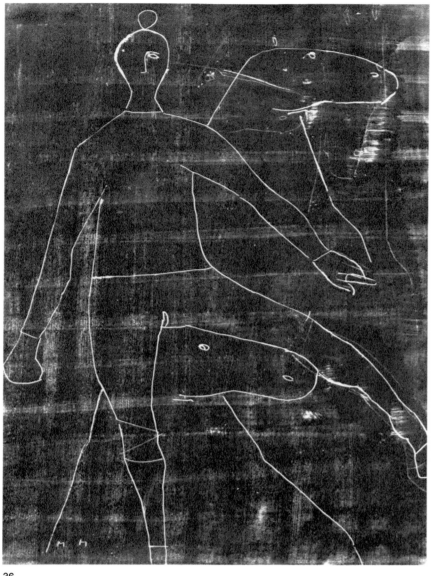

36

29

34

37

n° 25. *Horse and Rider.* Tempera.
10¹/₄ x 13³/₈ in: Private Coll. (p. 392).

n° 26. *Bathers.* Study. Gouache.
11³/₈ x 8⁵/₈ in:
Riccardo Jucker Coll., Milan. (p. 393).

n° 27. *Theater Wings.* Mixed media.
19¹/₈ x 13³/₈ in: Private Coll. (p. 394).

1943

n° 28. *Small Pomona.* Tempera and ink.
13 x 9³/₈ in:
Guido Sinigaglia Coll., Turin. (p. 394).

n° 29. *Nude and Horse.* Oil and tempera
on canvas. 38⁵/₈ x 26³/₄ in:
José Luis and Beatriz Plaza Coll., Caracas.
(p. 395).

1944

n° 30. *Portrait.* Gouache. 15⁷/₈ x 12⁵/₈ in:
W. and N. Bär Coll., Zurich. (p. 396).

n° 31. *Horse and Rider Lying Down.* Oil on
paper. 9³/₈ x 13⁵/₈ in:
Angela Rosengart Coll., Lucerne. (p. 396).

1945

n° 32. *Three Graces.* Oil on canvas.
31¹/₂ x 23⁵/₈ in:
Property of the artist. (p. 394).
*First version of " The Carriage Builder's
Daughters ". (p. 131).*

n° 33. *Small Pomona.* Oil. 19⁵/₈ x 15³/₈ in:
Guido Sinigaglia Coll., Turin. (p. 394).

1946

n° 34. *Rider.* Gouache. 13³/₄ x 10¹/₄ in:
Guido Sinigaglia Coll., Turin. (p. 395).

n° 35. *Riders.* Study. Water-color and ink.
19⁵/₈ x 13³/₈ in: Open Air Museum of Sculpture,
Middelheim, Antwerp. (p. 399).

1947

n° 36. *Horse and Rider.* Tempera on paper.
15 x 11 in: Emilio Jesi Coll., Milan. (p. 395).

n° 37. *Rider.* Tempera.
Approximately 17⁵/₈ x 9⁷/₈ in:
Private Coll., USA. (p. 395).

n° 38. *Horse and Rider.* Tempera on paper.
15³/₈ x 11⁷/₈ in:
Emilio Jesi Coll., Milan. (p. 398).

30

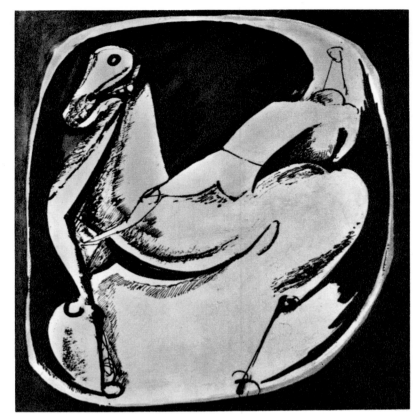

40

31

n° 39. *Horse and Rider.* Tempera on paper.
14³/₈ x 10⁵/₈ in: Emilio Jesi Coll., Milan. (p. 402).

1948

n° 40. *Horse and Rider.* Tempera on paper.
15³/₄ x 14⁵/₈ in: Feigel Coll., Basle. (p. 396).

n° 41. *Rider.* Study. Gouache. 11⁵/₈ x 8⁵/₈ in:
Guido Sinigaglia Coll., Turin. (p. 396).

n° 42. *In the Limelight.* Oil on canvas.
39³/₈ x 31¹/₂ in:
Luciano Pomini Coll., Castellanza, Italy.
(p. 397).

48

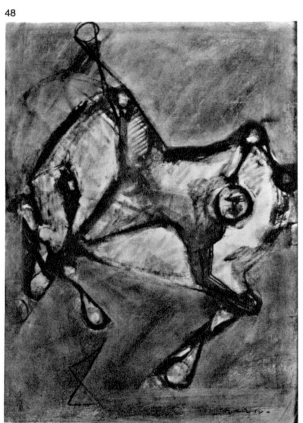

41

42

49

43

n° 43. *Four Women*. Water-color and pencil.
13 x 17 in: Manfred Behr Coll., Stuttgart.
(p. 397).

n° 44. *Rider*. Tempera on paper.
Approximately 15 x 12 in:
Museum of Fine Arts, Boston.
(Perry T. Rathbone Coll., Cambridge). (p. 398).

n° 45. *Horse and Rider*. Tempera on paper.
Approximately 9³/₈ x 11⁷/₈ in:
Sam Lewinson Coll., New York. (p. 398).

n° 46. *Rider*. Gouache. 19¹/₂ x 13 in:
Riccardo Jucker Coll., Milan. (p. 399).

n° 47. *Rider*. Pastel and ink on paper.
17⁷/₈ x 13³/₈ in: Tate Gallery, London. (p. 399).

50

51

44

52

45

38

53

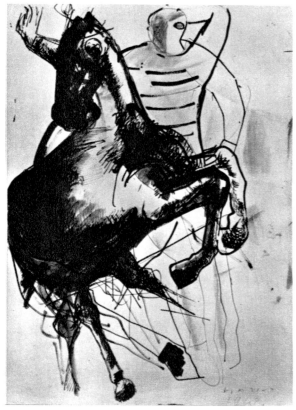

46

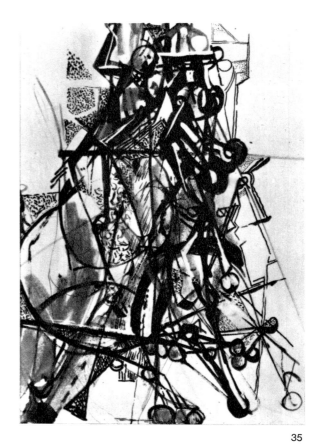

35

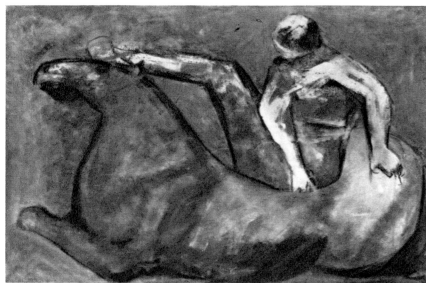

47

1949

n° 48. *The Fall.* Pastel and pencil.
Approximately 11 x 7 in:
Marina Marini Coll., Milan. (p. 396).

n° 49. *Nude.* Oil on canvas. 29$\frac{1}{8}$ x 24 in:
Property of the artist. (p. 397).

n° 50. *Reverse (Composition in Blue I).*
Oil on canvas. 39$\frac{3}{8}$ x 31$\frac{1}{2}$ in:
Property of the artist. (p. 397).

n° 51. *On the Stage (Composition in Blue II).*
Oil on canvas. 39$\frac{3}{8}$ x 30 in:
Renato Zevi Coll., Milan. (p. 397).

n° 52. *Horse and Man.* Tempera and pencil.
Approximately 11$\frac{7}{8}$ x 9$\frac{3}{8}$ in:
Mr. and Mrs. Grigant Coll., Detroit. (p. 398).

n° 53. *Rider on a Heavenly Background.*
Tempera. 14$\frac{5}{8}$ x 10$\frac{5}{8}$ in:
Riccardo Jucker Coll., Milan. (p. 398).

55

56

67

57

n° 54. *Rider.* Pastel and ink. 25⁵/₈ x 19⁵/₈ in: Riccardo Jucker Coll., Milan. (p. 387).

n° 55. *Horse and Rider.* Tempera. John Butler Coll., New York. (p. 399).

n° 56. *Rider.* Pastel and ink. 18¹/₂ x 12⁵/₈ in: Rijksmuseum Kröller-Müller, Otterlo, Holland. (p. 399).

n° 57. *Characters in a Circus.* Mixed media. 36¹/₈ x 28³/₈ in: Marina Marini Coll., Milan. (p. 400).

Toninelli dates this tempera 1951. We prefer to use the date 1949 which it bears in the book published by Deutsche Buch-Gemeinschaft where it is reproduced in color (Plate II).

n° 58. *Acrobats.* Tempera. Paper remounted on canvas. 27¹/₂ x 20 in: Marina Marini Coll., Milan. (p. 400).

n° 59. *The Cavalcade.* Tempera. Paper remounted on canvas. 33³/₄ x 24³/₈ in: Riccardo Jucker Coll., Milan. (p. 401).

n° 60. *Imaginary Games.* Oil on canvas. 83³/₈ x 60¹/₈ in: Private Coll., Milan. (p. 401).

n° 61. *Riders.* Oil on canvas. 39 x 29¹/₂ in: Art Gallery of Ontario, Toronto. (p. 401).

n° 62. *Imaginary Character.* Tempera. 17 x 14¹/₈ in: Private Coll. (p. 403).

58

68

69

59

91

n° 63. *Sorrowful Character.* Tempera.
17 x 14$^1/_8$ in: Private Coll. (p. 403).

n° 64. *Portrait of a Woman.* Tempera on
paper. 16$^7/_8$ x 16$^3/_8$ in:
Emilio Jesi Coll., Milan. (p. 403).

n° 65. *Rider Falling from his Horse.*
Gouache on cardboard. 19$^1/_8$ x 25$^3/_8$ in:
S. Rosengart Coll., Lucerne. (p. 404).

n° 66. *Pomona, Composition.*
Oil on canvas. 63 x 39$^3/_8$ in: Kunsthaus, Zurich
(gift of W. and N. Bär). (p. 122).

60

61

70

71

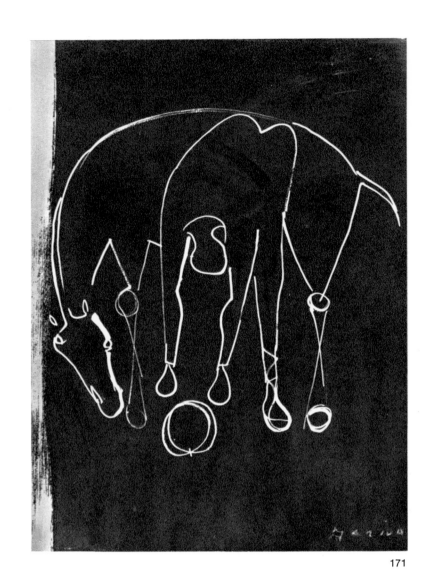

171

39

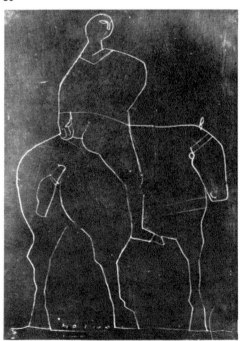

72

73

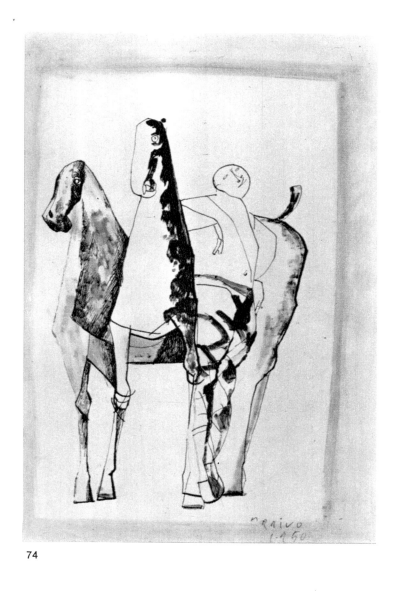

74

75

n° 71. *Juggler between two Horses.*
Tempera on paper. Height: approximately
11⁷/₈ in: Max Kahn Coll., New York. (p. 402).

n° 72. *Juggler.* Tempera on paper.
18⁷/₈ x 12⁵/₈ in:
Manfred Behr Coll., Stuttgart. (p. 402).

n° 73. *Horse.* Pastel and ink. 24¹/₈ x 17 in:
Private Coll. (p. 402).

n° 74. *Acrobat and Horses.* Tempera and
ink. 24³/₈ x 17 in: Private Coll. (p. 403).

n° 75. *Acrobat and Horses.* Pastel and ink
on paper. 24³/₈ x 17 in:
J. Pulitzer Jr. Coll., St. Louis. (p. 403).

n° 76. *Black Rider.* Oil. Paper remounted
on masonite. 39³/₈ x 30 in:
G. Lizzola Coll., Milan. (p. 404).

n° 77. *Composition with Rider.* Oil.
Approximately 38¹/₈ x 29¹/₈ in:
Pierre Matisse Gallery, New York. (p. 404).

n° 78. *Intuitive Truth.* Oil on canvas.
39³/₈ x 31¹/₂ in: Property of the artist. (p. 405).

n° 79. *Caryatid.* Oil on canvas.
80 x 35⁷/₈ in: Property of the artist. (p. 405).

n° 80. *Female Figure.* Oil on canvas.
37³/₈ x 31⁷/₈ in:
Property of the artist. (p. 405).

62

63

64

92

76

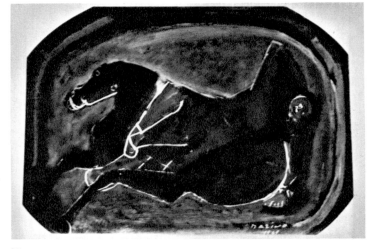

65

n° 81. *Pomona.* Oil on canvas.
46³/₈ x 35³/₈ in: Property of the artist. (p. 405).

n° 82. *Composition with a Green Horse.*
Oil. Approximately 58⁵/₈ x 35⁷/₈ in:
Pierre Matisse Gallery, New York. (p. 406).

n° 83. *Horse.* Mixed media.
Paper remounted on canvas. Length: approximately 39³/₈ in: Private Coll. (p. 408).

n° 84. *Small Rider.* Oil on canvas.
36⁵/₈ x 28³/₄ in:
Marina Marini Coll., Milan. (p. 409).

n° 85. *Juggler and Horse.* Tempera. Paper
remounted on canvas. 21 x 15³/₈ in:
Emilio Jesi Coll., Milan. (p. 409).

n° 86. *Dancer and Horse.* Tempera. Paper
remounted on canvas. 21 x 15³/₈ in:
Emilio Jesi Coll., Milan. (p. 409).

77

93

78

94

79

n° 87. *Horse and Rider.* Pastel and ink on paper. $9^7/_8$ x $13^7/_8$ in:
City Art Museum, St. Louis. (p. 413).

n° 88. *Horse and Rider.* Tempera. Paper remounted on canvas. 21 x $13^3/_4$ in:
Emilio Jesi Coll., Milan. (p. 415).

n° 89. *Rider.* Gouache. $15^3/_4$ x $11^7/_8$ in:
Rich. Furuholmen Coll., Oslo. (p. 388).

n° 90. *Horse and Rider.* Tempera. Paper remounted on canvas. 21 x $15^3/_8$ in:
Emilio Jesi Coll., Milan. (p. 417).

1951

n° 91. *Yellow and Blue.* Tempera.
Paper remounted on canvas. $37^3/_8$ x $26^3/_4$ in:
Marina Marini Coll., Milan. (p. 401).

80

81

405

82

95

n° 92. *Rider.* Oil on paper.
Approximately 63³/₈ x 39 in: City Art Museum,
St. Louis (gift of Mr. and Mrs. Morton May).
(p. 404).

n° 93. *Rider.* Gouache and ink on paper.
24¹/₈ x 16¹/₂ in:
Baron Lambert Coll., Brussels. (p. 404).

n° 94. *Physiognomy.* Oil on canvas.
59 x 31¹/₂ in: Property of the artist. (p. 405).

n° 95. *Horse.* Tempera and oil.
Paper remounted on canvas. 16 x 20¹/₂ in:
Max Stern Coll., New York. (p. 406).

n° 96. *Small Acrobat.* Oil on canvas.
15³/₄ x 20⁷/₈ in: Property of the artist. (p. 409).

n° 97. *Rider on a Chestnut Colored Ground.*
Oil. Approximately 38¹/₈ x 29¹/₈ in:
Pierre Matisse Gallery, New York. (p. 412).

107

108

109

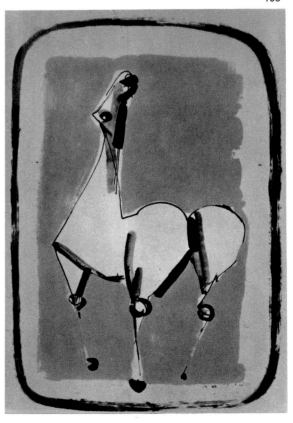

406

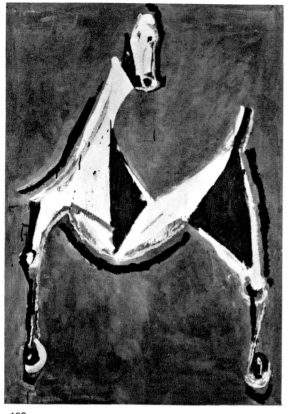

139

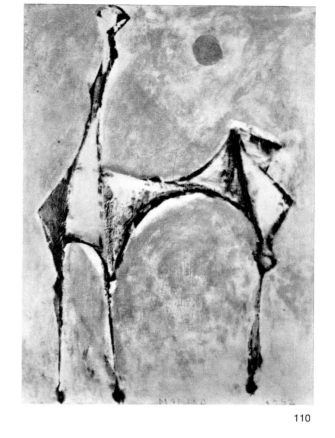

110

n° 98. *Miracle*. Study. Water-color and ink.
24³/₈ x 17 in: Open Air Museum of Sculpture,
Middelheim, Antwerp. (p. 412).

n° 99. *Man between Two Horses.* Tempera.
13 x 9⁷/₈ in:
Riccardo Jucker Coll., Milan. (p. 413).

n° 100. *Acrobats and Horse.* Mixed media.
38¹/₈ x 28¹/₄ in:
Albright-Knox Art Gallery, Buffalo, New York
(gift of Seymour H. Knox). (p. 415).

n° 101. *Jugglers and Horse.* Oil on paper.
Approximately 64¹/₂ x 45 in:
Pierre Matisse Gallery, New York. (p. 415).

n° 102. *Horse and Rider.* Oil.
Paper remounted on canvas. 39⁹/₈ x 27¹/₂ in:
G. Lizzola Coll., Milan. (p. 415).

140

141

111

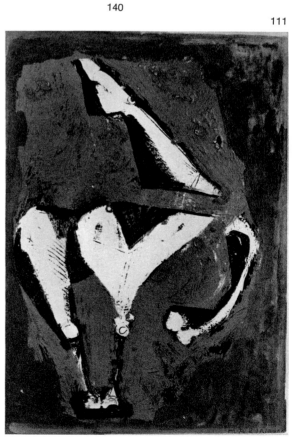

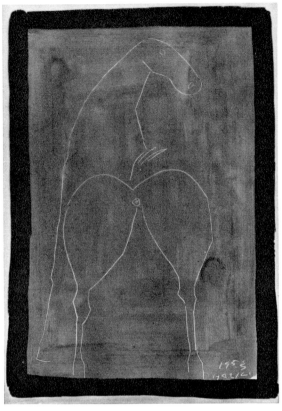

142

143

n° 103. *Acrobat and Horse.* Mixed media. Paper remounted on canvas. 40¹/₈ x 28¹/₈ in: Nelson Gallery-Atkins Museum (Nelson Fund), Kansas City, (gift of Mr. and Mrs. Robert S. Everitt). (p. 415).

n° 104. *Horse and Rider.* Tempera on paper. 33³/₄ x 26³/₄ in: Mr. and Mrs. Werner E. Josten Coll., New York. (p. 417).

n° 105. *The Meeting.* Oil on canvas. 79¹/₂ x 47³/₈ in: Property of the artist (p. 171).

Marino Marini reworked this painting in 1966.

n° 106. *The Dream.* Tempera. 59 x 47¹/₄ in: Property of the artist (p. 173).

Marino Marini reworked this painting in 1966.

83

144

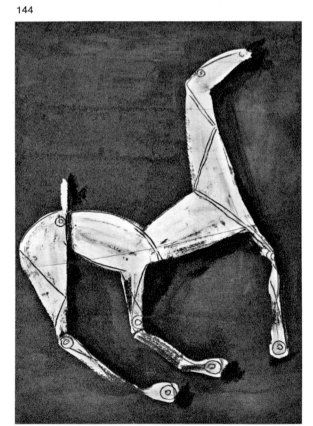

145

84

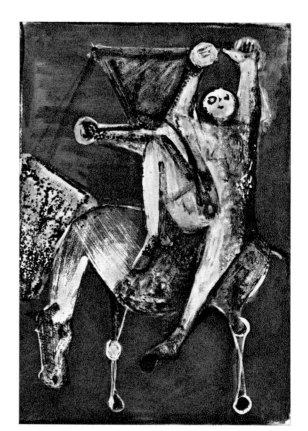

85

1952

n° 107. *Horse and Section.* Mixed media. 17 x 24³/₈ in: Private Coll., Rome. (p. 406).

n° 108. *Horse.* Oil on canvas. 39³/₈ x 29¹/₂ in: Rijksmuseum Kröller-Müller, Otterlo. (p. 406).

n° 109. *Horse with a Blue Circle.* Tempera. 24³/₈ x 17 in: Private Coll. (p. 406).

n° 110. *Horse.* Oil on canvas. 39³/₈ x 29¹/₈ in: C. Levi Coll., Turin. (p. 407).

n° 111. *Rearing Horse.* Oil on cardboard. 24³/₈ x 17 in: Dr. Arturo Mascetti Coll., Lugano, Switzerland. (p. 407).

n° 112. *Juggler and Horse.* Oil and tempera. 26³/₄ x 38⁵/₈ in: José Luis and Beatriz Plaza Coll., Caracas. (p. 409).

96

86

112

113

203

n° 113. *Composition.* Tempera. 7$^1/_8$ x 5$^1/_8$ in: Galleria del Milione, Milan. (Destroyed during the war?) (p. 410).

n° 114. *Rhythm II.* Mixed media. 24$^3/_8$ x 17 in: Property of the artist. (p. 410).

n° 115. *Dancer.* Tempera. 19$^1/_8$ x 13$^1/_8$ in: Dr. Max Fischer Coll., Stuttgart. (p. 411).

n° 116. *Dancer.* Mixed media on paper. 24 x 16$^1/_2$ in: Baron Lambert Coll., Brussels. (p. 411).

n° 117. *Horse and Rider.* Tempera. 20$^1/_8$ x 15$^3/_8$ in: Dr. Max Fischer Coll., Stuttgart. (p. 412).

n° 118. *Composition in Black.* Mixed media. 24$^3/_8$ x 17 in: Property of the artist. (p. 413).

n° 119. *Composition in Red.* Oil and gouache on masonite. 39$^3/_8$ x 29$^1/_2$ in: Sergio Grandini Coll., Lugano, Switzerland. (p. 414).

n° 120. *Jugglers.* Tempera. 27$^1/_8$ x 16 in: Mr. and Mrs. E. Mendoza Coll., Caracas. (p. 414).

n° 121. *Horse and Rider.* Water-color. 24 x 16$^3/_4$ in: Albright-Knox Art Gallery, Buffalo, New York (gift of M. A. Conger Goodyear). (p. 414).

n° 122. *Pink Horse and Rider.* Gouache. Approximately 16$^1/_2$ x 24$^3/_4$ in: Sergio Grandini Coll., Lugano, Switzerland. (p. 414).

n° 123. *Small Equestrian Composition II.* Mixed media. 24$^3/_8$ x 17 in: Private Coll., Milan. (p. 414).

114

146

178

115

116

n° 124. *Composition, Rider.* Oil.
$39^3/_8$ x $31^7/_8$ in: Private Coll. (p. 416).

n° 125. *Composition, Pink and Blue Rider.*
Oil. 39 x $31^1/_2$ in:
Pierre Matisse Gallery, New York. (p. 416).

n° 126. *Triangular Composition.* Oil.
Approximately $39^5/_8$ x $29^7/_8$ in:
Pierre Matisse Gallery, New York. (p. 422).

n° 127. *Composition in Green I.*
Oil on masonite. $39^3/_8$ x $29^7/_8$ in:
Private Coll., USA. (p. 422).

n° 128. *Composition in Green II.*
Oil on masonite, $39^3/_8$ x $29^7/_8$ in:
Private Coll., USA. (p. 422).

147

148

149

411

97

117

n° 129. *Small Equestrian Composition I.*
Mixed media. 24³/₈ x 17 in:
Private Coll., Udine, Italy. (p. 423).

n° 130. *Parade.* Oil on canvas.
50³/₄ x 37³/₈ in:
Pietro Campilli Coll., Rome. (p. 425).

n° 131. *Blue Rider.* Oil.
Paper remounted on canvas. 39 x 31¹/₄ in:
Pierre Matisse Gallery, New York. (p. 426).

n° 132. *Horse and Nude.* Gouache.
13³/₄ x 9⁷/₈ in:
Rich. Furuholmen Coll., Oslo. (p. 388).

n° 133. *Horse and Riders.* Gouache.
36 x 24 in:
Benjamin Watson Coll., Danbury. (p. 168).

n° 134. *Red Horse.* Oil on canvas.
78³/₄ x 55¹/₈ in:
A. M. Mees Coll., Noordwijk, Holland (p. 184).

150

98

168

99

151

118

87

n° 135. *Horse and Rider (Il Lambicco)*.
Oil on canvas. $39^3/_8$ x $39^3/_8$ in:
Pierre Matisse Gallery, New York (p. 186).

n° 136. *False Fall*. Oil on canvas.
$39^3/_8$ x $29^7/_8$ in: Galleria Gissi, Turin. (p. 429).

n° 137. *A Vision*. Tempera. 59 x $47^1/_4$ in:
Property of the artist (p. 174).
Marino Marini reworked this painting in 1966.

n° 138. *Performers*. Oil on canvas.
59 x $47^1/_4$ in: Property of the artist (p. 176).
Marino Marini reworked this painting in 1966.

1953

n° 139. *Red Horse, Composition*. Oil.
59 x 39 in:
Pierre Matisse Gallery, New York. (p. 407).

n° 140. *Brown Horse*. Mixed media.
$15^3/_4$ x $22^3/_8$ in:
Max Stern Coll., New York. (p. 407).

152

119

120

n° 141. *Horse.* Oil on paper. 23⅝ x 19⅝ in: Baltimore Museum of Art, Baltimore (Garrison Siemonn Coll.). (p. 407).

n° 142. *Horse.* Tempera. 24⅜ x 16½ in: Oppenhejm Coll., Copenhagen. (p. 408).

n° 143. *Horse.* Oil. 25⅛ x 17½ in: Pierre Matisse Gallery, New York. (p. 408).

n° 144. *Horse.* Tempera. 20 x 16½ in: Mr. and Mrs. E. Mendoza Coll., Caracas. (p. 408).

n° 145. *Horse.* Tempera. 20 x 16½ in: Private Coll. (p. 408).

n° 146. *Rhythm I.* Mixed media. 24⅜ x 17 in: Property of the artist. (p. 410).

121

122

123

414

100

101

n° 147. *Sea of Light.* Oil on canvas.
52 x 38¹/₈ in: Property of the artist. (p. 411).

n° 148. *Orange Blossom.* Oil on canvas.
39³/₈ x 29⁷/₈ in: Property of the artist. (p. 411).

n° 149. *Small Stage.* Oil on canvas.
39³/₈ x 29⁷/₈ in: Property of the artist. (p. 411).

n° 150. *Horse, Composition.* Tempera.
24³/₈ x 27 in:
Wallraf Richartz Museum, Cologne. (p. 412).

n° 151. *Horse and Rider.* Tempera on paper.
24 x 16¹/₂ in: Emilio Jesi Coll., Milan. (p. 413).

n° 152. *Horse and Rider.* Tempera.
24 x 16¹/₂ in: Mr. and Mrs. E. Mendoza Coll.,
Caracas. (p. 413).

n° 153. *Horse and Rider.*
Mixed media on paper. 24¹/₈ x 17 in:
Philadelphia Museum of Art, Philadelphia
(Louis E. Stern Coll.). (p. 417).

n° 154. *Horse and Rider.* Mixed media.
24³/₈ x 17 in: Dr. W. A. Bechtler Coll., Zollikon,
Switzerland. (p. 418).

n° 155. *Horse and Rider.* Tempera.
22³/₈ x 15³/₄ in: Manfred Behr Coll., Stuttgart.
(p. 418).

n° 156. *Horse and Rider.* Oil.
Approximately 22¹/₂ x 18⁷/₈ in:
Pierre Matisse Gallery, New York (p. 418).

n° 157. *Rider beside his Horse.*
Mixed media. 23⁵/₈ x 16¹/₂ in:
Baron Lambert Coll., Brussels. (p. 420).

102

88

103

179

180

124

n° 158. *Contemporaries.* Oil on canvas.
59 x 47¼ in: Emilio Jesi Coll., Milan. (p. 420).

n° 159. *Horse and Rider Standing.*
Oil on paper. 24½ x 17 in:
Galerie Rosengart, Lucerne. (p. 420).

n° 160. *Equestrian Composition.* Oil on
canvas. 47¼ x 39⅜ in: Private Coll. (p. 420).

n° 161. *Horses.* Tempera and ink.
Length: approximately 11⅞ in:
Private Coll. (p. 421).

n° 162. *Two Riders.* Oil on canvas.
47¼ x 35⅜ in:
Former Gustav Stein Coll., Cologne. (p. 423).

n° 163. *Back-cloth.* Oil on canvas.
59 x 47½ in: Property of the artist. (p. 425).

n° 164. *The Warrior and the Dance.*
Oil on canvas. 78¾ x 70½ in:
Mr. and Mrs. Rolf Weinberg Coll., Zurich.
(p. 425).

n° 165. *Horses and Rider.* Tempera.
18⅛ x 15 in:
Pierre Matisse Gallery, New York. (p. 426).

n° 166. *Acrobats and Horse.* Tempera on
paper. 16½ x 24⅜ in: Private Coll. (p. 428).

n° 167. *Acrobats.* Oil on masonite.
39⅜ x 29⅞ in:
Mrs. G. Falck-Devoto Coll., Milan. (p. 432).

n° 168. *Rider.* Mixed media. 27½ x 23⅝ in:
Riccardo Jucker Coll., Milan. (p. 412).

125

181

416

182

90

204

n° 169. *Juggler.* Tempera on paper.
24 x 16¹/₂ in: Emilio Jesi Coll., Milan (p. 155).

n° 170. *Juggler.* Oil on cardboard.
Approximately 39³/₈ x 23⁵/₈ in: ◁ This painting was stolen from
Marina Marini Coll., Milan. (p. 295).   the artist at Forte dei Marmi.

n° 171. *Juggler and Horse.*
Tempera on paper. 18¹/₈ x 12⁵/₈ in:
Emilio Jesi Coll., Milan. (p. 402).

n° 172. *Horse.* Oil. 17 x 24³/₄ in:
Peter and Ellen Keckeis-Tobler Coll., Zurich.
(p. 388).

n° 173. *Horse and Rider.*
Tempera on paper. 18¹/₈ x 13 in:
Dr. and Mrs. Sarnoff Coll., Bethesda. (p. 426).

104

153

154

205

n° 174. *Horse and Rider.* Water-color and ink. Paper remounted on canvas. Length: approximately 39³/₈ in: Private Coll. (p. 426).

n° 175. *Horse and Juggler.* Tempera on paper. Private Coll. (p. 427).

n° 176. *Battle.* Tempera on paper. 17 x 18¹/₈ in: Manfred Behr Coll., Stuttgart. (p. 434).

Study for a large picture (71 x 71 in:), sold in the United States. Its whereabouts is unknown.

n° 177. *Spectacle.* Oil on canvas. 39³/₈ x 31⁷/₈ in: Property of the artist (p. 175).

Marino Marini reworked this painting in 1966.

206

155

156

207

208

1954

n° 178. *Architecture in Gray I.*
Oil on canvas. 38¹/₈ x 28⁹/₈ in:
Property of the artist. (p. 410).

n° 179. *Fall of a Rider.* Oil on masonite.
39⁹/₈ x 29⁷/₈ in: P. Guarini Coll., Milan. (p. 416).

n° 180. *Rider's Game.* Oil on masonite.
39⁹/₈ x 29⁷/₈ in:
C. F. Bilotti Coll., New York. (p. 416).

n° 181. *Horse and Rider.* Gouache.
Paper remounted on canvas. 29⁷/₈ x 21¹/₄ in:
H. C. Bechtler Coll., Zurich. (p. 416).

n° 182. *Horse and Rider.*   Tempera on paper.
31¹/₂ x 23⁵/₈ in:
Hamburger Kunsthalle, Hamburg. (p. 417).

n° 183. *Three Horses.* Oil on paper.
24³/₈ x 17 in:
Galerie Rosengart, Lucerne. (p. 421).

n° 184. *Horse.* Mixed media.
Model for a lithograph. 20⁷/₈ x 14⁵/₈ in:
Manfred Behr Coll., Stuttgart. (p. 421).

n° 185. *Horse.* Oil. 24³/₈ x 17 in:
Pierre Matisse Gallery, New York. (p. 421).

n° 186. *Profile.* Oil on masonite.
39⁹/₈ x 29⁷/₈ in:
K. Pearlman Coll., New York. (p. 422).

n° 187. *Equestrian Composition.*
Oil on canvas. 51¹/₈ x 43¹/₄ in:
Adriano Barbieri Coll., Milan. (p. 423).

209

210

201

157

158

n° 188. *Acrobats and Horse*. Oil on canvas.
59 x 47¹/₂ in:
Museum of Art, Carnegie Institute, Pittsburgh
(gift of G. David Thompson). (p. 424).

n° 189. *Jugglers*. Oil on canvas.
59 x 47¹/₄ in: Property of the artist. (p. 425).

n° 190. *Horse and Rider*. Oil on canvas.
64¹/₈ x 39³/₈ in:
Pierre Matisse Gallery, New York. (p. 426).

n° 191. *Horse and Rider*. Tempera.
Pierre Matisse Gallery, New York. (p. 427).

n° 192. *Horse and Rider*. Tempera.
Private Coll., Milan. (p. 428).

n° 193. *Composition*. Oil.
Paper remounted on canvas. 39¹/₄ x 29¹/₈ in:
Pierre Matisse Gallery, New York. (p. 429).

n° 194. *Equestrian Figure II*. Mixed media.
24³/₈ x 17 in:
P. Ghitti Coll., Brescia, Italy. (p. 433).

196

159

160

420

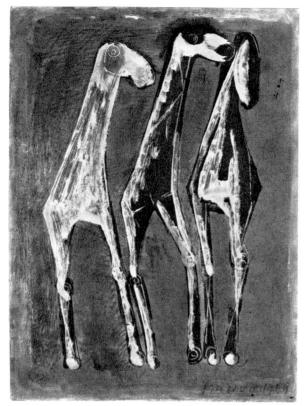

183

161

n° 195. *Horse and Rider.*
Tempera on paper. 24¹/₈ x 17 in: Bridgestone Museum, Ishibashi Found., Tokyo. (p. 435).

n° 196. *Blue Rider.* Oil on canvas.
78³/₄ x 71 in:
Walter H. Herdeg Coll., Zurich. (p. 420).

n° 197. *Jugglers.* Oil on canvas.
59 x 47¹/₄ in: Property of the artist. (p. 172).

n° 198. *Resurrection.* Oil on canvas.
43¹/₄ x 31¹/₂ in: Nathan Coll., Zurich. (p. 199).

n° 199. *Polychrome Trio.* Oil on canvas.
59 x 47¹/₄ in:
The Noockey Foundation, Toronto. (p. 224).

n° 200. *Black Miracle.* Mixed media.
Paper remounted on canvas. 50³/₈ x 33³/₄ in:
Private Coll., Milan. (p. 255).

211

184

185

126

231

127

128

186

212

232

n° 205. *Horse and Rider.*
Oil and tempera on cardboard. 33 x 23⁷/₈ in:
José Luis and Beatriz Plaza Coll., Caracas.
(p. 418).

n° 206. *Miracle.* Tempera. 24³/₈ x 17 in:
Private Coll., Milan. (p. 418).

n° 207. *Horse and Rider.*
Tempera on paper. 28⁵/₈ x 22³/₈ in:
Emilio Jesi Coll., Milan. (p. 419).

n° 208. *Horse and Rider.* Oil.
33³/₄ x 25 in:
Pierre Matisse Gallery, New York. (p. 419).

n° 209. *Blue Horse and Rider.* Tempera.
32¹/₂ x 23⁵/₈ in:
Pierre Matisse Gallery, New York. (p. 419).

n° 210. *Rider.* Tempera on paper.
31¹/₂ x 24³/₄ in:
Manfred Behr Coll., Stuttgart. (p. 419).

n° 211. *Horse in Harmony.* Oil on paper.
24³/₈ x 33³/₄ in: Private Coll., Milan. (p. 421).

n° 212. *Rider.* Tempera. 33 x 23⁵/₈ in:
W. and N. Bär Coll., Zurich. (p. 423).

n° 213. *Acrobat on Horseback.*
Oil on canvas. 78³/₄ x 71 in:
H. Abrams Coll., New York. (p. 424).

n° 214. *Horse and Rider.*
Wurtzburger Coll., Baltimore. (p. 427).

162

129

187

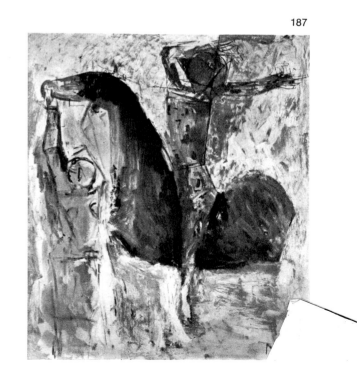

226

188

233

213

234

424

130

163

164

189

235

190

131

n° 215. *Horse and Figure.*
Oil on cardboard, 34³/₈ x 25¹/₈ in:
Riccardo Jucker Coll., Milan. (p. 427).

n° 216. *Horse and Rider.* Oil. 33³/₄ x 24³/₈ in:
Pierre Matisse Gallery, New York. (p. 427).

n° 217. *Acrobat.* Tempera. 30¹/₄ x 22⁷/₈ in:
Oppenhejm Coll., Copenhagen. (p. 428).

n° 218. *Small Horse.* Oil on paper.
10³/₈ x 7¹/₂ in:
Angela Rosengart Coll., Lucerne. (p. 428).

n° 219. *The Promise.* Oil on canvas.
59 x 59 in:
C. Djerassi Coll., Palo Alto, California. (p. 428).

165

173

174

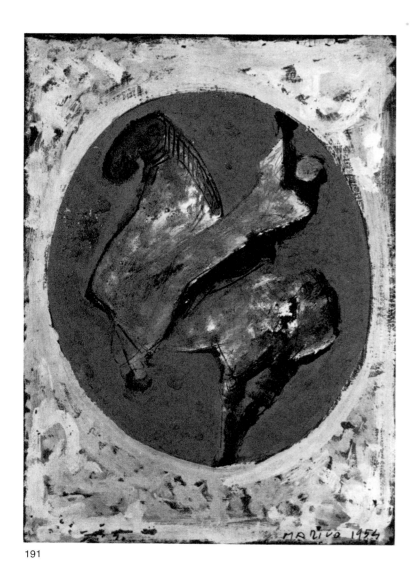

191

175

n° 220. *Composition in Harmony.*
Oil on canvas. 78³/₄ x 71 in:
Property of the artist. (p. 429).

n° 221. *Familiar Games.* Oil on canvas.
43¹/₄ x 33¹/₂ in:
J. Nehmad Coll., Milan. (p. 429).

n° 222. *Rider and Space.* Oil on canvas.
33³/₄ x 24³/₈ in: Falsetti Coll., Cortina d'Am-
pezzo, Italy. (p. 429).

n° 223. *The Limits of Fantasy.*
Oil on canvas. 38¹/₈ x 28³/₈ in:
Property of the artist. (p. 431).

n° 224. *Study in Forms.* Oil on canvas.
27¹/₂ x 19⁵/₈ in:
Marina Marini Coll., Milan. (p. 431).

n° 225. *Miracle in Color.* Oil.
Paper remounted on canvas. 47⁵/₈ x 33¹/₂ in:
C. F. Bilotti Coll., New York. (p. 433).

n° 226. *Juggler.* Oil on canvas.
31¹/₂ x 25⁵/₈ in:
Marina Marini Coll., Milan. (p. 424).

n° 227. *Blue Rider.* Oil on canvas.
55¹/₈ x 33³/₄ in: Emilio Jesi Coll., Milan. (p. 200).

n° 228. *Invocation.* Oil on canvas.
78³/₄ x 71 in: Nationalgalerie, Berlin. (p. 210).

n° 229. *Miracle.* Study. Tempera.
Paper remounted on canvas. 33 x 24³/₈ in:
Marina Marini Coll., Milan. (p. 257).

214

215

216

427

217

192

1955 - 1956

n° 230. *Architecture in Grey.*
Oil on canvas. 38¹/₈ x 28⁹/₈ in:
Property of the artist. (p. 431).

1956

n° 231. *Heroic Imagination.* Oil on canvas.
82⁵/₈ x 55¹/₈ in: J. Nehmad Coll., Milan. (p. 422).

n° 232. *Group of Jugglers.* Oil on canvas.
39⁹/₈ x 31¹/₂ in:
Leopoldo Zorzi Coll., Bari, Italy. (p. 423).

n° 233. *Jugglers.* Oil on canvas.
59 x 47¹/₄ in:
H. W. Rudhart Coll., Oberhausen, Federal
Republic of Germany. (p. 424).

n° 234. *Project for a Mosaic.* Mixed media.
24³/₈ x 16¹/₂ in:
Private Coll., Brescia, Italy. (p. 424).

n° 235. *Theater with Masked Figures.* Study.
Oil on canvas. 59 x 47¹/₄ in:
Property of the artist. (p. 425).

n° 236. *Horse.* Gouache. 24³/₄ x 18⁷/₈ in:
H. C. Bechtler Coll., Zurich. (p. 430).

n° 237. *Form and Color.* Oil on canvas.
26 x 19⁵/₈ in: Property of the artist. (p. 430).

n° 238. *Composition and Architecture.*
Oil on canvas. 26 x 19⁵/₈ in:
Galleria Gissi, Turin. (p. 430).

218

219

166

193

220

n° 239. *Architectural Composition.*
Mixed media. Paper remounted on canvas.
23⁵/₈ x 19⁵/₈ in: Property of the artist. (p. 430).

n° 240. *Composition II.* Tempera.
Paper remounted on canvas. 24³/₈ x 33 in:
Property of the artist. (p. 431).

n° 241. *Light, Composition.*
Oil on canvas. 27¹/₂ x 19⁵/₈ in:
Property of the artist. (p. 431).

n° 242. *Horse and Rider.* Oil. 19⁵/₈ x 15³/₄ in:
Pietro Papi Coll., Rome. (p. 432).

n° 243. *Dancer in Green.* Mixed media.
24³/₈ x 17 in: A. Totah Coll., Milan. (p. 432).

n° 244. *Composition.* Oil. 24³/₄ x 34¹/₄ in:
Galerie d'Art Moderne Marie-Suzanne Feigel,
Basle. (p. 438).

136

221

222

236

237

n° 245. *Miracle.* Tempera on paper.
32⁷/₈ x 24³/₈ in:
W. and N. Bär Coll., Zurich. (p. 250).

n° 246. *Theater with Masked Figures.*
Oil on canvas. 78³/₄ x 94¹/₂ in:
Greenwin Construction Company, Toronto.
(p. 178).

n° 247. *Farce in the Theater.* Oil on canvas.
59 x 47¹/₄ in: Alejandro Zaffaroni Coll.,
Palo Alto, California. (p. 225).

n° 248. *Orpheus.* Oil on canvas.
96³/₈ x 118 in: Property of the artist. (p. 226).

1957

n° 249. *Horse and Rider with Red and Black
Lines.* 33³/₄ x 24³/₈ in:
Pierre Matisse Gallery, New York. (p. 433).

n° 250. *Two Acrobats and a Horse.*
30³/₄ x 22¹/₈ in:
Pierre Matisse Gallery, New York. (p. 434).

202

238

239

430

223

230

240

224

241

242

167

n° 257. *Composition*. Tempera.
25⁷/₈ x 19⁵/₈ in:
Pierre Matisse Gallery, New York. (p. 437).

n° 258. *Abstract Composition*. 27³/₄ x 19⁵/₈ in:
Pierre Matisse Gallery, New York. (p. 437).

n° 259. *Two Figures and Color.*
Oil on canvas. 25⁵/₈ x 19⁵/₈ in:
Property of the artist. (p. 440).

n° 260. *The Carriage Builder's Daughters.*
Oil on canvas. 59 x 59 in:
Property of the artist. (p. 131).

n° 261. *Presentation of Jugglers.* Oil.
59 x 47⁵/₈ in:
A. Blum Coll., Zug, Switzerland. (p. 162).

263

243

432

264

249

225

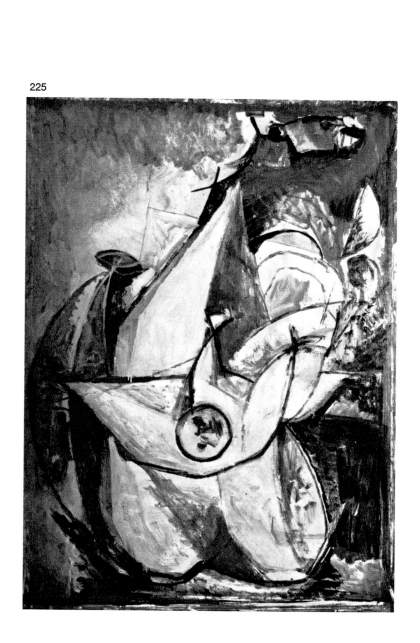

n° 262. *Representation in Blue.*
Oil on canvas. 59 x 47¹/₄ in:
J. L. Greene Coll., New York. (p. 227).

1958

n° 263. *Ecstasy in the Theater.*
Oil on paper. 30¹/₄ x 22 in:
Emilio Jesi Coll., Milan. (p. 432).

n° 264. *Horse and Juggler.* Oil on canvas.
47¹/₄ x 59 in:
Dominion Gallery, Montreal. (p. 433).

n° 265. *Idea for a Rider I.* Oil on paper.
71 x 59 in: Galleria Levi, Milan. (p. 434).

194

265

266

n° 266. *Sequences.* Tempera.
25⅝ x 19⅝ in: Ginobbi Coll., Rome. (p. 434).

n° 267. *Green and Red Abstract Composition.*
Tempera. 33⅜ x 24⅜ in:
Pierre Matisse Gallery, New York. (p. 436).

n° 268. *Figures in the Imagination.*
Oil on paper. 33¾ x 24 in:
Emilio Jesi Coll., Milan. (p. 437).

n° 269. *Mobility of Color.* Oil on canvas.
78¾ x 71 in: Property of the artist. (p. 437).

n° 270. *Research for a Composition.*
Oil on canvas. 24⅜ x 16½ in:
Property of the artist. (p. 440).

250

176

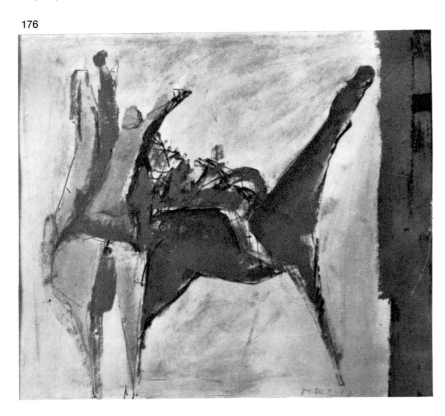

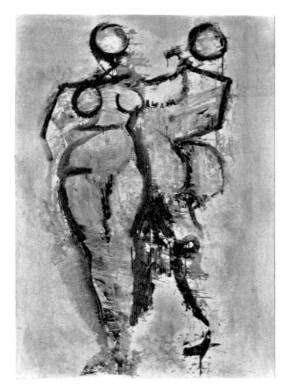

251

252

195

n° 271. *Juggler*. Oil on canvas.
59 x 47¼ in:
H. H. Tyssen Coll., Lugano, Switzerland.
(p. 167).

n° 272. *Idea for a Rider II*. Oil.
Paper remounted on canvas. 71 x 59 in:
Valente Coll., Zurich. (p. 220).

n° 273. *Representation in Green*.
Oil on canvas. 47¼ x 39⅜ in:
Emilio Jesi Coll., Milan. (p. 228)

n° 274. *Babylon*. Oil on canvas.
39⅜ x 31½ in: Property of the artist. (p. 229).

280

435

253

267

n° 275. *Gleams of Light in the Forest*.
Oil on canvas. 78³/₄ x 71 in:
C. Djerassi Coll., Palo Alto, California. (p. 230).

n° 276. *Miracle*. Mixed media.
Paper remounted on canvas. 52³/₄ x 32¹/₄ in:
St. Louis University Art Museum, St. Louis.
(p. 256).

1958 - 1959

n° 277. *Red Rider*. Oil on canvas.
78³/₄ x 71 in: P. Marinotti Coll., Milan. (p. 436).

n° 278. *The Orchestra*. Oil on canvas.
59 x 59 in: S. Cinicola Coll., Milan. (p. 438).

254

277

255

256

268

1958 - 1960

n° 279. *Grand Theater.* Oil on canvas.
71 x 71 in: A. Scamperle Coll., Rome. (p. 438).

1959

n° 280. *Composition.* Oil on paper.
59 x 46⁷/₈ in: Property of the artist. (p. 435).

n° 281. *Miracle.* Tempera. Paper remounted
on canvas. 28³/₄ x 39³/₈ in: (p. 440).
Work stolen from the Galleria Toninelli, Milan.

n° 282. *Finished Composition.*
Oil on paper. 24³/₈ x 16¹/₂ in:
Property of the artist. (p. 441).

n° 283. *Three Figures.* Oil on canvas.
59 x 47¹/₄ in: Property of the artist. (p. 132).

n° 284. *Dancer.* Oil on canvas. 59 x 47¹/₄ in:
Property of the artist. (p. 150).

1959 - 1960

n° 285. *Harlequin's Games.* Oil on canvas.
59 x 59 in: Galleria La Medusa, Rome. (p. 438).

n° 286. *The Vitality of Games.* Oil.
Paper remounted on canvas. 71 x 71 in:
F. Parisi Coll., Milan. (p. 438).

n° 287. *Living Theater.* Oil on canvas.
59 x 59 in: R. Toninelli Coll., Rome. (p. 177).

257

269

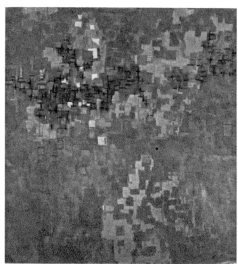

258

285

286

244

278

279

438

288

289

303

290

302

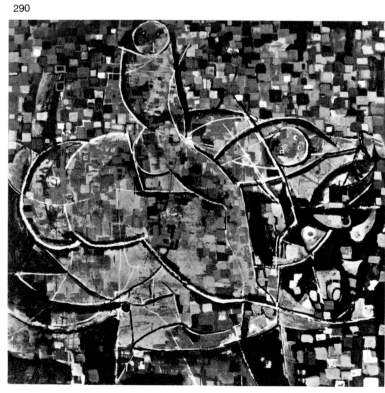

439

270

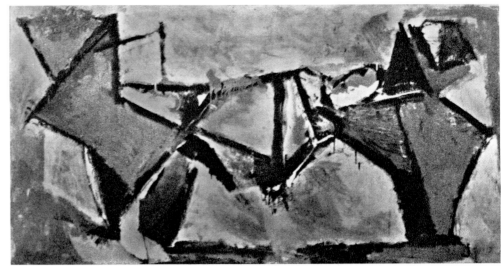

291

259

281

292

1960

n° 288. *Impressionability.* Mixed media.
Paper remounted on canvas. 59 x 59 in:
Albert White Gallery, Toronto. (p. 439).

n° 289. *Stage Set.* Oil on canvas.
74³/₄ x 74³/₄ in: Property of the artist. (p. 439).

n° 290. *Mosaic.* Painting. 71 x 59 in:
Property of the artist, Forte dei Marmi.
(p. 439).

n° 291. *The Warrior.* Oil on canvas.
Macchiati Coll., Milan. (p. 440).

n° 292. *The Cry.* Oil.
Paper remounted on canvas. 38⁵/₈ x 59 in:
Galleria Levi, Milan. (p. 440).

n° 293. *The Idea.* Mixed media. Paper.
28³/₄ x 59³/₈ in: Property of the artist. (p. 441).

n° 294. *The Cry II.* Oil on paper.
38³/₈ x 59 in: P. Marinotti Coll., Milan. (p. 441).

n° 295. *The Idea, Composition.* Tempera.
Paper remounted on canvas. 39³/₈ x 28³/₄ in:
D. Tega Coll., Milan. (p. 219).

440

304

282

293

328

294

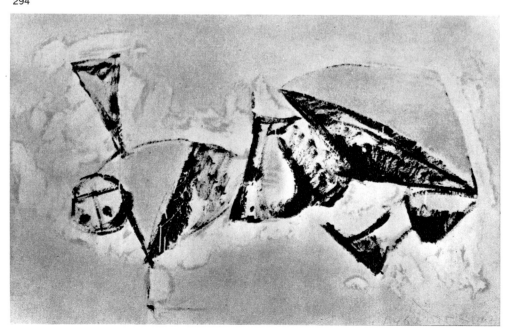

n° 296. *Iberia.* Mixed media. 29$^{7}/_{8}$ x 22 in:
A. Blum Coll., Zug, Switzerland. (p. 236).

n° 297. *Warrior.* Tempera.
Paper remounted on canvas. 59 x 59 in:
Property of the artist. (p. 277).

n° 298. *Synthesis.* Oil on canvas.
74$^{3}/_{4}$ x 74$^{3}/_{4}$ in: Property of the artist. (p. 278).

n° 299. *Composition.* Tempera.
Paper remounted on canvas. 49$^{1}/_{4}$ x 33 in:
Property of the artist. (p. 285).

n° 300. *Group of Elements IV.*
Mixed media. Paper remounted on canvas.
35$^{3}/_{8}$ x 65 in: Property of the artist. (p. 286).

n° 301. *The Fall of the Angel.*
Oil on canvas. 47$^{1}/_{4}$ x 59 in:
Property of the artist. (p. 235).

*Marino Marini reworked this painting in 1967
(see p. 378).*

1961

n° 302. *Poster.* Tempera on canvas.
59 x 47$^{1}/_{4}$ in: Property of the artist. (p. 439).

329

312

330

313

314

1962

n° 303. *The Warrior II.* Oil.
Paper remounted on canvas. 51$^1/_8$ x 59 in:
Galleria Levi, Milan. (p. 439).

n° 304. *Idea for a Composition.*
Mixed media. 22$^3/_4$ x 41 in:
Property of the artist. (p. 441).

n° 305. *Naked Women.*
Water-color on paper. 14$^1/_4$ x 10$^1/_8$ in:
Rijksmuseum Kröller-Müller, Otterlo. (p. 444).

n° 306. *Three Figures.*
Tempera on canvas. 78$^3/_4$ x 71 in:
Property of the artist. (p. 444).

n° 307. *The Warrior.* Oil.
Paper remounted on canvas. 51$^1/_8$ x 59 in:
Mrs. Michael M. Rea Coll., Sewickley. (p. 276).

1963

n° 308. *The Enchantment of the Dancers.*
Oil on canvas. 78$^3/_4$ x 71 in:
J. Nehmad Coll., Milan. (p. 238).

1964

n° 309. *Shooting.* Oil on canvas.
59 x 59 in: Property of the artist. (p. 237).

n° 310. *Composition.* Oil on paper.
39$^3/_8$ x 59 in: Property of the artist. (p. 286).

442

319

331

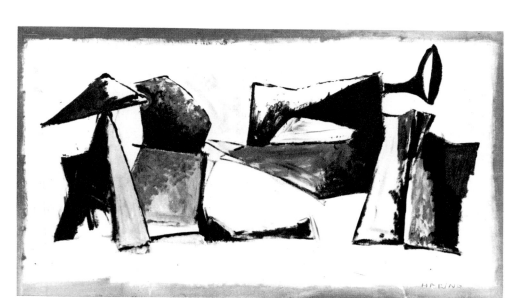

320

315

332

1965

n° 311. *Group of Elements I.* Mixed media.
Paper remounted on canvas. 35¹/₂ x 75 in:
Property of the artist. (p. 287).

1966

n° 312. *Group of Elements.* Tempera.
Paper remounted on canvas. 38¹/₈ x 70 in:
Property of the artist. (p. 442).

n° 313. *Composition.* Tempera.
Paper remounted on canvas. 35¹/₂ x 61⁷/₈ in:
Property of the artist. (p. 442).

n° 314. *Group of Elements.* Tempera.
Paper remounted on canvas. 57⁷/₈ x 69⁵/₈ in:
Property of the artist. (p. 442).

n° 315. *Group of Elements.* Tempera.
Paper remounted on canvas. 57 x 70 in:
Property of the artist. (p. 443).

n° 316. *The Minstrel.* Tempera.
59 x 47¹/₄ in: Property of the artist. (p. 444).

n° 317. *The Happy Wife.* Tempera.
59 x 47¹/₄ in: Property of the artist. (p. 444).

n° 318. *Dance in the Theater.* Tempera.
59 x 47¹/₄ in: Property of the artist. (p. 444):

n° 319. *Composition.* Mixed media.
34⁵/₈ x 65 in: Property of the artist. (p. 443)

316

317

n° 320. *Group of Elements*. Tempera. Paper remounted on canvas. 36¹/₄ x 63 in: Property of the artist. (p. 443).

n° 321. *Composition*. Tempera. Paper remounted on canvas. 31¹/₂ x 60⁷/₈ in: Property of the artist. (p. 287).

n° 322. *Group of Elements*. Tempera. Paper remounted on canvas. 35³/₈ x 67 in: Property of the artist. (p. 378).

1967

n° 323. *Passion for the Game*. Oil on wood. 78³/₄ x 78³/₄ in: Property of the artist. (p. 288).

n° 324. *The Cry*. Study. Tempera on paper. 25⁵/₈ x 36¹/₄ in: Marina Marini Coll., Milan. (p. 296).

n° 325. *The Cry*. Study. Tempera on paper. 25¹/₈ x 35⁷/₈ in: Marina Marini Coll., Milan. (p. 296).

n° 326. *Mobile - Immobile*. Tempera. Paper remounted on canvas. 53⁵/₈ x 76 in: Property of the artist. (p. 301).

n° 327. *Intensity*. Tempera. Paper remounted on canvas. 35³/₈ x 70¹/₂ in: Property of the artist. (p. 301).

1967 - 1968

n° 328. *Sketch for a Composition*. Oil on canvas. 39³/₈ x 31¹/₂ in: Property of the artist. (p. 441).

n° 329. *The Meaning of Cubism*. Oil on canvas. 21³/₄ x 17³/₄ in: Property of the artist. (p. 442).

n° 330. *Searching for an Idea*. Oil on canvas. 21³/₄ x 17³/₄ in: Property of the artist. (p. 442).

n° 331. *Decomposition*. Oil on canvas. 19⁵/₈ x 15³/₄ in: Property of the artist. (p. 443).

n° 332. *A Dialogue*. Oil on canvas. 19⁵/₈ x 15³/₄ in: Property of the artist. (p. 443).

1968

n° 333. *Vivacity*. Tempera. Paper remounted on canvas. 32⁵/₈ x 70¹/₂ in: Property of the artist. (p. 302).

n° 334. *Energy*. Tempera. Paper remounted on canvas. 33³/₄ x 70¹/₂ in: Property of the artist. (p. 302).

305

306

318

444

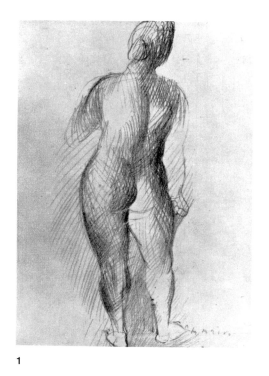

1

GENERAL CATALOGUE
OF THE
LITHOGRAPHS

(1941-1969)

2

For a book written by his friend, the painter-poet Filippo De Pisis in 1941, about his sculpture (Ed. della Conchiglia, Milan), Marino Marini executed his first two lithographs. The following year, having taken refuge in Switzerland and using the lithographic stones of the printer Salvioni, in Bellinzona, he drew nudes, Pomonas, horses and horsemen, bathing them in a delicate chiaroscuro which, far from enfeebling them, affirmed the vigor and purity of forms. It was, however, only after 1951, that his artistry acquired the personal character which places him in the front ranks among the great masters of contemporary lithography. For the first issue of the new series of XXᵉ Siècle, he engraved his work on ink-coated stone and in this same composition used a little color, very little. However, he immediately abandoned this process (nᵒˢ 35, 38), and used it only occasionally later (nᵒˢ 46, 57, 69, etc.), to draw freely on stone, either on a plain gray or white background. His art dealer, Curt Valentin, then commissioned him to do a series of seven lithographs, printed by F. Mourlot in Paris. With the exception of a "juggler," he repeated the theme of horses and horsemen, already treated in 1942, but this time his vigorous lines came to life

in an irresistible dynamism. We can also find in this series his need for expressive synthesis, at first purely geometric, to which he was to return later and which was, especially in 1952, a reflection of earlier research in the field of abstract painting (1937).

Thus, the mastery of Marino Marini, lithographer, asserted itself in Paris in 1952. The following year he worked in Switzerland with the printer Kratz (today Matthieu), commissioned by Klipstein & Kornfeld for the "Guilde de la Gravure" (directed at that time by Nesto Jacometti), as well as for Gérald Cramer. In 1954, he returned to Paris again, where he executed, with Mourlot, a lithograph in black, yellow and blue for the Art Institute of Chicago, but he returned frequently to Switzerland where he engraved, among others, with the printer Wolfensberger, for the Gallery of Modern Art of Basle, the portrait of Thomas Mann after an original drawing commissioned by the editor, Fischer, for an edition of the complete works of the author of The Magic Mountain.

The following year the Berggruen Gallery of Paris paid homage to the works of Marino Marini by exhibiting fifteen plates printed in Paris and Zurich, and edited a brochure on

the author. The artist drew two lithographs with the printer Mourlot, one for Berggruen, the other destined for the printer himself and which was not sold until 1968. Still with Mourlot, he composed lithographs for Cramer; but did not forget Switzerland, which shares with France the honor of having printed the greatest works of the master's golden age.

In 1957 and 1958, he created four plates for Nesto Jacometti's "L'Œuvre Gravée"; then, after an interruption of two years, he returned to the Kratz Printing House — now under the direction of Matthieu — and worked there for Jacometti and Kornfeld. In 1962, he agreed, for the "Association des Cent Bibliophiles", directed by Madame Madeleine de Harting, to create a few lithographs to illustrate a volume of poems by his sister, Egle. However, he completed only one, with Mourlot, suddenly preferring engraving to lithography. There was a new interruption of three years devoted exclusively to sculpture and painting in which he was becoming increasingly absorbed. In 1965, the theme of the "Miracle" inspired a first lithograph which he gave to the Philadelphia Museum of Art on the occasion of a large exhibition of his graphic works, and he then composed

3

4

5

6

1941

n° 1. Lithograph executed for the book "Marino Marini" by Filippo De Pisis, Edizioni della Conchiglia, Milan. 800 copies, numbered from I to L and from 1 to 750, 13 x 10¹/₈ in: 800 copies, not numbered but signed by the artist in an insertion at the top of the prints.

n° 2. Lithograph for the same work, 800 copies not numbered and not signed by the artist.

1942

The lithographs numbered from 3 to 25 were printed at Bellinzona by the Salvioni printing works.

n° 3. *Young Woman.* 17¹/₂ x 10⁷/₈ in: on a sheet measuring 21⁵/₈ x 14⁵/₈ in: 12 copies numbered and signed. *(Hofmann II).*

n° 4. *Study for Pomona.* 15¹/₈ x 11⁵/₈ in: on a sheet measuring 12¹/₈ x 15 in: 10 copies numbered and signed.

n° 5. *Young Woman.* 17³/₈ x 11⁷/₈ in: on a sheet measuring 22¹/₂ x 16⁵/₈ in: 8 copies numbered and signed.

7

8

9

10

11

a new lithograph on the theme of the "Miracle" for L'Œuvre Gravée. Most of this work consisted of compositions in black and white that were, in a way, imposed on him by his preoccupation at that time with plastics. However, though black expressed the dramatic power of the theme perfectly, color was not to be forgotten for long. After several lithographs for the Toninelli Gallery, as well as a new plate for XX° Siècle he undertook the album From Color To Form for which he dictated the preface and which includes ten large lithographs printed by Mourlot (commissioned by XX° Siècle and Leon Amiel, who had already edited jointly the Album N° 1 of engravings printed on the Lacourière presses by Frélaut).

Until now the lithographic works of Marino Marini include, in all, only one hundred plates. This is very little if one thinks of the impressive number of lithographs signed by Chagall, Picasso, Braque or Miró. However, their rareness does not in the least hamper their diffusion.

In the words of M. Carandente, author of the introduction to the catalogue of lithographs by Marino Marini (Toninelli, Editor, Milan), we can say that "rarely themes as limited in synthetic figurations have found in art vaster possibilities for precise expression." From the first works to the last, from the "Horsemen" and "Pomonas" to the "Warrior" and the "Cry," to the abstract interpretation of "Group of Elements," these themes express "a real adventure for modern visual consciousness". Their force moves from one work to the next by a dramatic, tragic and irresistible impulse and, beyond the novelty of figurative invention, we recapture the notion of something which existed in an absolutely free and eternal visual universe."

12

13

14

15

16

17

n° 13. *Chiaroscuro.* 13³/₄ x 9⁵/₈ in: on a sheet measuring 19³/₄ x 13³/₄ in: 10 copies numbered and signed. (Retouched by hand by the artist).

n° 14. *Seated Figure.* 15³/₈ x 9⁷/₈ in: on a sheet measuring 20¹/₂ x 12¹/₄ in: 13 copies numbered and signed.

n° 15. *Rest.* 11⁷/₈ x 15³/₄ in: on a sheet measuring 16⁵/₈ x 20¹/₂ in: 12 copies numbered and signed.

1943

n° 16. *Study for a Horse.* 14 x 10¹/₄ in: on a sheet measuring 20 x 15 in: 10 copies numbered and signed.

n° 17. *Back-cloth.* 12 x 16 in: on a sheet measuring 16 x 20 in: 10 numbered and signed.

n° 18. *The Announcement.* 15¹/₈ x 11⁵/₈ in: on a sheet measuring 20 x 15 in: 10 copies numbered and signed.

n° 19. *The Shield.* 15 x 11⁷/₈ in: on a sheet measuring 20 x 15 in: 10 copies numbered and signed.

n° 20. *Back-cloth.* 15¹/₈ x 11⁷/₈ in: on a sheet measuring 20 x 15¹/₈ in: 5 copies numbered and signed.

18

19

20

21

22

23

n° 21. *The Tournament I.* 15¹/₈ x 11⁵/₈ in: on a sheet measuring 20 x 15¹/₈ in: 10 copies numbered and signed.

n° 22. *Large Illustration.* 15³/₄ x 11⁵/₈ in: on a sheet measuring 19³/₄ x 15³/₄ in: 10 copies numbered and signed.

n° 23. *The Fable I.* 15³/₄ x 11⁷/₈ in: on a sheet measuring 19³/₄ x 15³/₄ in: 12 copies numbered and signed.

n° 24. *The Fable II.* 15³/₄ x 11⁷/₈ in: on a sheet measuring 19³/₄ x 15³/₄ in: Only a very few prints of this lithograph exist at the Salvioni printing works in Bellinzona, Italy.

n° 25. *The Tournament II.* 15³/₄ x 12³/₈ in: on a sheet measuring 20³/₈ x 16¹/₈ in: 6 copies numbered and signed.

1944

The lithographs numbered 26 to 32 were printed in Zurich by the J. C. Müller printing works.

n° 26. *The Fief.* 14⁵/₈ x 11¹/₄ in: on a sheet measuring 17 x 12³/₈ in: 8 copies numbered and signed.

n° 27. *Dancer.* 14⁵/₈ x 14¹/₄ in: on a sheet measuring 17 x 12⁵/₈ in: 11 copies numbered and signed.

24

25

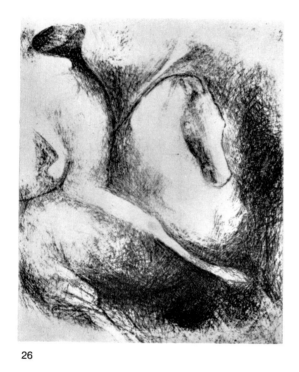

26

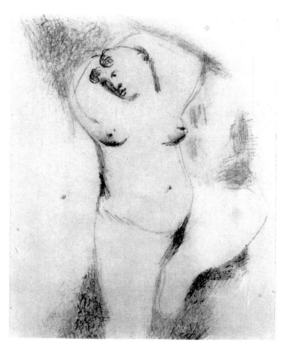

27

28

29

n° 28. *Study for Pomona.* 16¹/₂ x 12 in: on a sheet measuring 17 x 12⁵/₄ in: 10 copies numbered and signed.
With a brush, the artist added a wide black border on certain prints similar to n° 31.

n° 29. *Spring.* 14³/₄ x 8⁷/₈ in: on a sheet measuring 17¹/₂ x 13 in: 14 copies numbered and signed.

n° 30. *The Pilgrim.* 13³/₈ x 9⁷/₈ in: on a sheet measuring 19³/₄ x 13³/₄ in: 8 copies numbered and signed. (Lithograph retouched by hand by the artist).

n° 31. *Study for Pomona.* 14⁵/₈ x 9⁷/₈ in: on a sheet measuring 17 x 13³/₈ in: 10 copies numbered and signed.

1945

n° 32. *The Shape of a Horse.* 8⁵/₈ x 12¹/₂ in: on a sheet measuring 12 x 17 in: 10 copies numbered and signed.
This lithograph ends the first great period of Marino Marini's graphic work.

1947

n° 33. Lithograph designed for the periodical "L'Immagine," directed by Cesare Brandi, n° 1, 1st year, May 1947, 8¹/₂ x ¹/₄ in: 50 copies

30

31

32

33

34

35

on laid paper, signed and numbered from I to XX and from 1 to 30.

n° 34. Sketch of the lithograph for the periodical "L'Immagine," afterwards abandoned by the artist. Only two numbered prints are known. $13^{3}/_{4}$ x $9^{7}/_{8}$ in:

1951

n° 35. *Horse and Rider*. Original lithograph for the review "XX° Siècle," directed by G. di San Lazzaro. New series n° 1. $9^{5}/_{8}$ x $12^{3}/_{8}$ in: Colors: black and sienna. 1,500 copies, plus 30 copies for the limited edition signed and numbered by the artist.

n° 36. *Jugglers*. Published by Guilde de la Gravure, Geneva. Printed by Desjobert, Paris. $19^{1}/_{8}$ x $12^{1}/_{2}$ in: on a sheet measuring $22^{1}/_{8}$ x $15^{1}/_{8}$ in: Colors: pink, beige, black. Edition of 200 numbered and signed copies.

n° 37. Lithograph designed for the publication of "Marino Marini, due litografie e sei disegni," by Mario Ramous. Published by Licinio Cappelli, Bologna, Italy, 1951/. $12^{1}/_{8}$ x $7^{1}/_{8}$ in: on a sheet measuring $12^{1}/_{2}$ x $8^{1}/_{2}$ in: Colors: pink, gray, black. 100 copies numbered from 1 to 100 and signed by the artist.

n° 38. Lithograph designed for the same publication as n° 37. $12 \times 8^{5}/_{8}$ in: on a sheet measuring $12^{5}/_{8} \times 8^{5}/_{8}$ in: Colors: dark blue and black. 100 copies numbered from 1 to 100 and signed by the artist.

n° 39. *Acrobat with Two Horses.* $13^{3}/_{8} \times 9$ in: on a sheet measuring $15 \times 11^{3}/_{8}$ in:

n° 40. *Horse.* Lithograph which was abandoned by the artist and never published. Printed by Mourlot, Paris. $22^{7}/_{8} \times 16^{5}/_{8}$ in: on a sheet measuring $26 \times 19^{3}/_{4}$ in: A single copy exists. *(Hofmann 31).*

n° 41. *Riders and Horses, with a Green Border.* Published by the Curt Valentin Gallery, New York. Printed by Mourlot, Paris. $25^{7}/_{8} \times 19^{1}/_{4}$ in: on a sheet measuring $26 \times 19^{3}/_{4}$ in: Colors: light green, medium green, black. 50 signed and numbered copies. 5 artist's proofs. *(Berggruen 31).*
Douglas Cooper, in the preface to the book edited by Pizzi, emphasized the strength and dynamism of these lithographs as well as their bold use of color. Carendente admired especially the movement with which the artist endowed the figures drawn on stone.

n° 42. *Study for a Rider.* Lithograph which was abandoned by the artist and never

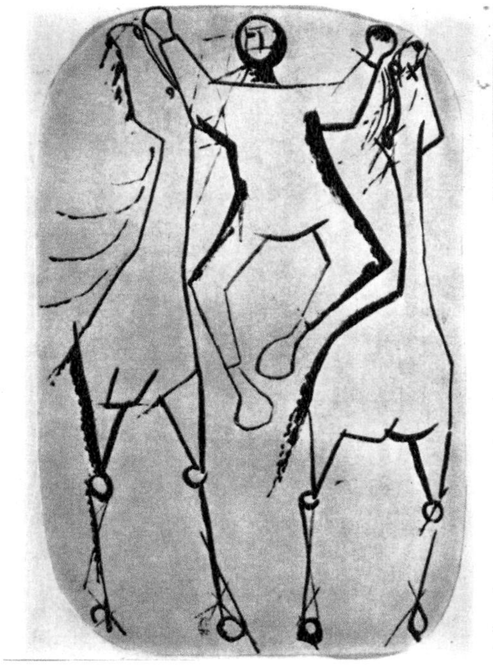

36

published. Printed by Mourlot, Paris. $22^{7}/_{8} \times 16^{7}/_{8}$ in: on a sheet measuring $25^{7}/_{8} \times 19^{3}/_{4}$ in: A single copy exists.

1952

n° 43. *Riders and Horses, on a Cream Ground.* Published by the Curt Valentin Gallery, New York. Printed by Mourlot, Paris, $22^{1}/_{8} \times 17$ in: on a sheet measuring $26 \times 19^{3}/_{4}$ in: Colors: cream and black. 40 numbered and signed copies. 5 artist's proof. *(Berggruen 9. Cooper I).*

n° 44. *Rider and Horse, in Yellow and Blue.* Published by the Curt Valentin Gallery, New York. Printed by Mourlot, Paris. $22^{1}/_{2} \times 16^{5}/_{8}$ in: on a sheet measuring $26 \times 19^{3}/_{4}$ in: Colors: yellow, light blue, black. 40 numbered and signed copies. 5 artist's proofs. *(Berggruen 29).*

n° 45. *Juggler.* Published by the Curt Valentin Gallery, New York. Printed by Mourlot, Paris. $24 \times 15^{1}/_{8}$ in: on a sheet measuring $26 \times 19^{3}/_{4}$ in: 25 numbered and signed copies, with a blue border. 25 numbered and signed copies, with a gray border. 5 artist's proofs. There are a few prints without a border. *(Berggruen 11: blue border. Cooper II: blue border).*

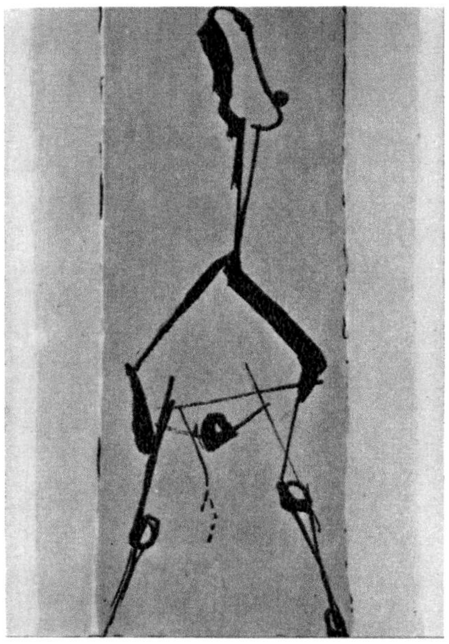

37

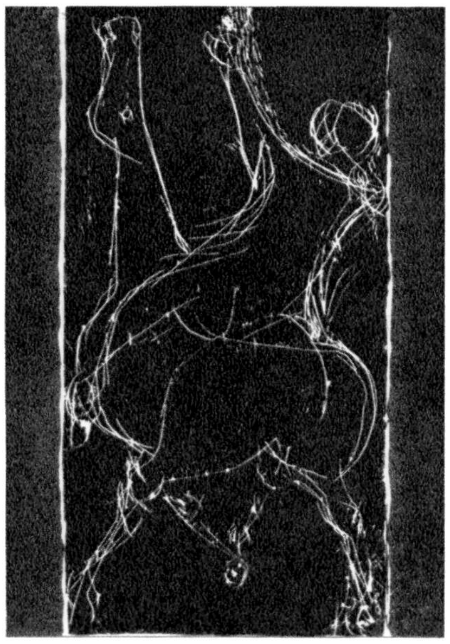

38

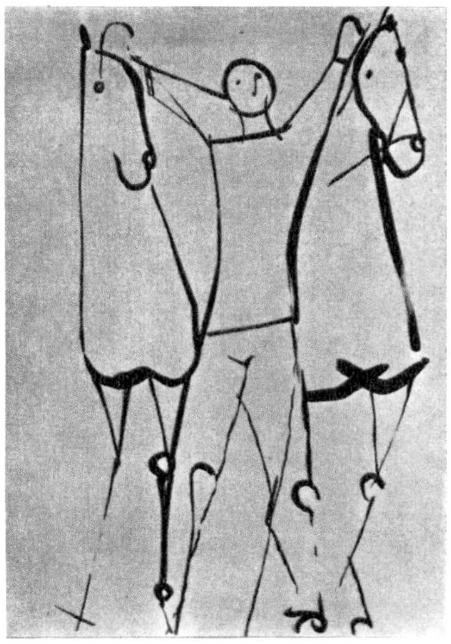

39

40

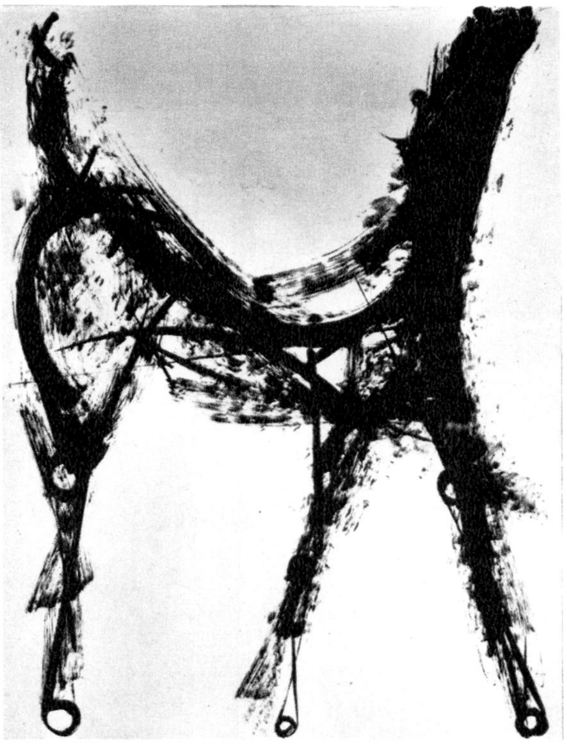

41

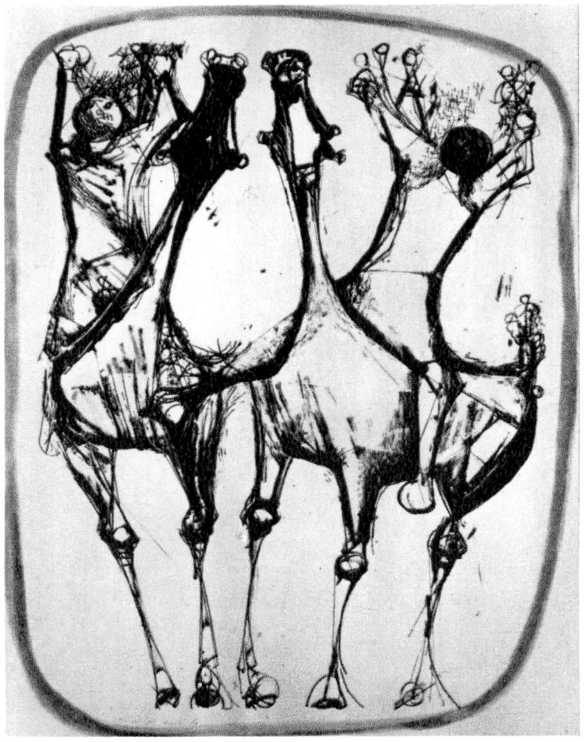

n° 46. *Rider and Horse, Orange and Yellow.* Published by the Curt Valentin Gallery, New York. Printed by Mourlot, Paris. 20¹/₂ x 12³/₈ in: on a sheet measuring 26 x 19³/₄ in: Colors: ochre, orange and black. 50 numbered and signed copies. 5 artist's proof. *(Berggruen 13).*

1953

n° 47. *Juggler and Horses, Green Ground, Yellow Border.* Published by Klipstein & Kornfeld, Berne. Printed by Kratz, Zurich. 24¹/₈ x 17⁵/₈ in: on Marais paper, measuring 25⁵/₈ x 19¹/₂ in: Colors: narrow yellow border, gray-green, black. 15 numbered and signed copies. 5 artist's proofs. Only 3 prints of these lithographs in the first stage in black exist. *(Berggruen 15).*

n° 48. *Games on Horseback.* Published by the Curt Valentin Gallery, New York. Printed by Mourlot, Paris. 22¹/₂ x 17 in: on a sheet measuring 25⁷/₈ x 19³/₄ in: 50 numbered and signed copies. 5 artist's proofs. *(Hofmann 51).*

n° 49. Lithograph done for the luxury edition of "Marino Marini, Scultore," by Umbro Apollonio, 2nd revised edition, Edizione del Milio-

42

ne, Milan 1953. 11 x 8³/₈ in: in a transparent cover. Colors: yellow and red. 25 copies numbered from 1 to 25 and signed in the Italian edition. 25 copies numbered from 26 to 30 and signed in the English edition. 3 artist's proofs for the 3 copies not for sale.

n° 50. *Horse Being Broken in.* Published by Gérald Cramer, Geneva. Printed by Mourlot. Paris. 22 x 15³/₄ in: on a sheet measuring 26 x 19³/₄ in: Colors: red, light blue, dark blue, black. 50 numbered and signed copies. 5 artist's proofs. *(Berggruen 19).*

n° 51. *Juggler and Two Horses, Blue, Yellow and Black.* Published by the Art Institute of Chicago, Chicago. Printed by Mourlot, Paris. 24 x 15¹/₂ in: on a sheet measuring 26 x 19³/₄ in: Colors: dark blue, ochre, black. 150 numbered and signed copies. *(Berggruen 33).*

n° 52. *Horse.* Published by Nesto Jacometti. Printed by Kratz, Zurich. 23¹/₂ x 16⁵/₈ in: on Zerkall-Bütten, measuring 28 x 20¹/₈ in: Colors: narrow pink border, black. 50 numbered and signed copies. 9 or 10 numbered artist's proofs. *(Berggruen 21).*
The Berggruen catalogue, contrary to the printer's view, indicates an edition limited to 45 examples and 5 artist's proofs.

43

44

45

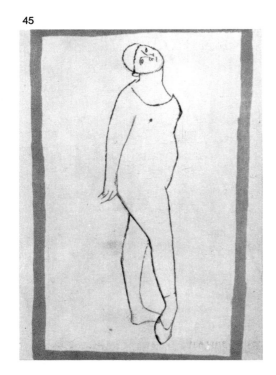

46

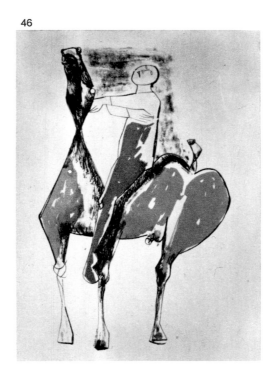

47

48

49

50

51

52

53

n° 53. *Red Rider.* Published by Klipstein & Kornfeld, Berne. Printed by Kratz, Zurich. 25⁵/₈ x 19³/₄ in: on Zerkall-Bütten measuring 28 x 20¹/₈ in: Colors: red, green, ochre, black. 65 numbered and signed copies. 5 artist's proof. *(Berggruen 27. Cooper IV).*

n° 54. *Horse.* Published by the Guilde de la Gravure, Geneva. Printed by Kratz, Zurich. 20¹/₂ x 13³/₈ in: on Lana Bütten, 22 x 15 in: Colors: gray, light blue, black. 220 numbered and signed copies. 5 artist's proofs. *(Hofmann 37).*

1954

n° 55. *Three Horses, with Yellow Border.* Published by Klipstein & Kornfeld, Berne. Printed by Mourlot, Paris. 23¹/₈ x 16⁷/₈ in: on a sheet measuring 26 x 19³/₄ in: Colors: yellow and black. 50 numbered and signed copies. 5 artist's proofs. *(Berggruen 25).*

1955

n° 56. *Jugglers.* Published by Gérald Cramer, Geneva. Printed by Mourlot, Paris. 24³/₄ x 17³/₈ in: on a sheet measuring 25⁷/₈ x 19³/₄ in: Colors: red border, yellow, orange, black. 50 numbered and signed copies. 5 artist's proofs. *(Berggruen 35).*

n° 57. *Composition.* Published by Schweizerische Graphische Gesellschaft, Berne. Printed by Kratz, Zurich. 24³/₈ x 17³/₈ in: on Marais paper measuring 26 x 19⁷/₈ in: Colors: gray border, black. Edition of 125 numbered and signed copies. 5 artist's proofs.

n° 58. *Rider on a Violet Ground with a Red border.* Published by Klipstein & Kornfeld, Berne. Printed Kratz, Zurich. 24⁵/₈ x 16⁵/₈ in: on Marais paper measuring 26 x 19³/₄ in: Colors: red, violet, black. 65 numbered and signed copies. 10 artist's proofs. *(Cooper III).*

n° 59. *Red Horse on a Green Ground.* Published by the Galerie d'Art Moderne, Basle. Printed by Wolfensberger, Zurich. 19⁷/₈ x 13³/₄ in: on a sheet measuring 25³/₈ x 19³/₄ in: Colors: green, red, black. 125 numbered and signed copies, intended for an album published on the occasion of the 10th anniversary of the Gallery. 25 numbered and signed copies. 25 copies reserved for the artist. *(Berggruen 17).*

n° 60. *Two Acrobats with a Horse.* Published by Berggruen et Cie. Paris. Printed by Mourlot, Paris. 23⁷/₈ x 16¹/₂ in: on a sheet measuring 26 x 19³/₄ in: Colors: yellow ground,

453

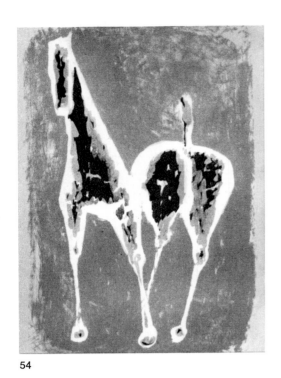

54

black. 50 numbered and signed copies. 8 artist's proofs. *(Hofmann 46. Cooper V).*

n° 61. *Family of Acrobats.* Published by Berggruen et Cie., Paris. Printed by Mourlot, Paris. 24³/₈ x 17³/₄ in: on a sheet measuring 26 x 19³/₄ in: Colors: dark blue border, ivory center, black. 50 numbered and signed copies. 8 artist's proofs. *(Hofmann 63. Cooper VII).*

n° 62. *Red and. Black Rider.* Published by Gérald Cramer, Geneva. Printed by Mourlot, Paris. 23⁵/₈ x 17¹/₈ in: on a sheet measuring 25⁷/₈ x 19¹/₂ in: Colors: red border, dark gray, black. 30 numbered and signed copies. *(Cooper VII).*

n° 63. *Rider and Horse, with Orange Border.* Published by Berggruen et Cie., Paris. Printed by Mourlot, Paris. 24³/₈ x 18¹/₈ in: on a sheet measuring 26 x 19³/₄ in: Colors: orange, dark blue, gray, black. 50 numbered and signed copies. 5 artist's proofs. Two copies of a first stage, uniquely in black, are known. *(Hofmann 47, under the title of "Acrobat on Horseback". Berggruen 7. Cooper VIII).*

n° 64. *Composition.* Published by Berggruen et Cie., Paris. Printed by Mourlot, Paris. 23⁷/₈ x 16¹/₂ in: on a sheet measuring 26 x 19³/₄

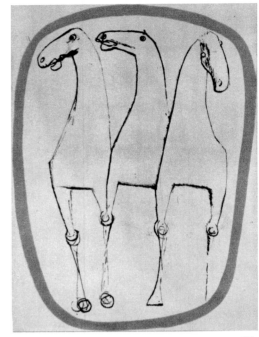

55

56

57

58

59

60

61

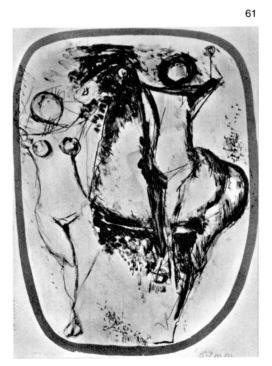

62

63

64

65

66

67

68

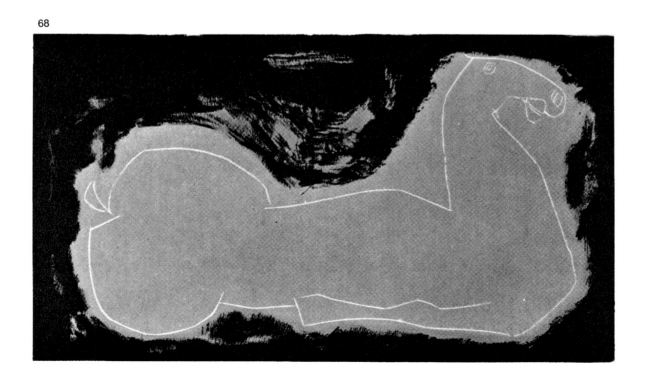

69

70

Colors: white slightly tinged with ochre and ivory ground, dark blue, chestnut, orange, black. 50 signed and numbered copies. 10 artist's proofs. (Cooper XI).

n° 72. *Acrobat.* Published by Berggruen et Cie., Paris. Printed by Mourlot, Paris. 24¹/₈ x 19 in: on a sheet measuring 26 x 19³/₄ in: Colors: light gray-blue border, dark blue, yellow, red, green, black. (Cooper XII).
In this new period of the artist's work, in which Marco Valsecchi discovered a "secret architectural aptitude," Marino Marini, according to Carandente, raised the level of his figurative work to that of pure form.

n° 73. *Acrobats.* Published by Berggruen et Cie., Paris. Printed by Mourlot, Paris. 24⁵/₈ x 18¹/₂ in: on a sheet measuring 26¹/₄ x 19⁷/₈ in: Colors: orange border, black. (Hofmann 49).

n° 74. *Miracle.* Published by Klipstein & Kornfeld, Berne. Printed by Kratz, Zurich. 25³/₈ x 18¹/₈ in: on Marais vellum measuring 26 x 19³/₄ in: Colors: red, gray, black. 50 numbered and signed copies. 8 artist's proofs. *Two copies of a first stage in black alone on a larger sheet are known to exist. (Hofmann 53. Cooper XIV).*

in: (The Berggruen catalogue gives the measurements as 22⁷/₈ x 15 in:) Colors: yellow, orange, pale green, dark green, brown, ivory, white slightly tinged with ochre. 50 numbered and signed copies. 5 artist's proofs. *(Berggruen 23. Cooper IX).*

n° 65. *Rider.* Published by Berggruen et Cie., Paris. Printed by Mourlot, Paris. 25⁷/₈ x 17³/₄ in: on a sheet measuring 26 x 19³/₄ in: Colors: red border, gray, dark gray, black. 50 numbered and signed copies. 7 artist's proofs. *(Hofmann V: reproduced in color. Cooper X).*

n° 66. *Ceramic I.* Published by Berggruen et Cie., Paris. Printed by Mourlot, Paris. 23⁵/₈ x 18⁷/₈ in: on a sheet measuring 26 x 19³/₄ in: Colors: ochre, pink, green, black. 50 numbered and signed copies. 8 artist's proofs.

n° 67. *Ceramic II.* Lithograph done for an album published by Mourlot, achieved by blocking out the outer black halo in "Ceramic I" and by using chestnut instead of red, and ochre instead of green. Published by Mourlot, Paris. 21 x 16⁷/₈ in: on a sheet measuring 26 x 19³/₄ in: 80 numbered and signed copies. 10 numbered and signed copies on Japanese vellum. Published in 1956. *(Cooper XIII).*

n° 68. *Horse.* Published by Berggruen et Cie., Paris. Printed by Mourlot, Paris. 12³/₄ x 22¹/₈ in: on a sheet measuring 19³/₄ x 26¹/₈ in: Colors: violet-blue and black. 50 numbered and signed copies. 5 artist's proofs.

n° 69. *Composition.* Lithograph done for the poster designed for the exhibition at the Galerie Berggruen et Cie., Paris. Published by Berggruen et Cie., Paris. Printed by Mourlot, Paris. 25¹/₈ x 17 in: on a sheet measuring 29³/₄ x 20¹/₂ in: Colors: orange-red and black. 200 unnumbered and unsigned copies besides the posters. 10 artist's proofs. Reproduced on the cover of the Berggruen catalogue.

n° 70. *Portrait of Thomas Mann.* Published by Fischer Verlag, Frankfurt-am-Main. Printed by Wolfensberger, Zurich. 13¹/₈ x 10³/₈ in: on a sheet measuring 22³/₄ x 17³/₄ in: Colors: white slightly tinged with ochre, black. 200 numbered and signed copies. 20 copies reserved for the artist.

1956

n° 71. *Games.* Published by Berggruen et Cie., Paris. Printed by Mourlot, Paris. 25⁵/₈ x 19³/₄ in: on a sheet measuring 26 x 19³/₄ in:

71

72

73

74

75

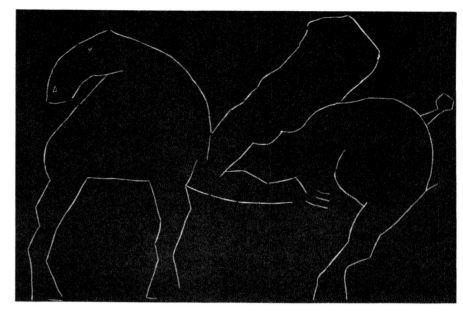

76

77

78

79

80

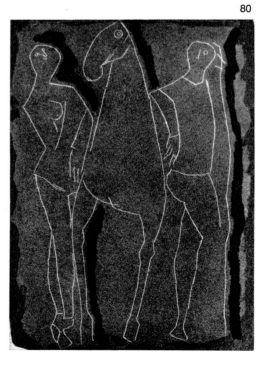

n° 75. *Horse and Rider.* Published by Gérald Cramer, Geneva. Printed by Kratz, Zurich. Toninelli noted in his catalogue of the lithographs of Marino Marini that even though Cramer believed that this particular lithograph had been printed by Mourlot in Paris, Emil Matthieu found an exact reference amongst the papers of his predecessor, Kratz. $15^1/_2$ x $12^1/_8$ in: on pearl Japanese vellum, measuring $16^3/_4$ x 13 in: Colors: dark blue border, black. 30 numbered and signed copies. 5 artist's proofs. *(Cooper XVI).*

n° 76. *Rider on a Black Ground.* Published by Klipstein & Kornfeld, Berne. Printed by Kratz, Zurich. $13^3/_4$ x 20 in: on Marais vellum $19^3/_4$ x $25^5/_8$ in: 50 numbered and signed copies. 5 artist's proofs. *(Hofmann 42).*

1957

n° 77. *Rider on a Gray Ground.* Published by L'Œuvre Gravée, Zurich-Paris. Printed by Kratz, Zurich. $22^3/_8$ x $15^3/_4$ in: on Rives BFK Raisin vellum, measuring $25^5/_8$ x $19^3/_4$ in: Colors: light gray, yellow, red, black. 50 numbered and signed copies. 5 artist's proofs. *(N° 109 in the catalogue of L'Œuvre Gravée. Cooper XV).*

n° 78.   *Rider.*   Lithograph done for l'Action Internationale de l'Union Suisse des Lithographes "Sept artistes de six pays dessinent au profit des réfugiés hongrois". (Drawings of seven artists from six countries for the benefit of Hungarian refugees, organised by International Action of the Swiss Union of Lithographers). 17³/₄ x 22 in: on Rives BFK Coquille vellum. 50 copies signed on the stone. 4 artist's proofs, of which certain ones have a dark blue oval painted in tempera around the subject. Six copies, "artist's proofs," obtained by printing the black outline on a white sheet, are known.

n° 79.   *Rider on a Green Ground.*   Published by L'Œuvre Gravée, Zurich-Paris. Printed by Kratz, Zurich 23¹/₈ x 16⁵/₈ in: on Rives BFK Raisin vellum measuring 25⁵/₈ x 19³/₄ in: Colors: green, pale red, dark red, black. 50 numbered and signed copies. 8 artist's proofs. *(N° 108 in the catalogue of L'Œuvre Gravée. Hofmann 68. Cooper XVII).*

n° 80.   *Composition.*   Published by Klipstein & Kornfeld, Berne. Printed by Kratz, Zurich. 25⁵/₈ x 19¹/₂ in: on Rives BFK Raisin vellum. Colors: ochre border, brown, black. 25 copies with a light brown center. 25 copies with a

81

82

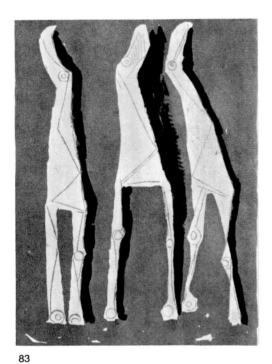

dark brown center. All numbered and signed. 6 artist's proofs. *(Cooper XVIII).*

n° 81.   *Rearing Figure.*   Published by Klipstein & Kornfeld, Berne. Printed by Kratz, Zurich. 23³/₄ x 16¹/₈ in: 50 numbered and signed copies. 7 artist's proofs.

n° 82.   *Rider on an Ochre Ground.*   Published by L'Œuvre Gravée, Zurich-Paris. Printed by Kratz, Zurich. 25 x 18 in: on Rives BFK Raisin vellum measuring 26 x 19³/₄ in: Colors: ochre, red, orange, brown, black. 50 numbered and signed copies. 8 artist's proofs. Published in 1958. *(N° 191 in the catalogue of L'Œuvre Gravée. Cooper XX). The geometric compositions of Marino Marini have, in our opinion, no relationship with Cézanne and Cubism. It is the "movement" with which the artist endows his figures which makes them "machines," but the elements into which the figure is broken up and which become in the end almost abstract, reacquire their humanity when the artist comes back to his basic figure.*

1958

n° 83.   *Three Horses.*   Published by L'Œuvre Gravée, Zurich-Paris. Printed by Kratz, Zurich.

83

84

85

86

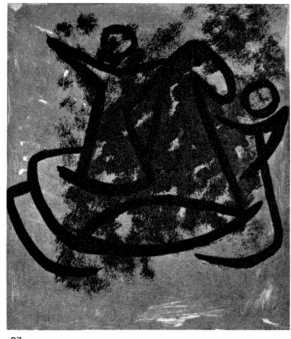

87

88

89

90

24 x 17 in: on Rives BFK Raisin vellum, measuring 25⁵/₈ x 19³/₄ in: Colors: gray ground, yellow, black. 50 numbered and signed copies. 8 artist's proofs. *(N° 192 in the catalogue of L'Œuvre Gravée, Cooper XIX).*

1960

n° 84. *Two Clowns and a Horse.* Published by Klipstein & Kornfeld, Berne. Printed by Emil Matthieu, Zurich. 25¹/₄ x 19 in: Rives BFK Jésus vellum 29⁷/₈ x 22 in: Colors: gray, dark gray, red, black. Edition of 50 numbered and signed copies. 7 artist's proofs.

n° 85. *Horse and Rider.* Published by Klipstein & Kornfeld, Berne. Printed by Emil Matthieu, Zurich. 25⁵/₈ x 19¹/₄ in: on Rives BFK Jésus vellum, measuring 30¹/₈ x 22 in: Colors: light gray, dark gray, black. 50 numbered and signed copies. 7 artist's proofs.

n° 86. *The Black Rider.* Published by "L'Œuvre Gravée", Zurich-Paris. Printed by Emil Matthieu, Zurich. 22³/₈ x 18¹/₈ in: on Rives BFK Raisin vellum, measuring 25⁵/₈ x 19³/₄ in: Colors: yellow, red, green, black. 50 numbered and signed copies. 5 artist's proofs. *(N° 285 in the catalogue of L'Œuvre Gravée).*

n° 87. Lithograph done for the luxury editions of the volume "L'Opera grafica di Marino Marini," by Werner Hofmann. Joint publication in 1960 by Verlag Gerd Hatje, Stuttgart and Il Saggiatore, Milan. Printed by Emil

91

92

93

94

459

Matthieu, Zurich. 12³/₈ x 10³/₈ in: on Zerkall-Bütten, measuring 28 x 20¹/₈ in: Colors: red, gray, black. The details printed in the colophon justifying the edition indicate 300 copies numbered from 1 to 300 and signed by the artist. The luxury edition in Italian contains the lithographs n°ˢ 11-20, 41-50, 71-80, 101-110, 131-140, 161-170, 191-200, 221-230, 251-260, 281-290. Emil Matthieu indicates that in all 520 copies were printed as well as 9 artist's proofs. Two proofs without gray are known. *(Toninelli H - 1960).*

1961

n° 88. Lithography intended for the volume "Marino Marini, Plastik". Publisher: Gerd Hatje, Stuttgart. No print of this lithograph has been made. Only a few rare copies of the proof are known. *(Toninelli I - 1961).*

n° 89. Lithograph done for the luxury editions of "Marino Marini, Plastik," with photographs by Helmut Lederer and introduction by Eduard Trier. Published by Gerd Hatje, Stuttgart 1961. Printed by Emil Matthieu, Zurich. 11⁵/₈ x 9¹/₂ in: on Japanese vellum. 400 copies including 350 numbered and signed, 10, not for sale, numbered from I to X and 6 artist's proofs. *(Toninelli J - 1961).*

95

n° 90. *Horseman on a Starry Black Ground.* Published by L'Œuvre Gravée, Zurich-Paris. Printed by Emil Matthieu, Zurich. 27⁵/₈ x 19³/₄ in: on Rives BFK Couronne vellum, measuring 35³/₈ x 25¹/₄ in: Colors: red, yellow, black. 50 numbered and signed copies. Only one artist's proof is known. *(N° 306 in the catalogue of L'Œuvre Gravée, Toninelli 79).*

n° 91. *Black and Red Rider on a Brown Ground.* Published by L'Œuvre Gravée, Zurich-Paris. Printed by Emil Matthieu, Zurich. 27⁵/₈ x 19³/₄ in: on Rives BFK Couronne vellum, measuring 35⁵/₈ x 25¹/₄ in: Colors: yellow, chestnut, red, black. 50 numbered and signed copies. Only one artist's proof is known on Japanese vellum.
(N° 327 in the catalogue of L'Œuvre Gravée. Toninelli 80).

1962

n° 92. *The Black Rider.* Published by Les Cent Bibliophiles de France et d'Amérique, Paris. Printed by Mourlot, Paris. 16³/₈ x 12³/₄ in: on Rives vellum. Colors: chestnut, yellow, dark blue, gray, black. 50 numbered and signed copies. About 5 artist's proofs on Japanese vellum. Published in 1963. *(Toninelli 81).*

1963

n° 93. *Rider.* Lithograph done for the luxury edition of the volume "Marino Marini,

pitture e disegni," with text by Franco Russoli, published by Toninelli Arte Moderna, Milan 1963. Printed by Giorgio Upiglio, Milan. 11³/₈ x 9¹/₂ in: Colors: red and black. 25 copies numbered from 1 to 25 and signed by the artist. 4 artist's proofs.

n° 94. Lithograph done for the luxury edition of the volume "Marino Marini, Bilder und Zeichnungen," with text by F. Russoli, published by Gerd Hatje, Stuttgart 1965. Printed by Giorgio Upiglio, Milan. 11³/₈ x 9⁷/₈ in: Colors: brown, red, black. 75 copies numbered from 1 to 75 and signed by the artist. 4 artist's proofs.

n° 95. *Horse and Rider* (The exact title should be *The Warrior*). Lithograph done for the review "XXᵉ Siècle" n° 21, May 1963. 9⁵/₈ x 12¹/₈ in: Colors: white slightly tinged with ochre, yellow, orange, black. 3,000 copies of the review, neither numbered nor signed. 50 copies published separately with wide margins, numbered from 1 to 50 and signed.

1965

n° 96. *Miracle.* Published by the Philadelphia Museum of Art. Philadelphia. Printed by Emil Matthieu, Zurich. 30¹/₄ x 21³/₄ in: on a

96

97

98

99

100

460

sheet measuring 35³/₈ x 25 in: 125 numbered and signed copies. 3 artist's proofs. *(Toninelli 82).*

n° 97. *The Miracle.* Published by L'Œuvre Gravée, Zurich-Paris. Printed by Emil Matthieu, Zurich. 32⁵/₈ x 22¹/₈ in: on a sheet measuring 35³/₈ x 24³/₄ in: Colors: chestnut and black. 60 numbered and signed copies. A few proofs in brown exist. *(N° 421 in the catalogue of L'Œuvre Gravée).*

n° 98. *The Stars.* Published by L'Œuvre Gravée, Zurich-Paris. Printed by Emil Matthieu, Zurich. 26¹/₈ x 19 in: (one proof on a sheet 35 x 24⁷/₈ in:) *(Toninelli 85).*

n° 99. *Waiting.* Published by Toninelli Arte Moderna, Milan. Printed by Emil Matthieu, Zurich. 29 x 19³/₄ in: on a sheet measuring 35¹/₂ x 25 in: 60 copies. 2 artist's proofs. *(Toninelli 86).*

n° 100. *Space.* Published by Toninelli Arte Moderna, Milan. Printed by Emil Matthieu, Zurich. 26 x 18⁵/₈ in: on a sheet measuring 35¹/₄ x 24⁷/₈ in: 60 copies. 2 artist's proofs, *(Toninelli 87).*

n° 101. *The Scream.* Published by L'Œuvre Gravée, Zurich-Paris. Printed by Emil Matthieu, Zurich. 21¹/₄ x 31¹/₂ in: on a sheet meas-

101

Emil Matthieu, Zurich. 20 x 30⁷/₈ in: (one proof on a sheet measuring 24⁷/₈ x 35¹/₄ in:) Colors: narrow pale yellow border, dark yellow, red, dark blue, pink, black. A single artist's proof in black and white also exists.

1968

n° 105. Lithograph published by Felix Man and the Ketterer Gallery, Munich, for the "Portefeuille de Dessins et Lithos de sculpteurs". Printed by Emil Matthieu, Zurich.

102

103

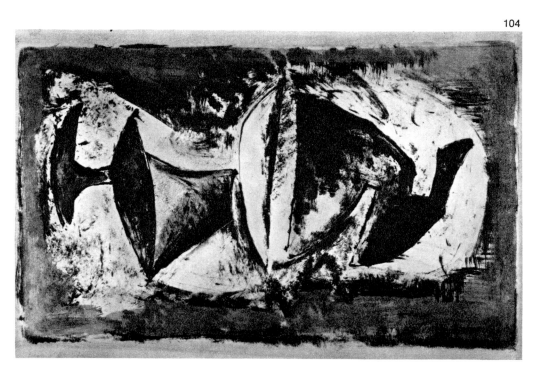

104

uring 25 x 35¹/₄ in: 50 numbered and signed copies.

Carandente wrote that "the hundred lithographs of Marino Marini afford yet another confirmation of his way of showing how tragedy overshadows the whole world..." It seems to us, however, that Marino Marini cannot be considered merely as an artist representative of his time—even as an artist of genius like Picasso—for he himself lives this tragedy, he identifies himself with the tragedy of his time. After the anguished protest of "The Miracle," we find "The Scream" monstrous but resigned; for it is no more than a mysterious symbol of a wonderfully modelled beauty.

n° 102. *Horse and Rider.* Published by Toninelli Arte Moderna, Milan. Printed by Emil Matthieu, Zurich. 24¹/₈ x 27¹/₈ in: (one proof on a sheet measuring 29¹/₂ x 34³/₈ in:) Colors: pink, lilac, black.

n° 103. *Group of Elements.* Published by Toninelli Arte Moderna, Milan. Printed by Emil Matthieu, Zurich. This lithograph accompanied the special edition of 100 copies of "Les Lithographies de Marino Marini".

n° 104. *Group of Elements.* Published by Toninelli Arte Moderna, Milan. Printed by

105

n° 108 a. Colors: Red, blue, green, ochre, yellow, pink, black.

n° 108 b. Colors: Dark blue, light blue, red, black, orange.

n° 108 c. Colors: White, dark blue, light blue, yellow, green, red, brown, black.

n° 108 d. Colors: Black and gray ground, blue, red, green, violet, pink, yellow, ochre.

n° 108 e. Colors: Yellow, ochre, red, blue, green, violet, black.

n° 108 f. Colors: White slightly tinted with ochre, very pale stone, red, orange, blue, green, yellow, violet, gray, brown, black.

n° 108 g. Colors: Green, dark blue, black, red, ochre, violet, yellow.

n° 108 h. Colors: White slightly tinted with ochre, light blue, dark blue, orange, green, ochre, yellow, black.

n° 108 i. Colors: Ochre, pink, white, gray, light blue, dark blue, yellow.

n° 108 j. Colors: Red, violet, white, dark blue, black, green, yellow.

n° 106. *Warrior.* Original lithograph for the review "XXᵉ Siècle" n° 30, June 1968. 12¹/₈ x 18¹/₈ in: Colors: dark blue ground, green, violet, red, black. 3,000 copies plus 50 exclusive signed examples with a margin, 25²/₈ x 17³/₄ in:

1969

n° 107. *Rider.* Original lithograph for the poster for this volume. Dimensions: 20¹/₂ x 15¹/₂ in: on a sheet measuring 25³/₄ x 20 in: Colors: light gray, pink, red, green, yellow, orange, black. Separate edition on Japanese vellum: 50 copies numbered from 1 to 50, plus 8 artist's copies numbered from I to VIII.

n° 108. *From Color to Form.* 10 original lithographs by Marino Marini. English and French texts by Marino Marini. Album first published by XXᵉ Siècle, Paris and by Leon Amiel, New York, on 30th January, 1969, the lithographs printed by Fernand Mourlot, Paris and the text by Fequet and Baudier.
50 copies numbered from 1 to 50 on Arches vellum, plus 6 copies numbered from E. C. I to E. C. VI reserved for collaborators and 15 copies (not for sale) numbered from H. C. I. to H. C. XV reserved for the artist and his friends, were printed. Dimensions: 20¹/₂ x 15¹/₂ in: on a sheet measuring 25³/₄ x 20 in:

106

107

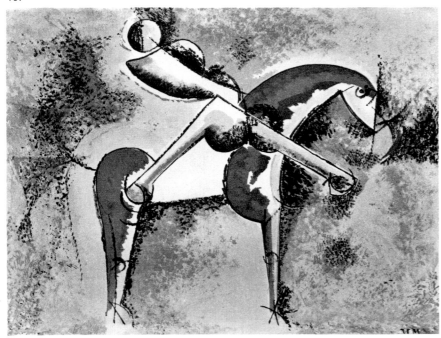

The references Hofmann, Cooper, Berggruen, Toninelli, followed by Arabic or Roman numerals relate to illustrations or plates included in the following publications devoted to Marino Marini's lithographs: "L'Opera Grafica de Marino Marini," by Werner Hofmann; Il Saggiatore, Milan, 1960.
"Marino Marini," by Douglas Cooper; Editoriale Silvana, Milan, 1959.
"15 Lithographs of Marino Marini," Exhibition catalogue; Galerie Berggruen et Cie., Paris, 1955.
"La Litografia di Marino Marini (1942-1965)". Introduction by Giovanni Carandente, catalogue and notes by L. F. Toninelli. Published by Romeo Toninelli, Milan.

108 a

108 b

108 c

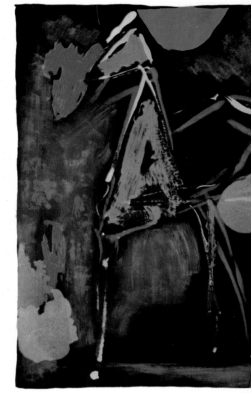

108 e

108 f

108 d

108 g

108 h

108 i

108 j

Marino Marini at Mourlot's workshop (1969).

Marino Marini with Fernand Mourlot (1969).

1

GENERAL
CATALOGUE
OF THE
ENGRAVINGS

1914 - 1969

2

1914 - 1915

n° 1. *Seated Woman.* Etching. $5^5/_8$ x $6^1/_2$ in: Unique copy.

n° 2. *The World War in 1914.* Etching. $15^1/_2$ x $14^3/_8$ in: Unique copy.

Marino Marini was attracted by engraving from his adolescence onwards. Although his early designs as a student are unknown, his etchings from the same period have been preserved. The artists under whose influence he first came were his teachers at the Academy of Fine Arts in Florence and some artists with a purely local reputation—for the city strangely ignored the great European artists of the day. His early works, wavering between Symbolism and Realism, the ephemeral sovereigns of the period, were already marked by the sureness of their composition and the vigor of their line. At that time, Italy remained artistically dependent on Central Europe, in spite of the resounding manifestations of emerging Futurism. Inspiration did not come from Paris but from Munich, and not from the Munich of Kandinsky and Klee but from that of the teachers from whom these two great innovators had obtained

n° 3. *The Builders.* Etching. 4 x 5 in: Unique copy.

1916

n° 4. *Summer.* Etching. $9^1/_2$ x $6^3/_4$ in:

4

5

3

8

7

6

9

his works in other media and based on his favorite themes, are exceptional in the sense that they were carried out in his own workshop (unlike the lithographs on which he had to work with various printers either in Paris or in Switzerland). The experimental proofs were made either on the small presses of the Academy of Monza or on those of the Brera Academy of Milan (where he was one of their well-known teachers until his resignation in 1968) under the supervision of the laboratory assistant of the Academy. It was necessary to wait until 1963 for the publication of Idea e Spazio in which he illustrated the poems of his sister Egle, and then in 1968 for the Album N° 1, in order that these zinc plates had the good fortune to be entrusted respectively to the Crommelynck brothers and to Jacques Frélaut (Imprimerie Lacourière).

their training. The engravings, as much as his modeling, pictorial or lithographic works, interpret Marino Marini's efforts to free himself from these obsolete influences and to reveal himself to himself. The plates which are reproduced here are almost entirely unpublished works, for the artist, who created them for his own pleasure, has always obdurately refused to sell them. It was only with the publication of Idea e Spazio (1963) and particularly with Album N° 1 (1968), that it became possible to appreciate to what extent his line could remain individual on a zinc plate and how much more incisive it is in his engravings than in his lithographs, in which he is limited in some degree by the material. His engravings, therefore, contemporary with

10

11

12

13

470

16

15

14

18

n° 5. *Engraving*. Etching. $9^1/_2$ x $7^1/_4$ in: Unique copy.

n° 6. *The Tree*. Etching. $3^3/_8$ x $3^3/_8$ in: Unique copy.

1917

n° 7. *The Mine*. Etching. $8^1/_8$ x $7^7/_8$ in: Unique copy.

17

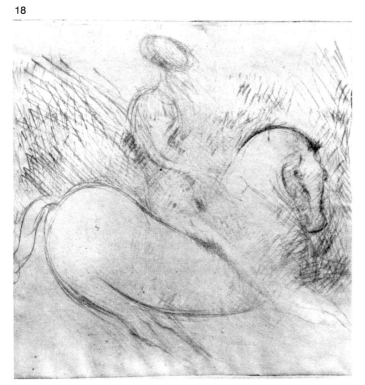

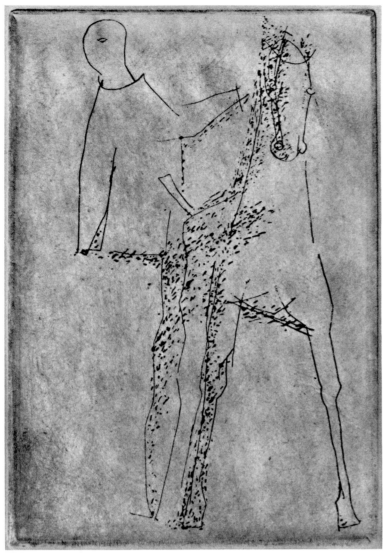

20

21

n° 11. *Crouching Nude.* Dry-point engraving.
$7^1/_8$ x $9^1/_2$ in. $13^3/_4$ x $19^1/_2$ in: Edition of 6 copies.

n° 12. *Crouching Nude.* Dry-point engraving.
$7^1/_8$ x $9^1/_2$ in. $13^3/_4$ x $19^3/_8$ in:
Experiment. Unpublished plate.

n° 13. *Crouching Nude.* Dry-point engraving.
$7^1/_4$ x $9^1/_2$ in. $13^3/_4$ x $19^3/_8$ in: Edition of 6 copies.

n° 14. *Three Graces.* Dry-point engraving.
$7^1/_8$ x $7^7/_8$ in. $9^1/_4$ x $12^5/_8$ in:
Experiment. Unpublished plate.

n° 15. *Pomonas.* Dry-point engraving.
$5^1/_8$ x $6^3/_4$ in. $9^1/_4$ x $12^5/_8$ in: Edition of 12 copies.

1923

n° 8. *Deposition.* Etching. $12^5/_8$ x $18^1/_2$ in:
Contessa Margherita Marcaldi Pistonsi Coll.
Egle Marini Guintoli Coll., Pistoia, Italy.

1940

n° 9. *The Two Friends.* Dry-point engraving.
$5^3/_4$ x $7^5/_8$ in. $13^7/_8$ x $18^1/_4$ in:
Experiment. Unpublished plate

n° 10. *The Friends.* Dry-point engraving.
$6^1/_8$ x $7^5/_8$ in. $9^1/_4$ x $12^5/_8$ in:
Experiment. Unpublished plate.

19

22

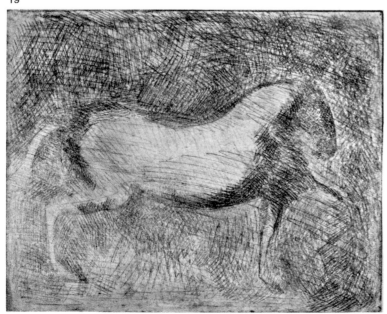

23

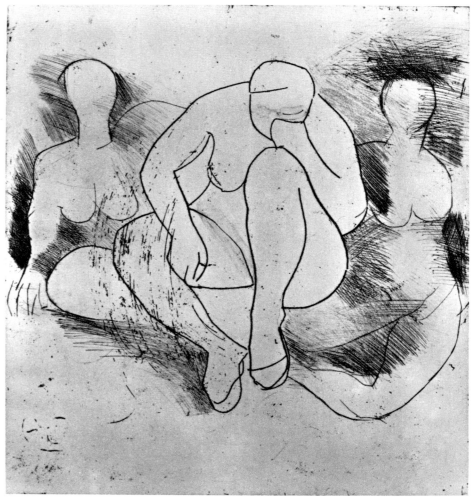

25

n° 16. *Two Pomonas.* Dry-point engraving.
6⁷/₈ x 7⁷/₈ in. 13³/₄ x 19¹/₂ in:
Experiment. Unpublished plate.

n° 17. *Rider.* Dry-point engraving.
6¹/₄ x 7⁷/₈ in. 9 x 12⁵/₈ in: Edition of 6 copies.

n° 18. *Rider.* Dry-point engraving.
6³/₄ x 7⁷/₈ in. 9¹/₄ x 12 in:
Edition of 12 copies.

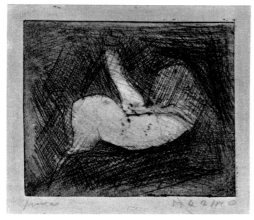

24

1941

n° 19. *Horse.* Dry-point engraving.
6¹/₄ x 7⁵/₈ in. 9¹/₂ x 13 in:
Experiment. Unpublished plate.

1942

n° 20. *Rider.* Etching.
4³/₄ x 7¹/₈ in. 9⁷/₈ x 14⁵/₈ in:
Experiment. Unpublished plate.

n° 21. *Rider.* Dry-point engraving.
7¹/₈ x 9⁵/₈ in. 13³/₄ x 19¹/₂ in: Edition of 6 copies.

n° 22. *Nude.* Dry-point engraving.
7¹/₈ x 9¹/₂ in. 13³/₄ x 19¹/₂ in:

1949

n° 23. *The Bathers.* Etching. 13 x 9³/₄ in:
Experiment.

1950

n° 24. *Small Rider.* Etching. 3⁷/₈ x 3¹/₈ in:
Experiment.

n° 25. *Composition.* Etching. 15³/₈ x 17³/₈ in:
Experiment. Unpublished plate.

n° 26. *Pomona.* Etching. 14 x 11⁷/₈ in:
Experiment.

n° 27. *Juggler.* Etching. 13³/₄ x 11⁷/₈ in:
Experiment.

26

27

28

29

30

31

1951

n° 28. *Juggler.* Etching. 13³/₄ x 11⁷/₈ in: Experiment.

n° 29. *Jugglers.* Etching. 13 x 9⁷/₈ in: Taken from an album published by the Galerie Gérald Cramer, Geneva.

n° 30. *Miracle.* Etching. 14 x 11⁷/₈ in: Experiment.

n° 31. *Jugglers.* Etching. 14 x 11⁷/₈ in: Experiment.

1952

n° 32. *Rider.* Etching. 14 x 11⁷/₈ in: Experiment.

n° 33. *Rider.* Etching. 14¹/₄ x 11⁷/₈ in: Experiment.

32

33

34

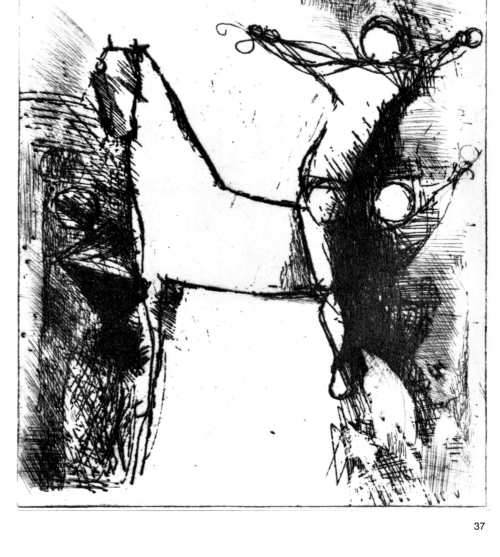

37

35

38

1954

n° 34. *Juggler.* Etching. 14 x 11⁷/₈ in: Experiment.

n° 35. *Juggler.* Etching. 13 x 9⁵/₈ in: Experiment.

n° 36. *Jugglers: a Composition.* Etching. 11³/₈ x 9⁵/₈ in: Experiment.

1955

n° 37. *Jugglers.* Etching. 11¹/₂ x 9⁵/₈ in: Experiment.

n° 38. *Jugglers and Horse.* Etching. 9¹/₂ x 11¹/₂ in. 15¹/₂ x 20⁵/₈ in: Experiment.

36

39

40

1956

n° 39. *Masked Players in the Theater.*
Etching. 17¹/₄ x 15¹/₂ in:
Experiment. Unpublished plate.

n° 40. *Composition.* Etching. 11³/₄ x 15⁵/₈ in:
Experiment.

n° 41. *Horse.* Etching. 14³/₈ x 11⁷/₈ in:
Experiment.

n° 42. *Two Pomonas.* Etching. 10¹/₄ x 7¹/₄ in:
Experiment. Unpublished plate.

41

42

43

44

45

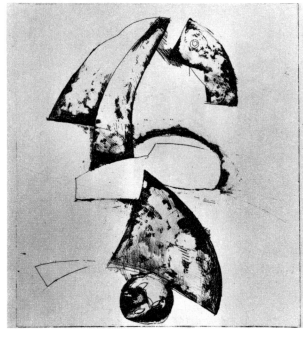

46

1960

n° 44. *Miracle: a Composition.* Etching.
11³/₈ x 9⁷/₈ in: Experiment.

n° 45. *Miracle.* Etching. 11³/₈ x 9⁵/₈ in:
Experiment.

47

1957

n° 43. *Miracle.* Etching. 10¹/₄ x 7¹/₄ in:
Experiment. Unpublished plate.

48

49 a

49 b

1962

n° 46. *The Cry.* Etching. 14 x 11⁷/₈ in: Experiment.

n° 47. *The Cry.* Etching. 11³/₈ x 9⁷/₈ in: Experiment.

n° 48. *The Cry.* Etching. 11³/₈ x 9⁷/₈ in: Experiment. Unpublished plate.

1963

n° 49. *Idea e Spazio.* Poems by Egle Marini illustrated by 12 etchings by Marino Marini. Album published by "Les Cents Bibliophiles de France et d'Amérique," first edition of 12 etchings, March 7, 1963, Crommelynck; first edition of the text, Fequet and Baudier.
Limited Edition: 100 copies on Rives Vellum, plus 28 copies for the artist and his collaborators, as well as a few copies of the engravings.
Dimensions of the copperplates:
15³/₄ x 11⁷/₈ in:
Dimensions of the leaves: 19⁷/₈ x 14⁷/₈ in:

49 d

49 c

49 e

49 f

n° 49 a. *Horses.* Colors: white line, black ground, red triangle.

n° 49 b. *Juggler.* Colors: blue-gray ground, black line, blue butterfly, ochre butterfly.

n° 49 c. *Juggler.* Colors: black ground, white line, orange spots.

n° 49 d. *Fossil of a Horse.* Colors: gray ground, black line, white and ochre spots.

n° 49 e. *Destruction and Reconstruction.* Colors: black ground, red line, brown horse, three gray triangles, one blue triangle.

n° 49 f. *Morning.* Colors: black ground, white line, blue spot.

n° 49 g. *The Surviving Rider.* Colors: white and brown ground, black line.

n° 49 h. *The Rider's Dream.* Colors: black ground, white line, two red triangles.

49 g

49 h

49 j

49 i

n° 49 i. *Warrior.* Colors: black ground, black line, gray horse and rider.

n° 49 j. *Performance.* Colors: black ground, white line, three blue, one brown and two white triangles..

n° 49 k. *Acrobat.* Colors: gray ground, black line, red triangle, brown spot.

n° 49 l. *In Secret.* Colors: black and blue-gray ground, pale blue line, blue spots.

49 k

49 l

n° 50. *Album N° 1*. (Introduction by G. di San Lazzaro). 12 original etchings by Marino Marini. Album published by XXème Siècle, Paris, an by Leon Amiel, New York. First edition, may 15, 1968; the text printed by Fequet and Baudier and the etchings by Lacourière.

Limited edition: 15 copies, numbered 1 to 15, on paper produced by Moulin Richard-de-Bas, Auvergne, plus 3 presentation copies, including the 12 original etchings by Marino Marini, plus a reserve of 18 copies on Auvergne paper; 35 copies numbered 16 to 50 on Rives Vellum, plus 15 copies numbered I to XV consisting of the 12 etchings only, not intended for sale.

Dimensions of the copperplates: 11⅝ x 14 in: Dimensions of the leaves: 15 x 20¼ in:

brothers by the force of the geometry of their contours.

For tragedy, in both the graphic and the plastic work of Marino Marini, is expressed only by the essential, by the extreme economy of form. Tragedy is not comedy: it cannot wait: it cannot bear the slightest burden.

It is incredible how even the most disciplined artists betray themselves in outlining the beginning of a breast or the curve of a belly, in plunging into the sacred preserve of the thighs. Marino Marini is not blameless in the terracottas of his youth. In the etchings in this Album, the first which he has allowed to be printed, nothing however weighs down or embellishes their graphic purity. Stendhal, who so greatly loved the city of Milan where these plates were engraved before being brought to Paris to be printed, had to reconsider this conception of the modern nude. Should I say that these plates which were engraved by the artist at the time when he was carving or painting in oil the same subjects, are not drawn but cut out, that shadows intervene simply to heighten the value of the whites, to make them « sing out loud » as Henri Matisse would have said,

and that the roughness of the forms does not exclude their grace — and may even, on the contrary, emphasize it?

We might perhaps notice that Marini's expressive line is not dissolved by softening in this decorative expressionism, whether abstract or figurative, in which too many artists, even the greatest, have fallen. Marini's sensuality has not become thicker, heavier, sexualized, as it were, in order to keep its flashing vitality, as in the work of Picasso: on the contrary it is always transfigured and made lighter by acquiring an aerial transcendency. In these etchings which date from 1950 to 1962, the play of love is no longer only the play of light and shade. The limited number of connaisseurs for whom these etchings are destined do not need to trouble themselves with these subtleties. May I be excused rather if I have slightly delayed their pleasure in order to indulge my own, in detaining them for a moment on the threshold of this moving and talented imagery, created by the meeting of Marini's eloquent lines — lines of an undeniable strength, which are nevertheless endowed with tenderness.

INTRODUCTION TO ALBUM No. 1

One line departs to meet another line: it takes the shortest way possible, and is often ahead so that it has to move in circles, like the serpent which enclosed the earth in its mythical coil.

These circles are heads — almost always lunar but occasionally solar — for Marino's riders are moon riders. These circles are horses' rumps, bathed in a light of which it is difficult to judge whether it spurts from the chariot of Apollo or the chariot of Diana, for ambiguity reigns supreme. These lines which seem so hurried to join together finally define characters such as Pomonas, riders, jugglers, actors, warriors — in short, all the characters of Marini's tragedy —, outline thighs, torso, legs and arms often spread out in the form of an X. In a few strokes, first on a zinc plate, then on a sheet of paper, a tragedy bursts forth: for the birth of a living being, whether a work of art or of the flesh, is always a tragedy. Is not our role, since we regard these images as spectators, that of a Greek chorus? We are not only spectators but also powerless and compassionate witnesses, bowing our heads before the raised arms of these tragic heroes.

We must not forget that Marino Marini was born in the land of the Etruscans. He belongs to a world which was not obliged to indulge in incest as the primitive world of Levi-Strauss, in order to reach a certain level of culture and of trade. The world of Marino Marini is that of the Etruscans in which a cultivated society seeks perfection in the worship of death. Even sport — like all heroic games — is a challenge to death. These horses have never helped men in their work in the fields. These « Pomonas » have sung, danced an given birth, but they have never washed their men's dirty clothes on the river bank. These riders have never borne arms like the riders of Paolo Uccello — their

50 a

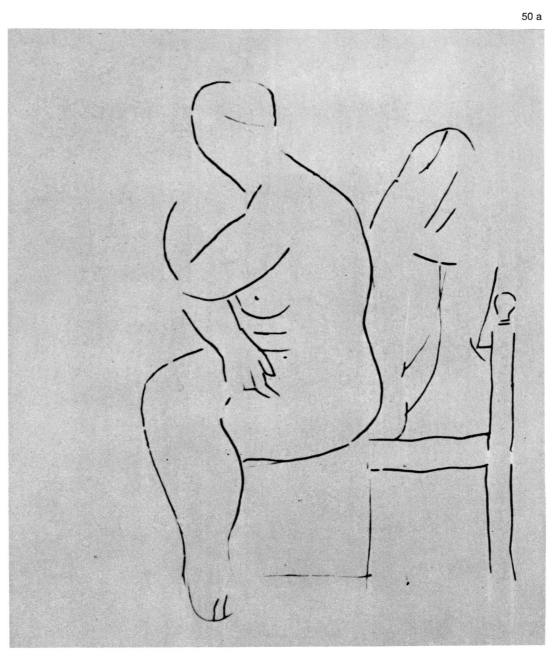

50 b

50 c

n° 50 a.   *Rest.*   1940.

n° 50 b.   *Idea.*   1950.

n° 50 c.   *Horseman.*   1954.

n° 50 d.   *Trio.*   1954.

n° 50 e.   *Invocation.*   1955.

50 d

50 e

50 f   50 g

n° 50 f. *Masked Players in the Theater.* 1956.

n° 50 g. *Jugglers.* 1956.

n° 50 h. *Idea for a Rider.* 1958.

n° 50 i. *The Annunciation.* 1958.

50 h   50 i

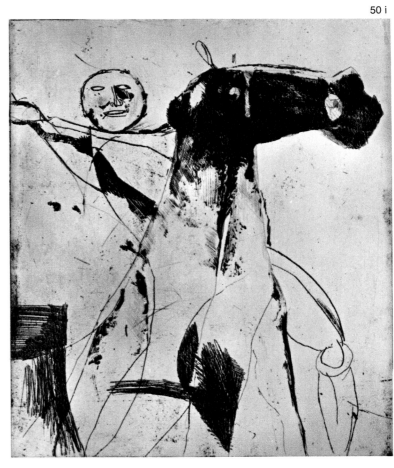

50 j

50 k

n° 50 j. *The Miracle.* 1960.

n° 50 k. *The Rider's Dream.* 1960.

n° 50 l. *Composition.* 1961.

n° 50 m. *Warrior.* 1962.

50 l

50 m

26 a

27 a

Recent Edition of Engravings

28 a

30

31 a

32 a

1970

23 original etchings have been collected in an album by the Crommelynck Brothers, who, for this occasion, have published several engravings already included in this catalogue. 7 engravings have been reproduced in our catalogue on preceding pages (nᵒˢ 23, 24, 35, 36, 37, 38, 44).

33 a

34 a

40 a

41 a

13 engravings, already reproduced in our catalogue, have been reworked by the artist (nᵒˢ 26, 27, 28, 30, 31, 32, 33, 34, 40, 41, 45, 46, 47).
3 engravings have so far been unpublished (nᵒˢ 51, 52, 53).
Edition on Rives Vellum:
65 copies numbered in Arabic numerals from 1 to 65.
15 copies of « Chapelle » numbered from I to XV.
Dimensions of the leaves: 21 x 16³/₄ in:
Introduction by Douglas Cooper.

45 a

46 a

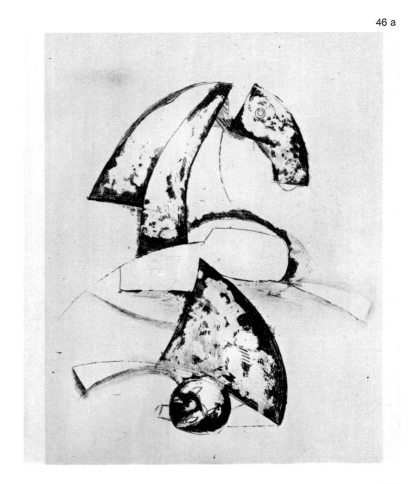

47 a

51

n° 51. *Composition.* Etching. 14 x 11$^{7}/_{8}$ in:

n° 52. *Juggler.* Etching. 14$^{1}/_{4}$ x 11$^{7}/_{8}$ in:

n° 53. *Juggler on Horseback.* Etching.
14$^{1}/_{4}$ x 11$^{7}/_{8}$ in:

52

53

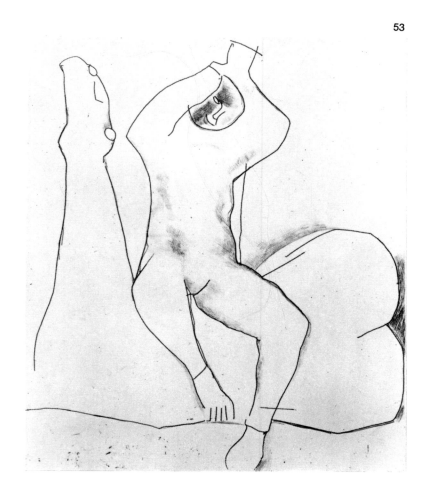

GENERAL DOCUMENTATION

MARINO MARINI'S NOTES

MY SCULPTURES

San Lazzaro told me that when Matisse found himself face to face with one of his paintings or one of his sculptures, he seemed to look at it and judge it as if it were the work of someone else; he no longer recognized it as his own work. In short, he no longer felt himself bound to it by the bonds which should be as indestructible between an artist and his work as between a father and his child.

I do not know if such a thing generally happens in middle age, but it seems to me that it is only at this time that an artist can speak about his own work—when he can appreciate it freely, without emotion,—almost, I might say, with detachment.

I do not wish to say that, when I see one of my bronzes, I really feel like a father with his young son or a mother with her small child—who is always the most beautiful in the world. I must even admit that one of my statues, portraits or even a simple drawing rarely gives me this happiness, this self-pride of the creator: more often, even though I cannot say they revolt me, I cannot see them again without a certain sense of boredom. It is almost painful for me to talk about my work.

I can distinguish in myself three different preoccupations, of which the principal is the portrait. In this medium, I have always tried to interpret the poetry rather than the expression or the character of the model —even in the most communicative of models. There is no human face in which this poetry does not appear, lodged somewhere, characterized in a single line, a protruberance or a slight hollow. The artist should be able to recognize it and free it. In this, he is guided by his sensitivity, and by his qualities of observation and of penetration. The artist should reconstitute this poetry by plastic means, and, in the particular case of sculpture (truly a primitive art), he can only express it in his chosen material—bronze, stone or wax—and, according to the nature of the material, by its form.

The figure or the statue demand, in contrast, a wider research into form, line and mass. My figures of women, which some people find awkward, reply to this preoccupation: in the figure I intend to deepen in a more united and stable whole which remains, however, free and supple, the natural play of volume. This research for volume is not the only aim of the sculptor who should nevere forget that the most moving factor in a sculpture is its poetry.

Now I must speak about the "Riders"—a search for (what should I call it?) a combination of bodies in space. I forgot space—every figure has its own space and it cannot be said that it should be either a kind of cage or infinity.

But, in the end, what is a statue, a portrait, a group? It is a toy which represents for a civilization what a wooden horse represents for a child. We must know how to caress a bronze as lovingly as a child caresses a doll. Art is a refined game.

("Tempo," December 14th, 1939)

The artist with his wife at Forte dei Marmi (1960).

Marini with his sister Egle (1960).

(Photo, Marina Marini)

With Henry Moore (1961).

With Lipchitz (1962).
With Nogushi (1964).

(Photos, Marina Marini)

THE BEGINNING OF MY CAREER

At the beginning of my career I rented, by chance, a studio belonging to the owners of a riding-school. Consequently, I had an opportunity to draw and model horses every day; but at the time they were still far from giving me inspiration for a subjective or apocalyptic vision. Moreover, my work remained classical, restrained and realist, until the end of Fascism and the second World War. For a long time afterwards, the purified style of Etruscan tombs or of some slightly archaic Roman sculptures remained immensely important to me. I reacted against the imperial pathos of official Fascist art by consciously basing my art on my private life and by avoiding all conventions. For example, I made anonymous busts comparable to the monuments of the unknown dead which, after two thousand years, move us so deeply because of their purely human aspect, apart from any feeling of historical tragedy. I think my nudes dating from this period also possess this classical and anonymous character, for I tried to suppress all subjective feeling in them. They show no autobiographical element, in contrast to certain works of Renoir or even of Maillol, in which, instead of classical or immortal beauty, the subject either is the woman beloved by the artist or at least the contemporary type of woman who especially pleased him.

(Extract from an interview, 1958)

MODELS

My nudes can be attributed to Greek sculpture. My busts, on the contrary, have been influenced by Etruscan and Roman art and also by medieval Christian realism as it appears in sculptures on sarcophagi. You will certainly know the masterpiece of Bonino da Campione at the Castelle Sforzesco here in Milan, the equestrain statue of Bernabo Visconti.
In the past, sculptors were happy to carve blooming, sensitive or powerful faces; but for the last fifteen years, sculpture has inevitably attained decomposing forms. Here in Italy, our whole being is still impregnated by our artistic past, for we live in the midst of its works. I myself was born in Tuscany, where the discovery of Etruscan art during the last fifty years has been an outstanding event. It is for this reason that my art relies more on themes taken from the past—such as the relationships between man and horse—than on modern subjects such as, for example, the relations between man and machine.

(Extract from an interview, 1958)

MY REALISM

I owe my love of reality to the Etruscans: it is a realism which is demonstrated by forms which possess a primitive density but which are rejuvenated by smooth surfaces in which light plays its full part.
It is only on the surface that simplification becomes distant from nature, in fact, since it searches essential truth, it comes much nearer to nature.
Destroyed and decomposed forms,—dead bodies, fallen horses, broken ends lying on the ground, shreds of flesh—once more become matter when they are transformed into a shapeless mass; but these broken-down masses have to be freshly rearranged. The decomposition of forms demands a new creation of complete and compact masses. From the moment when every superfluous element has been eliminated, realism disappears, absorbed by the form which it maintains henceforth as a skeleton bears its flesh. Is it thus marked out by chance? Is this the way towards abstraction?

(1957)

ABSTRACT OR FIGURATIVE?

I make no difference between figurative and abstract art, on condition that, in both cases, we are dealing with the plastic arts. What is supremely important is the quality of a work of art. Personally, as a Latin, I can only express myself freely in a figurative way; but I accept and admire every other artistic form, provided that the artist wishes to express something. We can be as moved by a single match as by a Doric column, but it would be absurd to consider from this reasoning that a box of matches has as much value as the Parthenon...

(1951)

THE IMAGE OF THE RIDER

For many centuries, the image of the rider has maintained an epic character. Its object was to pay homage to a conqueror, as, for example, Marcus Aurelius whose statue on the Capitol, inspired the majority of the equestrian statues of the Italian Renaissance, as well as that of Louis XIV, which ornaments the "Place des Victoires" in Paris. However, the nature of the relations which have existed for so long between men and horses—whether they concern the farm-horse which the ploughman leads to the drinking-trough in a painting by one of the Le Nain brothers, or the mount of a merchant by Rosa Bonheur, or the rearing stallion spurred by a warrior by Gericault—has been greatly changed during the last half century:—the horse has been replaced in its economic and military functions by the machine—the tractor, the car and the tank. It has quickly become a sign of luxury. It can even be said that, for the majority of our contemporaries, the horse has acquired a mythical character. Every artist is in some way a prophet. Almost a century before the invention of the automobile, romantic painters did not always paint their horses with the same objectivity as the majority of their predecessors: they remained faithful to the external appearance of the horse, but in compensation beautified that of the rider. Romantic painters indulged in a kind of worship of the horse, which they considered an aristocratic animal, a symbol of luxury, of sport and of adventure, and not simply as a means of transport or of work. From Gericault to Constantin Guys to Degas and Dufy, this worship was increasingly developed as a kind of military or athletic dandyism. On the contrary, with Odilon Redon, Picasso and Chirico, the horse has been transformed into a kind of dream, into a fabulous animal.

(Extract from an interview, 1958)

SUMMARY

Marini: Personally, I no longer have the intention of celebrating the victory of a hero. I would like to express something tragic, almost the twilight of humanity, a defeat rather than a victory. If you consider, one after another, my statues of nudes of the last twelve years, you will notice that each time the rider becomes less capable of mastering his horse and the animal becomes increasingly intractable and wilder instead of yielding. Quite seriously, I believe that we are approaching the end of the world.
Interviewer's Question: What do you understand by the world of humanism which forms the basis of our Western European art and which lasted from the Carolingian pre-Renaissance to the beginning of abstract art?

With Henry Miller (1961).

With the publisher Gottfried B. Fischer (1967).
With Mies Van Der Rohe in Berlin (1967).

(Photos, Marina Marini)

491

Marini in The Hague during the installation of his monument (1957).

Marini: I do not want to be involved in a major artistic controversy. The feeling of which I am speaking resembles the impressions which the Romans had when, at the end of their Empire, they witnessed the collapse of a civilization established for several centuries caused by Barbarian invasions. My statues of riders express the anguish provoked by the events of my age. With every new work, the movements of my horses increase; the riders, increasingly less powerful, have lost their former domination over animals, and the catastrophes which strike them are similar to those which destroyed Sodom and Pompei. Thus I am trying to symbolize the last phase of the decomposition of a myth—that of the heroic and victorious man, of the "uomo di virtù" of the humanists. For the last fourteen years, my works have been intended to be tragic rather than heroic.

(Extract from an interview, 1968)

These texts are drawn from the small volume on Marino Marini, with an introduction by Egle Marini, Edited by Ernst Scheidegger and published by Verlag der Arche in Zurich.

FROM COLOR TO FORM

To conceive a form is, for me, to seize upon its color —vision of color, aggressiveness of color, aggressiveness of life—aggressiveness of the form.

The elements of my Art do not count—everyone has his own loves—what counts is to give them reality in art.

I have always had a need to paint and I never begin a sculpture without having first pictorially explored its essence.

A part of me lives intensely in graphic expression; the line gives a precise observation and the taste for graphic art is almost Nordic.

Painting is born in me like a spontaneous and keen need to a search for color.

There is no sculpture which has not passed through this experience.

The Warrior. A reality, a tragic and impassioned vision, without possibility of joy.

My artistic vision is part of reality—an imagined reality. I do not combat the abstract expression of cerebral art.

This very free architecture found in me in its early period a fervent defender and I do not reject it except when it becomes academic.

No work of art exists which is not achieved by these two expressions.

If these elements blend together, they give life—to what is Art.

At the origins of painting and sculpture there are intellectualistic tendencies which should blend and amalgamate into the true artistic expression.

For me, when one speaks of Art with a capital A, it must mean all that nature which intensifies the different ideas composed of living forms, emotions and the other vital sources of the spirit.

The Miracle. It is not defined by a form or a line— everything lies in a more lyrical, poetic imagination.

Personality is unconsciously acquired through the continual experiencing of poetic emotions intensely lived. I admire all the painting and sculpture of the Primitives, for the Moderns I require a delay for reflection.

Portraits. The subjects do not live under their own name but under the one which the artist imposes on them.

The principal problem in sculpture can consist in the relationship of volumes, provided that to the latter there is added a movement, a life—then, the object becomes Art.

Expressionism, at a certain moment, is the desire for a more precise conquest, especially in the expression of things it is the sum of different emotions and of an entity of form and color.

In sculpture, the last period is constructive—by constructive I mean an orientation towards architecture: it is to seek an idea farther from the human form but all the closer to the constructive and static line.

Projects cannot be described—to describe and discuss them is to lose them—there is nothing to do but wait. The theme of the "horseman" is a pretext for recounting and imagining the emotions in plastic language—the theme of the "horseman" is modeled by that poetic image and is transformed by it.

The living reality, "realistic," of the "horseman"—the principal theme which I treated—decomposes itself to become a constructive unreality.

An unreality which may be termed "constructive," because the work, in its deepest sense, draws closer to architecture and because reality fades away before the cubic structure of forms.

The poetic idea does not die out but continues through the successive compositions of the years 1958-1959-1960.

(Extract from the album of lithographs « From Color to Form », XXᵉ Siècle Ed., Paris, 1969)

492

MONOGRAPHS

1936 - Paul Fierens
Marino Marini (Art Italien Moderne), Chroniques du Jour, Paris, Hoepli, Milan.
1937 - Lamberto Vitali
Marino Marini (Arte Moderna Italiana), Ed. Hoepli, Milan.
1939 - G. Cesetti
Marino Marini (Quaderni del disegno), Ed. del Cavallino, Venice.
1941 - Filippo De Pisis
Marino Marini, Ed. della Conchiglia, Milan.
1942 - L. Anceschi
Marino Marini (Quaderni del Disegno Contemporaneo), Ed. della « Galleria della Spiga e Corrente », Milan.
1944 - G. Contini
20 sculture di Marino Marini, Ed. della Collana, Lugano.
1946 - Lamberto Vitali
Marini (Quaderni d'Arte a cura di G. Raimondi e di C. L. Ragghianti), Ed. U., Florence.
1948 - Raffaele Carrieri
Marino Marini, Ed. del Milione, Milan.
1950 - Enzo Carli
Marino Marini (Arte Moderna Italiana), Hoepli, Milan.
1951 - Mario Ramous
Marino Marini, Cappelli, Bologna.
1951 - Mario Ramous
Marino Marini - Due litografie e sei disegni, Cappelli, Bologna.
1953 - Umbro Apollonio
Marino Marini, Ed. del Milione, Milan, 2nd and 3rd editions revised.
1954 - Eduard Trier
Marino Marini, Galerie Der Spiegel, Cologne.
1954 - Sinagra (E. Marini)
Marino, sei tavole a colori, Ed. del Milione, Milan.
1954 - Emil Langui
Marini, Albert de Lange, Amsterdam.
1959 - Douglas Cooper
Marino Marini, Silvana editoriale d'Arte, Milan.
1959 - Egle Marini
Marino Marini, der Arche, Zurich.
1960 - P. M. Bardi
Marini - Graphic Work and Paintings, Harry N. Abrams, New York.
1960 - Werner Hofmann
Marini - Malerei und Graphik, Gerd Hatje, Stuttgart.
1960 - Werner Hofmann
L'opera grafica di Marino Marini, Il Saggiatore, Milan.
1961 - Egle Marini
Marino Marini - Ein Lebensbild, ein Gesprach mit seiner Schwester Egle, Fischer Bücherei, Frankfurt-am-Main.
1961 - Eduard Trier
Marino Marini, Gerd Hatje, Stuttgart.
1961 - Eduard Trier
Marino Marini, Garzanti, Milan.
1961 - Eduard Trier
Marino Marini, Ed. du Griffon, Neuchatel.
1961 - Eduard Trier
Marino Marini, Praeger, New York.
1961 - Heinz Fuchs
Il Miracolo - Marino Marini, Ed. Philipp Reclam Jr., Stuttgart.
1961 - Eduard Trier
The Sculpture of Marino Marini, Thames and Hudson, London.
1963 - Hartmut Biermann
Marino Marini - Deutsche Buch Gemeinschaft Berlin-Darmstadt-Vienna.
1963 - Hartmut Biermann
Marino Marini, Emil Vollmer, Wiesbaden, Berlin.

With his niece Loraine at Forte dei Marmi (1967).
(Photo, Marina Marini)

1963 - Franco Russoli
Il Guerriero di Marino Marini, Aldo Martello, Milan.
1963 - Franco Russoli
Marino Marini - Dipinti e disegni, Toninelli, Milan.
1964 - Franco Russoli
Marino Marini - Paintings and Drawings, Harry N. Abrams, New York.
1964 - Franco Russoli
Marino Marini - Bilder und Zeichnungen, Gerd Hatje, Stuttgart.
1964 - Franco Russoli
Marino Marini - Paintings and Drawings, Thames and Hudson, London.
1966 - Giovanni Carandente
Le Litografie di Marino Marini, Toninelli, Milan.
1966 - Jiri Setlik
Marini, Odeon, Prague.
1966 - Giovanni Carandente
Marino Marini (I Maestri della Scultura), Fratelli Fabbri, Milan.
1968 - Alberto Busignoni
Marino Marini, Sadea Sansoni, Florence.
1968 - Giovanni Carandente
Marino Marini. Lithographs 1942-1965, Harry N. Abrams, New York,
1968 - Werner Haftmann
Marino Marini: Werk Ausgabe, Carl Schünemann, Bremen.
1969 - Werner Haftmann
Marino Marini. A suite of sixty-three re-creations of drawings and sketches, Harry N. Abrams, New York.

GRAPHIC WORK AND ILLUSTRATED BOOKS

1942 - Ugo Foscolo
Ultime lettere di Jacopo Ortis, Ed. della Conchiglia, Milan. (Drawings).

1942 - Salvatore Quasimodo
Il fiore delle Georgiche, Ed. della Conchiglia, Milan. (Drawings).

1951 - Mario Ramous
La memoria, il messaggio, Ed. Cappelli, Bologna (Drawings).

1957 - Egle Marini
Poesie, Ed. Del Milione, Milan. (Drawings).

1958 - Egle Marini
Gedichte, Fischer, Frankfurt-am-Main. (Drawings).

1963 - Egle Marini
Idea e Spazio - Original etchings, « Les Cent Bibliophiles de France et d'Amérique », Paris.

1968 - G. di San Lazzaro
L'Album N° 1. 12 original etchings. XXe Siècle, Paris. Amiel, New York.

1969 - Marino Marini
From Color to Form. 10 original lithographs in color. XXe Siècle, Paris. Amiel, New York.

1970 - Douglas Cooper
23 engravings of Marino Marini. Crommelynck, Paris.

In Nuremberg (1966).   *(Photo, Marina Marini)*

EXHIBITIONS

1923
IInd Biennal, *Rome.*

1927
IIIrd International Exhibition of Decorative Art. *Monza.* May-October.

1928
"Novecento Toscan" Group. *Milan*, Galleria Milano. December.

1929
Exhibition of the Italian "Novecento". *Nice*, Société des Beaux-Arts. March-April.
IInd Exhibition of the Italian "Novecento". *Milan.* 2nd March-30th April.
Exhibition of Modern Italian Art. *Paris*, Éditions Bonaparte. November.

1930
Exhibition of Italian Moderns. *Basle*, Kunsthalle. 5th-12th February.
The Development of Modern Art in Italy. *Berne*, Kunstmuseum. March-May.

1931
Exhibition of the Italian "Novecento". *Stockholm.* 9th September-4th October.

1932
Marino Marini. *Milan*, Galleria Milano. February.
Marino Marini. *Rome*, Galleria Sabatello. 6th-13th November.
XVIIIth Biennal, *Venice.*

1933
Campigli and Marino Marini Exhibition. *Milan*, Galleria Milano.

1934
XIX Biennal, *Venice.* June-October.
Exhibition of Italian Art. *Geneva.* 22nd September-18th November.

1935
IInd Quadriennal of National Art. *Rome.* February-July.
Contemporary Italian Sculpture. *Vienna.* November.

1937
Marino Marini. *Milan*, Galleria Barbaroux. December.

1940
Exhibition of Contemporary Italian Painters and Sculptors. *Zurich*, Kunsthaus. November-December.

1941
Marino Marini. *Genoa*, Galleria Genova. 15th-29th March.

1942
Marino Marini. *Rome*, Galleria dello Zodiaco. November-December.

1943
Marino Marini. *Venice*, Galleria del Cavallino.

1944
Four Foreign Sculptors in Switzerland. *Basle*, Kunstmuseum. 14th October-26th November.

1945
Marino Marini. Germaine Richier. Fritz Wotruba. *Berne*, Kunsthalle. 9th June-8th July.
Marino Marini. *Basle*, Gallery of Modern Art. 9th September-5th October.
Marino Marini. *Zurich*, Aktuaryus Gallery. 26th September-17th October.

1947
Forty Years of Italian Art. *Lausanne*, Musée Cantonal des Beaux-Arts. 15th February-15th March.
Forty Years of Italian Art. *Lucerne*, Kunstmuseum. 29th March-1st June.

1948
Exhibition of Contemporary Italian Art. *Madrid.* May.
XXIVth Biennal, *Venice* (own room). May-September.

Italian Art in our Time. *Stockholm*, Färg och Form Gallery. September.
Italian Art in our Time. *Gothenburg*, Konstmuseum. October.
Sculpture. *New York*, Buchholz Gallery. 28th September-16th October.

1949
The Works of Marino Marini. *Rome*, Galleria dell'Obelisco. March.
From Rodin to Brancusi. *Palm Beach*, Society of the Four Arts. 4th-27th March.
IIIrd International Exhibition of Sculpture. *Philadelphia*, Fairmount Park Art Association, Museum of Art. May.
Peggy Guggenheim Collection. *Milan*, Palazzo Reale. June-July.
Italian Art in the XXth Century. *New York*, Museum of Modern Art.
Exhibition of Contemporary Art. *Catania and Palermo*, Circolo Artistico.

1950
Contemporary Italian Art. *Brussels*, Palais des Beaux-Arts. 28th January-28th February.
Marino Marini. *New York*, Buchholz Gallery (Curt Valentin). 14th February-11th March.
35 drawings by Marino Marini. *Washington*, Watkins Gallery. 2nd-24th March.
European Sculpture. *Munich*, Haus der Kunst. 1st November-24th December.

1951
Marino Marini: Sculptures and Drawings. *London*, Hanover Gallery. 8th May-16th June.
Sculptures in Battersea Park. *London.* May-September.
Inaugural Exhibition of the Civic Museum of Open-Air Sculpture. *Antwerp*, Middelheim Park. 8th September-31st October.
The Werner Bär Collection of Sculpture. *Winterthur*, Kunstmuseum. 16th September-11th November.
Marino Marini. *Hanover*, Kestner Gesellschaft. November 1951-January 1952.

1952
Marino Marini. *Hamburg*, Kunstverein. February.
Marino Marini. *Munich*, Bayerische Staatsgemäldesammlungen, Haus der Kunst. 21st March-4th May.
Sonsbeek '52. International Exhibition of Sculpture. *Arnheim.* 30th May-15th September.
Exhibition of "Man and Form in our Time". *Recklinghausen*, Städtische Kunsthalle. 13th June-3rd August.
Marini. Moore. Wotruba. *Salzburg*, Welz Gallery. Summer.
XXVIth Biennal, *Venice* (own room). July-September.
Sculpture in the Twentieth Century. *Philadelphia*, Fairmount Park Art Association, Museum of Art. 11th October-7th December.
IInd International Biennal of Contemporary Color Lithographs. *Cincinnati*, Art Museum.
Contemporary Drawings 1945-1952. *Chicago*, The Art Institute.

1953
Marino Marini. *Gothenburg*, Kunstmuseum. January-February.
Sculpture in the Twentieth Century. *Chicago*, The Art Institute. 22nd January-8th March.
Marino Marini. *Stockholm*, Svensk-Franska Konstgalleriet. February-March.
Italian Art in Our Time. *Stockholm*, Liljevalchs Konsthall. March-April.
Marino Marini. *Copenhagen*, Statens Museum for Kunst. 14th March-7th April.
Marino Marini. *Oslo*, Nasjonalgelleriet. April-May.
Marino Marini, Sculptures and Drawings. *Cincinnati*, Art Museum. April-May.
Sculpture in the Twentieth Century. *New York*, The Museum of Modern Art. 29th April-7th September.
Open-Air Sculptures. *Hamburg.* 30th April-31st October.

IInd Biennal. *Antwerp,* Middelheim Park. 20th June-30th September.

Fantastic Art. *Ostend,* Kursaal. 5th July-31st August.

Marino Marini. *New York,* Curt Valentin Gallery. 27th October-21st November.

Seventy-Five Years of Sculpture. *Houston,* Museum of Fine Arts. November.

Young Italian Art. *Zurich,* Kunsthaus. 21st November 1953-10th January 1954.

IInd Biennal, *São Paulo.* 8th December 1953-8th February 1954.

1954

Marino Marini. *Helsinki,* Artek Gallery. 26th January-16th February.

Marino Marini. *Geneva,* Gérald Cramer Gallery. 10th March-1st April.

Marino Marini. *Berne,* Gutekunst and Klipstein. 13th-28th April.

Marino Marini. *Cologne,* Der Spiegel Gallery. May-June.

Sculpture in the Open Air. *London,* Holland Park. May-September.

Marino Marini. *Basle,* Gallery of Modern Art. 29th May-15th July.

Marino Marini. *Zurich,* Gallery 16. 29th November-24th December.

Contemporary Sculptors' Drawings. *Columbus, Ohio,* The School of Fine and Applied Arts, State University.

1955

Marino Marini. *Rotterdam,* Museum Boymans-Van Beuningen. 26th February-28th April.

Marino Marini. *Düsseldorf,* Kunstverein. 8th May-12th June.

Spring Exhibition. *New York,* Pierre Matisse Gallery. 11th-28th May.

IIIrd Biennal. *Antwerp,* Middelheim Park. 1st June-10th September.

Man's Image. *Recklinghausen,* Städtische Kunsthalle. 12th June-26th July.

Marino Marini. *Mannheim,* Kunsthalle. 25th June-31st July.

Documenta I. International Exhibition. *Kassel,* Fridericianum Museum. 15th July-18th September.

Marino Marini, 15 lithographs. *Paris,* Berggruen Gallery. 30th September-29th October.

Drawings by Marino Marini. *New York,* Martha Jackson Gallery. October.

Contemporary Italian Art. *St. Louis,* City Art Museum. 13th October-14th November.

International Exhibition. *Pittsburgh,* Carnegie Institute. October-December.

Marino Marini, Lithographs in color. *Hamburg,* Hoffman Gallery. December.

First Showing of Recent Works. *New York,* Pierre Matisse Gallery. December.

1956

International Exhibition. *Recklinghausen.* January.

Marino Marini, Sculptures and Drawings. *London,* Hanover Gallery. 8th May-16th June.

International Exhibition of Contemporary Sculpture. *Paris,* Musée Rodin. June.

From Rodin to Lipchitz. *New York,* Fine Arts Associates. 9th October-3rd November.

Modern Italian Art from the Estorick Collection. *London,* The Arts Council of Great Britain.

1957

Graphic Works of the Twentieth Century. Private Collections. *Erlangen,* The Orangery. 20th February-31st March.

Marino Marini. *New York,* The Contemporaries Gallery. 10th March-30 April.

Marino Marini. *Düsseldorf,* Vömel Gallery, 10th March-30th April.

Italian Art from 1910 until Today. *Munich,* Haus der Kunst. 6th June-15th September.

The Miracle. *Baden-Baden,* Staatliche Kunsthalle. August-September.

Italian Sculpture in the XXth Century. *Messina.* 1st August-15th September.

Italian Sculpture in the XXth Century. *Rome.* November-December.

Sculpture 1880-1957. *New York,* Fine Arts Associates. 10th December 1957-11th January 1958.

Contemporary Painting and Sculpture. *New York,* World House Galleries, 10th December 1957-25th January 1958.

Italian Sculptors. *Chicago,* The Arts Club. 10th December 1957-23rd January 1958.

Italian Sculpture in the XXth Century. *Bologna.* 22nd December 1957-3rd January 1958.

1958

Drawings by XXth Century Sculptors. *Duisburg,* Städtisches Kunstmuseum. 1st-30th March.

Marino Marini, Sculptures and Paintings. *New York,* Pierre Matisse Gallery, 11th-29th March.

"50 Years of Modern Art". World Exhibition. *Brussels.* 17th April-21st July.

Sculpture in Town. *Antwerp.* June-August.

Giacometti, Marini, Matisse, Moore. *London,* Hanover Gallery. 24th June-13th September.

Marino Marini. *Lausanne,* Vallotton Gallery. June-July.

Le Corbusier, Marino Marini. *Zurich,* Palette Gallery. July.

Morandi, Tosi, Marino Marini, Campigli, Sironi, De Pisis. *Caracas,* Gallery of Contemporary Art. September.

Some Contemporary Works of Art. *Cleveland,* Museum of Art.

Exhibition of Contemporary Painting and Sculpture. *Pittsburgh,* Carnegie Institute. 5th December 1958-8th February 1959.

1959

Masterpieces of Art. *Raleigh,* North Carolina Museum of Art. 6th April-17th May.

Environmental Sculpture. *Eskilstuna,* Sweden. 18th May-28th June.

Vth Biennal. *Antwerp.* Middelheim Park. May-September.

IIIrd International Exhibition of Engravings. *Ljubljana,* Gallery of Modern Art. 7th June-5th September.

Drawings by Sculptors of the XIXth and XXth Centuries. *Otterlo,* Rijksmuseum Kröller-Müller. 13th June-2nd August.

Documenta II. *Kassel.* 11th July-11th October.

The Werner Bär Collection of Sculpture. *Zurich,* Kunsthaus. 19th August-19th September.

"Vitality in Art". International Exhibition. *Venice.* Palazzo Grassi. August-October.

The Werner Bär Collection of Sculpture. *Berne,* Kunstmuseum. 26th September-15th November.

The Sculpture Collection of Mr. and Mrs. Ted Weiner. *Fort Worth,* Art Center. 5th-25th October.

Vitality in Art. *Recklinghausen,* Kunsthalle. October-December.

The 1959 Purchase Exhibition. *East Lansing,* Kresge Art Center, Michigan State University. November.

Vitality in Art. *Amsterdam,* Stedelijk Museum. December 1959-January 1960.

Contemporary Italian Water-Colors and Drawings. *Düsseldorf,* Kunsthalle. 18th December 1959-17th January 1960.

1960

Lithographs by Marino Marini. *Tokyo,* The National Museum of Modern Art. 29th January-21st February.

Exhibition of Floriade Sculpture. *Rotterdam,* Museum Boymans-Van Beuningen. 25th March-25th September.

Marino Marini, Drawings, Gouaches, Lithographs. *Erlangen,* The Orangery. 7th-20th April.

XXth Century Italian Art in American Collections. *Milan,*

Palazzo Reale. 30th April-26th June.
Woman. *Basle,* Beyeler Gallery. May-June.
1961
The James Thrall Soby Collection. *New York,* The Museum of Modern Art. 1st-25th February.
Italian Sculpture. *Tokyo,* National Museum of Modern Art. February.
VIth Biennal. *Antwerp,* Middelheim Park. 15th July-15th October.
Vith Biennal, *Tokyo.*
The Pittsburgh International Exhibition of Contemporary Painting and Sculpture. *Pittsburgh,* Carnegie Institute. 27th October 1961-7th January 1962.
1962
Marino Marini. Gouaches and Lithographs. *Francfurt-am-Main* Vonderbank Gallery. January.
Marino Marini. *Zurich,* Kunsthaus. 23rd January-25th February.
Art since 1950. World's Fair. *Seattle.* 21st April-21st October.
International Exhibition of Sculpture. *Spoleto.* June-September.
XXXIst Biennal, *Venice.* June-September.
Summer Exhibition. *Basle,* Gallery of Modern Art. Summer.
Art from 1900 until Today. *Vienna,* Museum of the XXth Century. 21st September-4th November.
International Exhibition of Contemporary Art. *London,* O'Hara Gallery. 15th-24th November.
Inaugural Exhibition. *Zurich,* Gimpel and Hanover Gallery. 16th November 1962-25th January 1963.
1963
Suggestion for a Collection of Modern Art. *Milan,* Toninelli Gallery. 23rd January-23rd February.
Modern Italian Drawings. *Ivrea,* Olivetti Cultural Center. February.
Arp, Calder, Marini. *Basle,* Gallery of Modern Art. 11th May-30th September.
International Symposium of Contemporary Sculpture. *Tokyo,* Museum of Modern Art. Summer.
Examples of Suffering in Modern Art. *Darmstadt,* Mathildenhöhe. 29th June-1st September.
Sculptures from the Bo Boustedt Collection. *Gothenburg,* Konstmuseum. 29th August-6th October.
The Hirshhorn Collection. *New York,* Guggenheim Museum.
Paintings by Marino Marini, *Milan,* Toninelli Gallery November 1963-February 1964.
Sculptures from the Milan School. *Milan,* Pirelli Cultural Center. 14th December 1963-12th January 1964.
1964
"Idea e Spazio". Poems by Egle Marini, Etchings by Marino Marini. *Milan,* Galleria Ciranna. 28th February-26th March.
VIIIth International Exhibition in Black and White. *Lugano.* 27th March-31st May.
"Painting and Sculpture of a Decade" (Exhibition organized by the Calouste Gulbenkian Foundation). *London,* Tate Gallery. 22nd April-28th June.
Marino Marini as a Painter. *Munich,* Günther Franke Gallery. 25th April-30th May.
Bo Boustedt Collection. *Amsterdam,* Stedelijk Museum. 1st May-7th June.
Masterpieces of Swiss Collections. *Lausanne,* Palais de Beaulieu. 1st May-25th October.
Sculptors' Drawings. *Munich,* Günther Franke Gallery. 8th June-15th July.
Synthesis. *Basle,* Gallery of Modern Art. 16th June-30th September.
XXXIInd Biennal, *Venice.* 20th June-18th October.
Documenta III. *Kassel.* 27th June-5th October.
The Bo Boustedt Collection of Modern Sculpture. *Lübeck,* Dommuseum. 4th July-2nd August.
Sculptures in Metal. *Turin,* The City Gallery of Modern Art. 19th September-18th October.
International Exhibition of Drawings. *Darmstadt,* Mathildenhöhe. 12th September-15th November.
Curatorial Retrospective. *Philadelphia,* Museum of Art. 21st September-1st November.
The Artist's Reality. An International Sculpture Exhibition. *New York,* New School Art Center. 14th October-14th November.
Pittsburgh International Museum of Art. *Pittsburgh,* Carnegie Institute. 30th October 1964-10th January 1965.
Marino Marini as a Painter. *Rotterdam,* Museum Boymans-Van Beuningen. 6th November-6th December.
1965
Religious Art in our Time. *Hamburg,* St. Jacob Kirche and Hamburger Kunsthalle. 3rd February-7th March.
Marino Marini as a Painter. *Antwerp,* Musée Royal des Beaux-Arts. 27th February-19th April.
Afro, Burri, Marini. *Milan,* Toninelli Arte Moderna. 4th March-5th April.
Great Contemporary Sculptures. *Amsterdam,* Vondelpark. 1st April-1st October.
European Sculpture. *Milan,* Galleria d'Arte Annunciata. 14th April-5th May.
Water-Colors and Drawings by Marino Marini. *Zurich,* Obere Zäune Gallery. 29th April-29th May.
The Billy Rose Art Garden. *Jerusalem,* The Israel Museum. 2nd May-2nd November.
The Garden of International Sculpture. Statuettes. *Odense,* City Hall Gallery. 19th June-31st August.
Pan-Athenes in World Sculpture. *Athens.* 8th September-8th November.
Rare Lithographs by Marino Marini. *Milan,* Galleria Ciranna. 30th September-29th October.
Contemporary Italian Sculpture. *Wellington* and *Auckland,* New Zealand. September 1965-January 1966.
The Sprengel Collection. *Hanover,* Kunstverein. 10th October-28th November.
Vth Design Fair. *Milan,* Galleria d'Arte Annunciata, December.
Marino Marini. Graphics and Related Works. *Philadelphia,* Museum of Art. 3rd December 1965-16th January 1966.
L'Atelier Mourlot. *London,* Redfern Gallery. 7th December 1965-31st January 1966.
1966
Marino Marini. *Rome,* Palazzo Venezia. 10th March-10th June.
The Figure. *Milan,* Toninelli Arte Moderna. 30th March-30th April.
Form and Truth. *Florence,* Palazzo Capponi. 7th-30th May.
The Figure. *Turin,* Galleria Narciso. 14th May-16th June.
Marino Marini. Painter and Drawer. *Darmstadt,* Kunsthalle. 21st May-3rd July.
Sonsbeek '66, Vth International Exhibition of Sculpture. *Arnhem.* 27th May-25th September.
Marino Marini, Painter and Drawer, *Nuremberg,* Fränkische Galerie am Marientor. 4th September-9th October.
Marino Marini, Painter and Drawer. *Kaiserslautern,* Pfalzgalerie. 15th October-15th November.
Contemporary Sculpture. *Erlangen,* The Orangery. 13th November-4th December.
Contemporary Italian Art. *Mexico City,* Museum of Modern Art.
Some Aspects of Contemporary Painting. *Milan,* Toninelli Arte Moderna. December 1966-January 1967.
1967
The Figure. *Milan,* Toninelli Arte Moderna. 24th February-20th March.
Modern Art in Italy. 1915-1935. *Florence,* Palazzo Strozzi. 26th February-28th June.
International Exhibition of Contemporary Sculpture. Expo '67. *Montreal.* April-October.

Masterpieces from Swiss Collections. *Paris*, Orangerie. May.

Arp, Léger, Marini, Matta, Severini, Zadkine. *Gratz*, Forum Stadtpark. 9th June-15th July.

Important European Sculptors. *New York*, La Boetie Gallery. 26th September-25th October.

International Exhibition of Engraving. *Vancouver*, Art Gallery. 5th-29th October.

Fifteen Unpublished Paintings by Marino Marini. *Milan*, Toninelli Arte Moderna. October - November.

From Picasso to Guttuso. *Milan*, Galleria Annunciata. 21st October-10th November.

Sculpture from Twenty Nations. Guggenheim International Exhibition. *New York*, Guggenheim Museum. 20th October 1967-4th February 1968.

The 1967 Pittsburgh International Exhibition of Contemporary Painting and Sculpture. *Pittsburgh*, Carnegie Institute. 27th October 1967-7th January 1968.

Masterpieces. *Turin*, Galleria La Bussola. December.

First Showing of Paintings, Sculpture and Drawings. *New York*, Pierre Matisse Gallery. 19th December 1967-25th January 1968.

1968

Marino Marini, Colored Lithographs. *Stockholm*, Italian Cultural Institute. 23rd April-4th May.

Exhibition of Photographs of the Sculptures of Marino Marini. *Pistoia*, Valiani. 8th June-8th August.

Sculptures from the Norton Simon Collection. *Los Angeles*, County Museum of Art. August.

Art Collections. *Berlin*, Nationalgalerie. September.

Images of Man. *Darmstadt*, Kunsthalle. 14th September-17th November.

Album N° 1 of Marino Marini; Twelve original engravings. *Milan*, Galleria Ciranna. 26th October-20th November.

Italian Sculptors: IInd International Exhibition of Small Bronzes. *Paris*, Musée d'Art Moderne de la Ville de Paris.

19th November-23rd December.

Collective Exhibition: Selected works. *Milan*, Galleria Toninelli. December.

Marino Marini. *New York*, Weintraub Gallery. December.

Suggestion for a Collection. *Rome*, Galleria Nuove Carpine. 6th December 1968-10th January 1969.

International Exhibition of Graphic Art. *Florence*, Palazzo Strozzi. 21st December 1968-30th January 1969.

1969

Masters of Modern Italian Art from the G. Mattioli Collection. *Washington*, National Gallery of Art. January.

Sculptors' Drawings. *Antwerp*, Middelheim Park. 22nd February-27th April.

An Epic of Vitality: Marini, Burri, Moreni. *Turin*, Galleria Gissi. March.

Marino Marini: From Color to Form. *Paris*, Bibliothèque Nationale. March.

American and European Painting. *Los Angeles*, Felix Landau Gallery. March.

Masters of the XXth Century. *Milan*, Galleria Levi. 13th March-30th April.

Marino Marini: Etchings and Lithographs. *London*, Graphic Arts Gallery. 1st-30th April.

Collective Exhibition. *Milan*, Toninelli Arte Moderna. April-May.

Marino Marini: Graphic Works. *Hamburg*, Lochte Gallery. 10th May-15th June.

Graphic Arts of the XXth Century. *Menton*, Biennal, Palais de l'Europe. July-September.

Masterpieces of Swiss Collections. *Munich*, Staatliche Graphische Sammlung. 8th August-19th October.

Italian Modern Art. *Haarlem*, Franz Hals Museum. 12th October-30th November.

1970

Marino Marini. Painting and Drawings. *Rome*, Toninelli Arte Moderna. February.

CATALOGUES OF EXHIBITIONS

1923
Il Biennale Romana. *Rome*.

1927
III Mostra Internazionale delle Arti decorative. *Monza*. May-October.

1928
Mostra del Gruppo Novecento Toscano. *Milan*, Galleria Milano. December. *(Raffaele Franchi)*.

1929
Exposition du Novecento Italien à la Société des Beaux-Arts. *Nice*. March-April. *(Antonio Maraini)*.

Il Mostra del Novecento Italiano. *Milan*. 2nd March-30th April.

Exposition d'Art Italien Moderne aux Éditions Bonaparte. *Paris*. November. *(Mario Tozzi)*.

1930
Ausstellung Moderne Italiener. *Basle, Kunsthalle*. 5th-12th February.

Die Entwicklung der Modernen Kunst in Italien. *Berne*, Kunstmuseum. March-May.

1931
Utställning Italiensk "Novecento". *Stockholm*. 9th September-4th October. *(Margherita Sarfatti)*.

1932
Marino Marini. *Milan*, Galleria Milano. February.

Marino Marini. *Rome*, Galleria Sabatello. 6th-13th November.

XVIII Esposizione Internazionale Biennale d'Arte. *Venice*.

1934
XIX Esposizione Internazionale Biennale d'Arte. *Venice*. June-October.

Exposition d'Art Italien. *Geneva*. 22nd September-18th November. *(G. de Reynolds)*.

1935
Il Quadriennale d'Arte Nazionale. *Rome*. February-July.

Italienischer Plastik der Gegenwart. *Vienna*. November. *(Leo Plasiscig)*.

1940
Ausstellung Zeitgenössischer Italienischer Maler und Bildhauer. *Zurich*, Kunsthaus. November-December. *(Antonio Maraini)*.

1941
Marino Marini. *Genoa*. Galleria Genova. 15th-29th March.

1942
Marino Marini. *Rome*, Galleria dello Zodiaco. November-December. *(Filippo De Pisis)*.

1944
Vier ausländische Bildhauer in der Schweiz. *Basle*, Kunstmuseum. 14th October-26th November.

1945
Marino Marini. Germaine Richier. Fritz Wotruba. *Berne*, Kunsthalle. 9th June-8th July. *(A. R.)*.

Marino Marini. *Zurich*, Galerie Aktuaryus. 26th September-17th October. *(Lamberto Vitali)*.

1947
Quarante Ans d'Art Italien. *Lausanne*, Musée Cantonal des Beaux-Arts. 15th February-15th March. *(Giovanni Ponti)*.

1948
Exposición de Arte Italiano Contemporaneo. *Madrid*. May.

Italiensk Nutidskonst. *Stockholm*, Färg och Form. September. (*Giuseppe Galassi*).
Italiensk Nutidskonst. *Gothenburg*, Konstmuseum. October. (*Giuseppe Galassi*).
Sculpture. *New York*, Buchholz Gallery. 28th September-16th October.

1949
Opere di Marino Marini. *Rome*, Galleria dell'Obelisco. March. (*Palma Bucarelli*).
Rodin to Brancusi. *Palm Beach*, Society of the Four Arts. 4th-27th March.
3rd Sculpture International. *Philadelphia*, Museum of Art, Fairmount Park Art Association. May.
La Collezione Guggenheim. *Milan*, Palazzo Reale. June - July. (*Francesco Flora*).
Twentieth Century Italian Art. *New York*, Museum of Modern Art. (*Soby and Barr*).

1950
Art Italien Contemporain. *Brussels*, Palais des Beaux-Arts. 28th January-28th February. (*Giuseppe Raimondi*).
Marino Marini. *New York*, Buchholz Gallery (Curt Valentin) 14th February-11th March. (*James Thrall Soby*).
35 Drawings of Marino Marini. *Washington*, Watkins Gallery. 2nd-24th March.
Werke Europäischer Plastic. *Munich*, Haus der Kunst. 1st November-24th December.

1951
Marino Marini. Sculpture and Drawings. *London*, The Hanover Gallery. 8th May-16th June (*James Thrall Soby*).
Sculpture at Battersea Park. *London*. May-September. (*Ruth Dalton*).
Exposition Inaugurale du Musée Communal de Sculpture en plein air. *Antwerp*, Middelheim Park. 8th September-31st October.
Die Plastiksammlung Werner Bär. *Winterthur*, Kunstmuseum. 16th September-11th November. (*Hermann Hubacher*).
Marino Marini. *Hanover*, Kestner Gesellschaft. November 1951-January 1952. (*Alfred Hentzen*).

1952
Marino Marini. *Hamburg*, Kunstverein. February. (*Alfred Hentzen*).
Marino Marini. *Munich*, Bayerische Staatsgemäldesammlungen, Haus der Kunst. 21st March-4th May. (*Bernhard Degenhart*).
Sonsbeek '52. International Tentoonstelling Beeldhouwkunst. *Arnhem*. 30th May-15th September. (*J. A. de Goeijen*).
Ausstellung Mensch und Form unserer Zeit. *Recklinghausen*, Städtische Kunsthalle. 13th June-3rd August. (*Franz Grosse Perdekamp*).
Marini. Moore. Wotruba. *Salzburg*, Galerie Welz. Summer. (*D´ Ernst Köller*).
Sculpture of the Twentieth Century. *Philadelphia*, Museum of Art, Fairmount Park Art Association. 11th October-7th December. (*Andrew C. Ritchie*).
Second International Biennal of Contemporary Color Lithographs. *Cincinnati*, Art Museum. (*Gustave von Groschwitz*).
Contemporary Drawings 1945-1952. *Chicago*, Art Institute. (*Carl O. Schniewind*).

1953
Marino Marini. *Gothenburg*, Konstmuseum. January-February. (*Christian Faerber*).
Sculpture of the Twentieth Century. *Chicago*, Art Institute. 22nd January-8th March. (*Andrew C. Ritchie*).
Marino Marini. *Stockholm*, Svensk-Franska Konstgalleriet. February-March. (*Christian Faerber*).
Nutida Italiensk Konst. *Stockholm*, Liljevalchs Konsthall. March-April. (*Umbro Apollonio*).

Marino Marini. *Copenhagen*, Statens Museum for Kunst. 14th March-7th April. (*Christian Faerber*).
Marino Marini. *Oslo*, Nasjonalgalleriet. April-May. (*Christian Faerber*).
Marino Marini. Sculpture and Drawings. *Cincinnati*, Art Museum. April-May.
Sculpture of the Twentieth Century. *New York*, The Museum of Modern Art. 29th April-7th September. (*Andrew C. Ritchie*).
Plastik im Freien. *Hamburg*. 30th April-31st October. (*Werner Haftmann, Carl Georg Heise*).
IIᵉ Biennal. *Antwerp*, Middelheim Park. 20th June-30th September. (*E. Baudouin*).
Art Fantastique. *Ostend*, Kursaal. 5th July-31st August. (*Emile Langui*).
Marino Marini. *New York*, Curt Valentin Gallery. 27th October-21st November. (*Sinagra*).
Seventy-five years of Sculpture. *Houston*, The Museum of Fine Arts. November.
Junge Italienische Kunst. *Zurich*, Kunsthaus. 21st November 1953-January 1954. (*R. Wehrli*).
Futuristas e Artistas Italianos de Hoye. Segunda Bienal de *São Paulo*. 8th December 1953-8th February 1954. (*Rodolfo Pallucchini*).

1954
Marino Marini. *Helsinki*, Galery Artek. 26th January - 16th February. (*Umbro Apollonio*).
Marino Marini. *Geneva*, Galerie Gérald Cramer. 10th March-1st April. (*Umbro Apollonio*).
Marino Marini. *Cologne*, Galerie Der Spiegel. May-June. (*Eduard Trier*).
Sculpture in the open air. *London*, Holland Park. May-September.
Contemporary Sculptors' Drawings. *Columbus*, Ohio State University, The School of Fine and Applied Arts. (*Joseph Schwarz*).

1955
Marino Marini. *Rotterdam*, Museum Boymans-Van Beuningen. 26th February-28th April. (*A. M. Hammacher*).
Marino Marini. *Düsseldorf, Kunstverein*. 8th May-12th June.
Spring Exhibition. *New York*, Pierre Matisse Gallery. 11th-28th May.
IIIʳ Biennal. *Antwerp*, Middelheim Park. 1st June-10th September. (*L. Craeybeckx*).
Das Bild des Menschen. *Recklinghausen*, Städtische Kunsthalle. 12th June-26th July.
Marino Marini. *Mannheim*, Kunsthalle. 25th June-31st July. (*Walter Passarge*).
Documenta I. Internationale Ausstellung. *Kassel*, Museum Fridericianum. 15th July-18th September. (*Werner Haftmann*).
Marino Marini. 15 lithographies. *Paris*, Galerie Berggruen. 30th September-29th October. (*Douglas Cooper*).
Drawings by Marino Marini. *New York*, Martha Jackson Gallery. October. (*Dorothy Norman*).
Contemporary Italian Art. *St. Louis*, City Art Museum. 13th October-14th November. (*W. N. Eisendrath Jr.*).
The 1955 Pittsburgh International Exhibition. *Pittsburgh*, Carnegie Institute. October-December. (*Gorden B. Washburn*).
First showing of recent works. *New York*, Pierre Matisse Gallery. December.

1956
Internationale Ausstellung. *Recklinghausen*. January.
Marino Marini. Sculpture and Drawings. *London*, The Hanover Gallery. 8th May-16th June (*James Thrall Soby*).
Exposition Internationale de Sculpture Contemporaine. *Paris*, Musée Rodin. June. (*Paul Léon*).
Rodin to Lipchitz. *New York*, Fine Arts Associates. 9th October-3rd November. (*John Coolidge*).

Modern Italian Art from the Estorick Collection. *London*, The Arts Council of Great Britain. *(Philip James).*

1957

Graphik des 20. Jahrhunderts aus Erlangen Privatbesitz. *Erlangen*, Orangerie. 20th February-30th March. *(Bernhard Meyer Rutz).*

Marino Marini. *Düsseldorf*, Galerie Vömel. 10th March-30th April. *(Christoph Bernoulli).*

Contemporary Art. *Buffalo*, Albright Art Gallery. 15th May-15th June. *(Gordon M. Smith).*

Ausstellung Italienischer Kunst von 1910 bis zur Gegenwart. *Munich*, Haus der Kunst. 6th June-15th September. *(Fortunato Bellonzi).*

Il Miracolo. *Baden-Baden*, Staatliche Kunsthalle. August-September. *(D' Mahlow).*

Scultura Italiana del XX Secolo. *Messina.* 1st August-15th September. *(Giovanni Carandente).*

Scultura Italiana del XX Secolo. *Rome.* November-December. *(Giovanni Carandente).*

Sculpture 1880-1957. *New York*, Fine Arts Associates. 10th December 1957-11th January 1958.

Contemporary Painting and Sculpture. *New York*, World House Galleries. 10th December 1957 - 25th January 1958. *(J. B. Neumann).*

Italian Sculptors. *Chicago*, The Arts Club. 10th December 1957-23rd January 1958.

Scultura Italiana del XX Secolo. *Bologna.* 22nd December 1957-3rd June 1958. *(Giovanni Carandente).*

1958

Bildhauer Zeichnungen des 20. Jahrhunderts. *Duisburg*, Städtisches Kunstmuseum. 1st-30th March. *(G. Händler).*

Marino Marini. Sculpture. Paintings. *New York*, Pierre Matisse Gallery. 11th-29th March.

50 ans d'Art Moderne. *Brussels*, Exposition Universelle et Internationale. 17th April-21st July. *(Emile Langui).*

La sculpture dans la Ville. *Antwerp. June-August.*

Giacometti. Marini. Matisse. Moore. *London*, The Hanover Gallery. 24th-13th September.

Morandi. Tosi. Marino Marini. Campigli. Sironi. De Pisis. *Caracas*, Galeria de Arte Contemporaneo. September. *(Edgardo Giorgi Alberti).*

Some Contemporary Works of Art. *Cleveland*, Museum of Art. *(Sherman E. Lee).*

Exhibition of Contemporary Painting and Sculpture. *Pittsburgh*, Carnegie Institute. 5th December 1958-8th February 1959. *(Gordon B. Washburn).*

1959

Masterpieces of Art. *Raleigh*, North Carolina Museum of Art. 6th April-17th May. *(James B. Byrnes).*

Skulptur i Miljö. *Eskilstuna* (Sweden). 18th May-28th June. *(Svante Lundkvist).*

Ve Biennale. *Antwerp*, Middelheim Park. May-September. *(L. Craeybeckx).*

IIIrd International Exhibition of Modern Engravings. *Ljubljana*, Moderna Galerija. 7th June-5th September. *(Zoran Krzisnik).*

Tekeningen van Beeldhouwers 19ͤ en 20ͤ eeuw. *Otterlo*, Rijksmuseum Kröller-Müller. 13th June-2nd August. *(A. M. Hammacher).*

Malerei. Documenta II. *Kassel.* 11th July-11th October. *(Werner Haftmann).*

Skulptur nach 1945. Documenta II. *Kassel,* 11th July-11th October. *(Eduard Trier).*

Druckgraphik nach 1945. Documenta II. *Kassel.* 11th July-11th October. *(Albrecht Fabri).*

Werner Bär Plastik. *Zurich*, Kunsthaus. 19th August-19th September. *(Werner and Nelly Bär).*

Vitalità nell'Arte. *Venice*, Palazzo Grassi. August-October. *(Henry Michaux).*

Plastiksammlung Werner Bär. *Berne*, Kunstmuseum. 26th September-15th November. *(Hugo Wagner).*

The Sculpture Collection of Mr. and Mrs. Ted Weiner.

Fort Worth, Art Center. 5th-25th October. *(H. B. Caldwell).*

The 1959 Purchase Exhibition. *East Lansing*, Kresge Art Center, Michigan State University. *November.* (Allen Leepa and Howard Church).

Italienische Aquarelle und Zeichnungen der Gegenwart. *Düsseldorf*, Kunsthalle. 18th December 1959-17th January 1960. *(Bernhard Degenhart).*

1960

Lithographs by Marino Marini. *Tokyo*, The National Museum of Modern Art. 29th January-21st February. *(Atsuo Imaizumi).*

Beeldententoonstelling Floriade. *Rotterdam*, Museum Boymans-Van Beuningen. 25th March-25th September.

Marino Marini. Zeichnungen. Gouachen. Lithographien. *Erlangen*, Orangerie. 7th-20th April.

Arte Italiana del XX Secolo da Collezioni Americane. *Milan*, Palazzo Reale. 30th April-26th June. *(James Thrall Soby).*

La Femme. *Basle*, Galerie Beyeler. May-June.

1961

The James Thrall Soby Collection. *New York*, The Museum of Modern Art. 1st-25th February. *(A. H. Barr Jr.).*

Italian Sculpture. *Tokyo*, The National Museum of Art. February.

VIᵉ Biennal. *Antwerp*, Middelheim Park. 15th July-1st October. *(L. Craeybeckx).*

The VIth Tokyo Biennal. *Tokyo.* *(Tsynelaka Ueda).*

The Pittsburgh International Exhibition of Contemporary Painting and Sculpture. *Pittsburgh*, Carnegie Institute. 27th October 1961-7th January 1962. *(Gordon B. Washburn).*

1962

Marino Marini. *Zurich*, Kunsthaus. 23rd January-25th February. *(Eduard Hüttinger).*

Art since 1950. *Seattle*, World's Fair. 21st April-21st October. *(Sam Hunter).*

Mostra Internazionale di Scultura. *Spoleto.* June-September.

Summer 1962. *Basle*, Galerie d'Art Moderne. Summer.

Kunst von 1900 bis heute. *Vienna*, Museum des 20. Jahrhunderts. 21st September-4th November. *(Werner Hofmann).*

International Exhibition of Contemporary Art. *London*, The O'Hara Gallery. November. *(Herbert Read).*

Eröffnungausstellung. *Zurich*, Gimpel et Hanover Gallery. 16th November 1962-5th January 1963.

1963

Proposta per una raccolta d'Arte Moderna. *Milan*, Galleria Toninelli. 23rd January-23rd Febraury. *(Guido Ballo).*

Disegni Italiani Moderni. *Ivrea*, Centro Culturale Olivetti. February. *(Giovanni Carandente).*

Arp. Calder. Marini. *Basle*, Galerie d'Art Moderne. 11th May-30th September.

International Symposium of Contemporary Sculpture. *Tokyo*, The National Museum of Modern Art. Summer. *(Soichi Tominaga).*

Zeugnisse der Angst in der Modernen Kunst. *Darmstadt*, Mathildenhöhe. 29th June-1st September. *(Hans Gerhart Evers).*

Skulptur, Bo Boustedts Samling. *Gothenburg*, Konstmuseum. 29th August-6th October. *(Alfred Westholm).*

The Hirshhorn Collection. *New York*, Guggenheim Museum.

Dipinti di Marino Marini. *Milan*, Galleria Toninelli. November 1963-February 1964. *(Franco Russoli).*

Scultori della Scuola di Milano. *Milan*, Centro Culturale Pirelli. 14th December 1963-12th January 1964. *(Marco Onorato).*

1964

"Idea e Spazio". Poemi di Egle Marini. Acqueforti di Marino Marini. *Milan*, Galleria Ciranna. 28th February-26th March.

VIII Esposizione Internazionale di Bianco e Nero. *Lugano*. 27th March-31st May. *(Giuseppe Martinola)*.
The Painting and Sculpture of a Decade. *London*, Tate Gallery. Organized by the Calouste Gulbenkian Foundation. 22nd April-28th June.
Marino Marini als Maler. *Munich*, Günther Franke Galerie. 25th April-30th May. *(Werner Haftmann)*.
Bo Boustedt Collection. *Amsterdam*, Stedelijk Museum. 1st May-7th June.
Chefs-d'œuvre des Collections Suisses. *Lausanne*, Palais de Beaulieu. 1st May-25th October.
Bildhauerzeichnungen. *Munich*, Günther Franke Galerie. 8th June-15th July.
Synthèse. *Basle*, Galerie d'Art Moderne. 16th June-30th September.
Documenta III. Malerei. Skulptur. Handzeichnungen. *Kassel*. 27th June-5th October. *(Werner Haftmann)*.
Moderne Skulptur Bo Boustedts Sammlung. *Lübeck*, Dommuseum. 4th July-2nd August. *(Alfred Westholm)*.
Sculture in metallo. *Turin*, Galleria Civica d'Arte Moderna. 19th September-18th October. *(G. C. Anselmetti)*.
Internationale der Zeichnung. *Darmstadt*, Mathildenhöhe. 12th September-15th November. *(H. W. Sabais)*.
Curatorial Retrospective. *Philadelphia*, Museum of Art. 21st September-1st November. *(Carl Zigrosser)*.
An International Sculpture Exhibition. The Artist Reality. *New York*, New School Art Center. 14th October-14th November. *(Paul Mocsanyi)*.
Pittsburgh International Museum of Art. *Pittsburgh*, Carnegie Institute. 30th October 1964-10th January 1965. *(Gustave von Groschwitz)*.
Marino Marini als Schilder. *Rotterdam*, Museum Boymans-Van Beuningen. 6th November-6th December. *(Raffaele Carrieri)*.

1965

Religiose Kunst unserer Zeit. *Hamburg*, St. Jakob Kirche and Hamburger Kunsthalle. 3rd February-7th March.
Marino Marini als Schilder. *Antwerp*, Koninklijk Museum voor Schone Kunsten. 27th February-19th April. *(L. Craeybeckx)*.
Afro. Burri. Marini. *Milan*, Toninelli Arte Moderna. 4th March-5th April.
Sculptuur in *Amsterdam*. Vondelpark. 1st April-1st October. *(Sandberg)*.
Scultura Europea. *Milan*, Salone Annunciata. 15th April-5th May. *(Mario de Micheli)*.
Marino Marini. Aquarelle und Zeichnungen. *Zurich*, Galerie Obere Zaüne. 29th April-29th May.
The Billy Rose Art Garden. *Jerusalem*, The Israel Museum. 2nd May-2nd November.
Skulptur i Eventyrhaven Statuetter i Rädhushallen. *Odense*. 19th June-31st August. *(Jan Zibrandtsen)*.
Litografie rare di Marino Marini. *Milan*, Galleria Ciranna. 30th September-29th October.
Contemporary Italian Sculpture. Arts Council Exhibition. *Wellington* and *Auckland* (New Zealand). September 1965-January 1966. *(Fortunato Bellonzi)*.
Sammlung Sprengel. *Hannover*, Kunstverein. 10th October-28th November. *(Alfred Hentzen)*.
V Fiera del Disegno. *Milan*, Galleria Annunciata. December.
Marino Marini. Graphics and Related Works. *Philadelphia*. Museum of Art. 3rd December 1965-16th January 1966. *(Giovanni Carandente)*.
L'Atelier Mourlot. *London*, Redfern Gallery. 7th December-31st January 1966. *(Jean Adhémar)*.

1966

Mostra di Marino Marini. *Rome*, Palazzo Venezia. 10th March-10th June. *(Giovanni Carandente)*.
La Figura. *Milan*, Toninelli Arte Moderna. 30th March-30th April.

Forma et Verità. I. *Florence*, Palazzo Capponi. 7th-30th May. *(Lorenzo Papi)*.
Marino Marini als Maler und Graphiker. *Darmstadt*, Kunsthalle. 21st May-3rd July. *(Werner Haftmann)*.
Sonsbeek '66. V° Internazionale Beeldententoonstelling. *Arnhem*. 27th May-25th September. *(Dr H. L. C. Jaffé)*.
Marino Marini als Maler und Graphiker. *Nuremberg*, Fränkische Galerie am Marientor. 4th September-9th October. *(Werner Haftmann)*.
Marino Marini als Maler und Graphiker. *Kaiserslautern*, Pfalzgalerie. 15th October-15th November. *(Werner Haftmann)*.
Plastik in unserer Zeit. *Erlangen*, Orangerie. 13th November-4th December. *(Helmut Lederer)*.
Arte Italiano Contemporaneo. *Mexico City*, Museo de Arte Moderno. *(Fortunato Bellonzi)*.
Alcuni aspetti della pittura contemporanea. *Milan*, Toninelli Arte Moderna. December 1966-January 1967.

1967

La Figura. *Milan*, Toninelli Arte Moderna. 24th February-20th March.
Arte Moderna in Italia 1915-1935. *Florence*, Palazzo Strozzi. 26th February-28th June. *(Carlo Ragghianti)*.
International Exhibition of Contemporary Sculpture. *Montreal*, Expo 67. Apri-October. *(Guy Robert)*.
Chefs-d'œuvre des Collections Suisses. *Paris*, Orangerie. May. *(Jean Chatelain, F. Daulte, Hélène Adhémar)*.
Arp. Léger. Marini. Matta. Severini. Zadkine. *Graz*, Forum Stadtpark. 9th June-15th July. *(Heribert Schwarzbauer)*.
International Exhibition of Engravings at *Vancouver*. The Vancouver Art Gallery. 5th-29th October. *(William S. Liebermann)*.
15 Dipinti inediti di Marino Marini. *Milan*, Toninelli Arte Moderna. October-November.
Da Picasso a Guttuso. *Milan*, Galleria Annunciata. 21st October-21st November.
Sculptures from Twenty Nations. International Exhibition. *New York*, Guggenheim Museum. 20th October 1967-February 1968. *(Edward F. Fry)*.
The 1967 Pittsburgh International Exhibition. *Pittsburgh*, Carnegie Institute. 27th October 1967 - 7th January 1968. *(Gustave von Groschwitz)*.
First Showing of Paintings, Sculptures, Drawings. *New York*, Pierre Matisse Gallery. 19th December 1967-25th January 1968.

1968

Mostra fotografica. Sculture di Marino Marini. *Pistoia*, Valiani. 8th June-8th August. *(Dr Corrado Gelli, Arrigo Valiani)*.
Kunstsammlungen. *Berlin*, Nationalgalerie. September. *(Werner Haftmann)*.
Menschenbilder. *Darmstdat*, Kunsthalle. 14th September-17th November. *(Arnold Gehlen)*.
L'Album N° 1 di Marino Marini. *Milan*, Galleria Ciranna. 26th October-20th November.
Mostra Biennale Internazionale della Grafica. *Florence*, Palazzo Strozzi, 21st December 1968-30th January 1969. *(Armando Nocentini)*.

1969

Tekeningen von Beeldhouwers. *Antwerp*, Middelheim Park, Orangerie. 22nd February-27th April.
Epica della Vitalità. Marini. Burri. Moreni. *Turin*, Galleria Gissi. March. *(Albino Galvano)*.
American and European Painting. *Los Angeles*, Felix Landau Gallery. March.
Europäische Meisterwerke aus Schweizer Sammlungen. *Munich*, Staatliche Graphische Sammlung. 8th August-19th October. *(H. R. Hahnloser)*.
Moderne Italiaanse Kunst. *Haarlem*, Franz Hals Museum. 12th October-30th November.

WORKS BY MARINO MARINI BELONGING TO MUSEUMS

AMSTERDAM
Stedelijk Museum

ANTWERP
Koninklijk Museum

ANTWERP
Middelheim, Openlichtmuseum

BALTIMORE
Museum of Modern Art

BASLE
Kunstmuseum

BERLIN
Nationalgalerie

BOCHUM, Federal Republic of Germany
Kunstmuseum

BRUSSELS
Musées Royaux des Beaux-Arts

BUFFALO, New York State
Albright-Knox Art Gallery

CARACAS
Museo de Arte Moderna

CHARLEROI, Belgium
Palais des Beaux-Arts, Musée Communal

CHICAGO
The Art Institute

CINCINATTI, Ohio
Cincinnati Art Museum

COLOGNE
Wallraf-Richartz Museum

COPENHAGEN
Statens Museum

CURAÇAO
Curaçao Museum

DETROIT
Institute of Arts

DUISBURG
Wilhelm-Lembruck-Museum

DUSSELDORF
Kunstverein

EDINBURGH
Scottish National Gallery of Modern Art

ESSEN
Folkwang-Museum

FLORENCE
Galleria d'Arte Moderna

FORT DODGE, Iowa
Blanden Memorial Art Gallery

FULLERTON, California
Norton Simon Inc. Museum of Art

GOTHENBURG, Sweden
Konstmuseum

HAMBURG
Kunsthalle

HANOVER,
Landesmuseum

HARTFORD, Connecticut
Wadsworth Atheneum

HELSINKI
Ateneumin Taidemuseo

KANSAS CITY
William Rockhill Nelson Gallery of Art

KYOTO, Japan
Museum of Modern Art

LINCOLN, Nebraska
University of Nebraska Art Gallery

LONDON
Tate Gallery

LONDON
National Portrait Gallery

LOS ANGELES, California
Los Angeles County Museum of Art

MANNHEIM
Kunsthalle

MILAN
Galleria d'Arte Moderna

MINNEAPOLIS, Minnesota
The Minneapolis Institute of Arts

MINNEAPOLIS, Minnesota
Walker Art Center

MUNICH
Bayerische Staatsgemäldesammlungen

NEW YORK
Museum of Modern Art

NORTHAMPTON, Mass.
Smith College Museum of Art

NUREMBERG
Germanisches Nationalmuseum

OSLO
Nasjonalgalleriet

OTTAWA, Canada
National Gallery of Canada

OTTERLO, Holland
Rijksmuseum Kröller-Müller

PARIS
Musée National d'Art Moderne

PERTH, Western Australia
The Western Australian Art Gallery

PHILADELPHIA
Museum of Art

PISTOIA, Italy
Museo Civico

PITTSBURGH, Penn.
Museum of Art, Carnegie Institute

PORTLAND, Oregon
Museum of Art

PROVINCETOWN, Mass.
The Chrysler Art Museum

RIO DE JANEIRO
Museu de Arte Moderna

(1968)

(Photo, Marina Marini)

ROCHESTER, New York State
Memorial Art Gallery of the University

ROME
Galleria Nazionale d'Arte Moderna

ROTTERDAM
Museum Boymans-Van Beuningen

St. LOUIS, Missouri
City Art Museum

St. LOUIS, Missouri
University Museum of Art.

SAN DIEGO, California
Museum of Modern Art

SAN FRANCISCO
Museum of Art

SÃO PAULO
Museu de Arte Contemporânea

STOCKHOLM
National Museet

THE HAGUE, Holland
Gemeentemuseum

TOKYO
Bridgestone Museum

TOLEDO, Ohio
Toledo Museum of Art

TORONTO
Art Gallery of Ontario

TRIESTE
Museo Civico Rivoltella

TURIN
Galleria d'Arte Moderna

UTICA, New York State
Munson-Williams-Proctor Institute

VIENNA
Albertina

VIENNA
Kunsthistorisches Museum

VIENNA
Museum des 20. Jahrhunderts

WASHINGTON
National Portrait Gallery

WINTERTHUR, Switzerland
Kunstmuseum

ZURICH
Kunsthaus

ACADEMIC HONORS

1932
Honorary Academician, Accademia Fiorentina delle Arti, Florence.

1947
Academician, Accademia Clementina, Bologna.

1950
Honorary Academician, Académie Royale Flamande, Brussels.

1951
Honorary Academician, Akademisches Kollegium, Munich.

1952
Member of the Kungliga Akademien för de Fria Konsterna, Stockholm.

1954
Honorary Member, International Mark Twain Society, Kirkwood, Missouri.

1957
Academician, Accademia Nazionale di San Luca, Rome.

1958
Corresponding Member, Bayerische Akademie der Schönen Künste, Munich.

1959
Member of the Accademia Latinitati Excolendae, Rome.

Corresponding Member, Academia Nacional de Bellas Artes, Buenos Aires.

1960
Associate Academician, Accademia Tiberina, Rome.

1961
Member of the Pontificia Insigne Accademia Artistica dei Virtuosi, Rome.

1962
Honorary Academician, Accademia 500, Rome.

Honorary Member, Akademie der Bildenden Künste, Nuremberg.

1965
Honorary Member, Associazione Incisori d'Italia, Turin-Milan-Rome.

1966
Member of the Istituto Accademico, Rome.

1967
Honorary Academician, Accademia Clementina, Bologna.

1968
Honorary Member, American Academy of Arts and Letters, New York.

Honorary Member, National Institute of Art and Letters, New York.

Honorary Academician, Accademia Pistoiese del Ceppo, Pistoia.

1969
Member of the Order für Wissenschaft und Künste: « Pour le Mérite », Göttingen.

Knight of the Mark Twain Society, Kirkwood, Missouri.

AWARDS AND DECORATIONS

1929
Diploma of Honor - International Exhibition, Barcelona

1933
Diploma with Silver Medal - V Triennale, Milan.

1935
First Sculpture Prize - II Quadriennale, Rome.

1936
Diploma of Honor - Exhibition of Italien Art, Budapest.

1937
« Grand Prix » - International Exhibition, Paris.

1952
First Sculpture Prize - XXVI Biennale, Venice.

1954
Gold Medal of the President of the Republic, Rome.

International Grand Prize - Accademia dei Lincei, Rome.

1961
Donatello Prize - Florence.

1962
Gold Medal of Merit - City of Milan.

1963
« City of Milan » Prize - Milan.

1964
« Europa Arte » Prize - Ancona.

1966
« Ibico Reggino » Prize for Sculpture - Reggio Calabria.

Diploma of the II Biennale of Contemporary Italian Engraving and Drawing - City of Padua and Association of Italian Engravers of Milan.

1967
Gold Medal for Services rendered - Florence.

Biancamano Prize - Milan.

Gold Medal for Great Civic Merit - Chamber of Commerce of Pistoia.

Diploma of Merit, First Class, Gold Medal - Ministry of Education, Rome.

1968
First Prize from the City of Venice for the VIII Biennale of Contemporary Italian Engravers - Venice.

1969
Medal of the Presidency of the Italian Chamber of Deputies.

DRAWINGS REPRODUCED IN THIS BOOK

The American Ambassador awarding to M.M. the insignia of the « Mark Twain Society » (Florence, 1969).

1947

506

TABLE OF CONTENTS

PRINTED THE 5th OF SEPTEMBER 1970
BY THE PRESSES OF AMILCARE PIZZI, S.p.A.
CINISELLO BALSAMO (MILAN).

THE FIRST FIFTY COPIES OF THIS WORK
INCLUDE AN ORIGINAL COLOR LITHOGRAPH
BY MARINO MARINI
SIGNED AND NUMBERED 1 TO 50.

The photographs of the works reproduced in this book were done by the following photographers:
Bacci, Hammacher, Mercurio, Savio, Sinigaglia, Lo Studio, Studio 22 (Milan) - Rampazzi (Turin) - De
Antonis (Rome) - Cancogni (Pietrasanta) - Bessi (Carrara) - Ferruzzi (Venice) - Paul Bijtebier (Brussels)
- Cianetti, Dietrich Widner (Basle) - Vicari (Lugano) - Michael Speich Winterthur) - Walter Dräyer
(Zurich) - Lederer (Erlangen) - List (Munich) - Bo Boustedt (Kungälv, Sweden) - Tom Scott (Edin-
burg) - Oliver Baker, Alex L. Hillmann, Peter July, O.E. Nelson, Eric Pollitzer, Walter J. Russel, John
D. Schiff, Adolph Studl, Soichi Sunami, Taylor and Dull, Charles Uht (New York) - A.J. Wyat (Phila-
delphia).